Key Stage 3
Classbook

Maths

  for September 2000

Alan
Smith

First published 1998
Reprinted 1998 (twice)
Second edition 2000

Letts Educational
Schools and Colleges Division
9–15 Aldine Street
London W12 8AW
Tel 020 8740 2270
Fax 020 8743 8451

Text: © Alan Smith 1998

Design and illustrations © Letts Educational Ltd 1998

Design and page layout: Ken Vail Graphic Design, Cambridge

Illustrations: Simon Girling & Associates (Mike Lacey),
Ken Vail Graphic Design

Colour reproduction by PDQ Repro Ltd, Bungay, Suffolk

British Library Cataloguing-in-Publication Data

A CIP record for this book is available from the British Library

ISBN 1 84085 417 0

Printed and Bound in Spain

Letts Educational Limited, a division of Granada Learning Limited.
Part of the Granada Media Group.

Contents

Introduction

Level 4

Contents

Level 5

Level 6

Introduction

This Letts Key Stage 3 Mathematics Classbook is designed to give complete coverage of the core skills required at Level 4, Level 5 and Level 6 of the National Curriculum for Mathematics.

The classbook has been written in 37 Units, set out in an order which closely follows the National Curriculum. Units 1 to 10 cover the various topics in AT2 (Number and Algebra), AT3 (Shape, Space and Measures) and AT4 (Data Handling), all at Level 4 (with a little revision of Level 3). These are followed by a Review Unit, comprising mental arithmetic and longer written exercises, again at Level 4.

Similarly Units 11 to 24 and a second Review Unit cover Level 5, and Units 25 to 37 and a Review Unit cover Level 6.

Each Unit begins with an overview of the key points to be covered and is followed by explanations, examples and exercises, and then a summary of what has been covered. Finally, the Unit closes with a Review Exercise which provides further practice at the standard level of difficulty. However, later questions marked with a star* are deliberately rather more challenging.

Calculators

Throughout the book the need for a calculator is indicated by the following symbols:

means that a calculator is prohibited;

means that a calculator is permitted.

The ability to solve certain types of question without using a calculator is tested both at Key Stage 3 and at GCSE. It is important to show all your working, so that the examiner can see exactly what you did in order to obtain your answer. Remember that incorrect answers can still score method marks, provided your working is clear and sensible.

Self-check answers

To allow you to check that you fully understand a topic, key questions have been marked with the symbol . This means that the answer to this question is in the back of the book. Once you have thoroughly attempted such a question, check the answer before completing the rest of the exercise. Ask your teacher for help if you do not understand any particular key question.

Using and applying mathematics

AT1 (Using and Applying Mathematics) is embedded within many of the activities within this book, but it is likely that your teacher will use coursework-style tasks to develop this further. Watch for the opportunity to describe number patterns using algebra when you write up your coursework; the skills you will need are rehearsed in Unit 26. Other Units with special relevance to coursework or GCSE examinations are indicated in the appropriate summary.

Finally, remember the importance of regular homework. You will work hard in class to master the skills covered in this book, but, like any skills, they are easily lost again unless you keep in practice. This Key Stage 3 Mathematics Classbook will give you plenty of opportunity to practise all the core skills up to Level 6. It will help you achieve a strong platform of mathematical skills across the syllabus by the time you reach the end of Key Stage 3.

Level 4 Unit 1
Place value and powers of 10

In this Unit you will learn how to:

- ■ write a number in words, if it is given to you in figures;
- ■ write a number in figures, if it is given to you in words;
- ■ add and subtract whole numbers without a calculator;
- ■ multiply and divide by 10 or 100 without a calculator.

A calculator should not be used in this Unit, except perhaps for checking.

1.1 Place value

Our number system works in base 10. Each figure in a number has a place value – units, tens, hundreds etc. The place values change by a factor of 10 as you move from one column to the next.

Example   Sarfraz looks at the number 3842.
He wants to read the number out loud. What should he say?

Solution

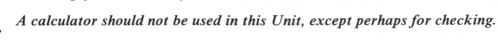

1000	100	10	1
3	8	4	2

> These are the place values.
> The units are on the right-hand end.
> Multiply by 10 each time you move one column to the left.

The 3 means three thousand.
The 8 means eight hundred.
The 4 means four tens or forty.
The 2 means two units.

Sarfraz should say 'three thousand, eight hundred and forty-two'.

Example   Write in figures 'twelve thousand, four hundred and thirty-two'.

Solution   Begin by drawing up a set of place value headings:

10 000	1000	100	10	1

Twelve thousand, …

10 000	1000	100	10	1
1	2			

... four hundred and thirty-two.

10 000	1000	100	10	1
1	2	4	3	2

The final answer is written 1 2 432.

> The figures (or digits) are grouped in blocks of three. Do not use commas.

Exercise 1.1

Write in figures:

1 Four thousand, two hundred and sixty-six
2 ✔ Thirteen thousand, five hundred and ninety-three
3 Eleven thousand, four hundred and five
4 Twenty thousand, nine hundred and seven
5 Thirty-three thousand, one hundred and eight
6 Nine thousand and eighty
7 Five thousand and forty-nine
8 Thirteen thousand, two hundred
9 ✔ Twenty thousand and three
10 Seven hundred thousand and fifty-six.

Write in words:

11 6394	**12** 7032	**13** 12 342	**14** ✔ 63 207
15 90 265	**16** 14 205	**17** 7073	**18** 10 005
19 67 256	**20** ✔ 32 067		

1.2 Addition and subtraction of whole numbers

You have probably had plenty of practice at adding or subtracting whole numbers, using 'carry' or 'exchange' where necessary. When adding and subtracting make sure that the place values line up, as in these examples.

Example   Add three hundred and sixty-five to seven thousand, nine hundred and eleven.

Give your answer in words.

Solution   The numbers are 365 and 7911.

1000	100	10	1
	3	6	5
7	9	1	1

> Write one number underneath the other.
> Make sure the place values line up.

1000	100	10	1
	3	6	5
7	9	1	1
1	2	7	6

Add the units, then the 10s, then the 100s and so on. Here $3 + 9 = 12$ so the 1 is carried across to the next column…

1000	100	10	1
	3	6	5
7	9	1	1
8₁	2	7	6

… and here is the final result.

The answer is eight thousand, two hundred and seventy-six.

Example Take 2391 away from 4672.

Solution There are two different methods for dealing with the 'exchange'. Use whichever one you have seen before.

Method 1

1000	100	10	1
4	6	7	2
2	3	9	1
			1

Start by subtracting in the units column …

1000	100	10	1
4	⁵6̸	¹7	2
2	3	9	1
			1

… then move to the 10s. An 'exchange' is needed here – there are two different ways of doing it.

1000	100	10	1
4	⁵6̸	¹7	2
2	3	9	1
2	2	8	1

Finish by subtracting the 10s, then the 100s, then the 1000s.

Method 2

1000	100	10	1
4	6	7	2
2	3	9	1
			1

1000	100	10	1
4	6	¹7	2
2	⁴3̸	9	1
			1

1000	100	10	1
4	6	¹7	2
2	⁴3̸	9	1
2	2	8	1

So $4672 - 2391 = \underline{2281}$

Exercise 1.2

Work out these additions and subtractions.

1 $2592 + 1377$ **2** $147 + 174$ **3** ✔ $39\,733 + 56\,882$

4 $2877 + 506$ **5** $5644 + 6729$ **6** $1277 - 1146$

7 $4672 - 1950$ **8** ✔ $12\,577 - 9769$ **9** $329 - 77$

Work out these additions and subtractions. In each case write the answer in words.

10 $471 + 229$

11 $6529 + 3382$

12 $176 - 92$

13 $3396 - 1839$

14 ✔ $12\,376 + 9428$

15 $2786 - 292$

16 $468\,774 + 399\,235$

17 ✔ $23\,967 - 4750$

18 $2785 - 1493$

19 $85\,113 + 24\,278$

20 $64\,307 - 4982$

1.3 Multiplying and dividing by 10 or 100

If you multiply a whole number by 10 then all the digits move one place to the left. If you multiply by 100 the digits move two places to the left. In division the digits move to the right instead.

Example   Work out 3753×100.

Solution   The digits all move two places to the left, like this:

100 000	10 000	1000	100	10	1
		3	7	5	3
3	7	5	3	0	0

Two extra zeroes come in here as the digits have all moved two places left.

$3753 \times 100 = \underline{375\,300}$

Example   Divide $23\,600$ by 10.

Solution $23\,600 \div 10 = \underline{2360}$
The digits move one place to the right

Example
Multiply 7000 by 200.

2 zeroes

3 zeroes

Solution $7 \times 2 = 14$
$\therefore 7000 \times 2 = 14\,000$
$\therefore 7000 \times 200 = \underline{1\,400\,000}$

$3 + 2 = 5$ zeroes

The symbol $\therefore$ means **therefore**.

Exercise 1.3

Work out these multiplications and divisions:

1 452×100 **2** 2506×10 **3** $13\,866 \times 100$

4 455×10 **5** ✔ 6370×100 **6** ✔ $23\,900 \div 10$

7 $9060 \div 10$ **8** $450\,000 \div 100$ **9** $12\,000 \div 10$

Work out these multiplications and divisions. In each case write the answer in words.

10 $93\,000\,000 \div 100$ **11** 1600×10 **12** 500×10

13 $1800 \div 10$ **14** $25\,000 \div 100$ **15** ✔ 830×100

16 ✔ $640\,000 \div 100$ **17** 2000×100 **18** $14\,000 \div 100$

19 $450\,000 \div 100$ **20** $20\,000 \times 10$

Summary

In this Unit you have practised writing numbers in figures and in words. You have practised adding and subtracting whole numbers without a calculator, ensuring that place values (e.g. the units) line up.

You have also learnt how to multiply and divide by 10 or 100 without a calculator. This is an important skill, which may be tested (without a calculator) as part of either a Key Stage 3 or GCSE examination.

Review Exercise 1

1 Write in figures:
   a) Twelve thousand, four hundred and one
   b) Sixty-five thousand, seven hundred and four
   c) Sixty-three thousand and ninety
   d) Four hundred and two thousand, six hundred and eleven
   e) Five thousand and forty.

2 Write in words:
   a) $22\,301$ **b)** $450\,207$ **c)** $50\,056$ **d)** $103\,246$ **e)** 7209

Work out these additions and subtractions:

3 $45\,203 + 2948$ **4** $8699 + 7546$ **5** $14\,203 - 9731$

6 $1577 - 899$ **7** $9622 + 1379$ **8** $12\,788 - 9949$

9 $23\,577 + 72\,845$ **10** $12\,003 - 9844$ **11** $1035 + 44\,396$

Work out these multiplications and divisions:

12 6000×100

13 800×10

14 5000×100

15 $4000 \div 100$

16 $6000 \div 10$

17 $226\,000 \times 100$

18 $226\,000 \div 100$

19 7000×100

20* $16\,000 \div 200$

21* The number of people attending each of four football matches are 26 409, 31 322, 17 488 and 29 277. Find the total number of people who attended.

22* The caterers at an open-air concert provided meals for 7500 people, but 11 277 people turned up. All the meals were sold. How many of the concert-goers were unable to buy a meal?

23* The three volumes of a set of guide books contain 686, 722 and 692 pages.
 a) How many pages are there in total?
 b) If the volumes are reprinted so that they are all the same length, how many pages will each volume contain?

24* A machine sorts plastic bricks into bags of 200. There are 46 000 bricks altogether. How many bags can be filled?

25* The Hundred Years War started in 1337 and finished in 1453. For how many years did it last?

26* An airline owns 20 aircraft, and each aircraft can carry 243 passengers. How many passengers can all the aircraft carry in total?

27* Huw has a broken calculator. Five of the eight digits on the LCD display are damaged and cannot be read; they are shown by # marks in the diagram. Huw keys in a four-digit number and this is what he sees on the display:

#	#	#	#	3	#	2	6

Huw multiplies this number by 100. Draw the result that he sees on the calculator display.

28* A toner cartridge in my office photocopier needs replacing every 8000 copies, on average. Last year it used 20 cartridges. Calculate the number of copies which were made during the year.

29* A ski resort charges 954 francs for an adult ski-pass and 816 francs for a child. Find the total cost for a family of two adults and three children. Give your final answer in francs, and also give a rough answer in pounds, using the fact that 10 francs is about £1.

30* The sizes of computer files are often measured in kilobytes (kB). I have six files, whose sizes are 232 kB, 154 kB, 277 kB, 449 kB, 185 kB and 228 kB. Find the total size of the six files in kilobytes.
 My hard disk has enough spare space to store 2 megabytes (a megabyte is 1000 kB). Explain carefully how you can tell whether there is enough spare space to store these six files.

Unit 2
Numbers and number patterns

In this Unit you will learn how to:
- use mental recall of multiplication facts up to 10×10;
- recognise factors and multiples;
- identify prime numbers;
- describe and extend number patterns.

A calculator should not be used in this Unit, except perhaps for checking.

2.1 Multiplication up to 10×10

You have probably learnt some of the basic 'times tables' – especially the $2 \times$ and $5 \times$ tables.

The tables up to $10 \times$ are shown in this multiplication square:

	1	2	3	4	5	6	7	8	9	10
1	1	2	3	4	5	6	7	8	9	10
2	2	4	6	8	10	12	14	16	18	20
3	3	6	9	12	15	18	21	24	27	30
4	4	8	12	16	20	24	28	32	36	40
5	5	10	15	20	25	30	35	40	45	50
6	6	12	18	24	30	36	42	48	54	60
7	7	14	21	28	35	42	49	56	63	70
8	8	16	24	32	40	48	56	64	72	80
9	9	18	27	36	45	54	63	72	81	90
10	10	20	30	40	50	60	70	80	90	100

Example Find the value of 3×7.

Solution Looking **along** the '3' row and **down** the '7' column:

	1	2	3	4	5	6	⑦	8	9	10
1	1	2	3	4	5	6	7	8	9	10
2	2	4	6	8	10	12	14	16	18	20
③	3	6	9	12	15	18	㉑	24	27	30

So $3 \times 7 = 21$.

Learn the tables in the multiplication square. Then cover up the square, and find the values of these:

1 ✔ 4×8 **2** 6×5 **3** 3×3 **4** 7×2

5 5×5 **6** 3×4 **7** 6×5 **8** ✔ 3×8

9 7×7 **10** 9×4 **11** 6×3 **12** 9×7

2.2 Factors and multiples

Multiples are found by looking along a multiplication square.
For example, the multiples of 2 are 2, 4, 6, 8, 10 and so on.

The multiplication square only gives the first ten multiples; they do carry on after this, without limit.

Example   Write down the first five multiples of 7.

Solution   Using the square, the multiples are 7, 14, 21, 28, 35.

Example   Is 44 a multiple of 8?

Solution   Look along the '8' row:

8	8	16	24	32	40	48	56	64	72	80

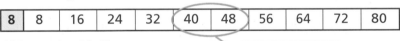

44 is not in this list.
Therefore 44 is not a multiple of 8.   44 is not here

Example   Is 72 a multiple of 6 ?

72 is beyond the end of these numbers.

Solution   Look along the '6' row:

6	6	12	18	24	30	36	42	48	54	60

Continuing past 60 in jumps of 6 we get more multiples of 6:
60, 66, 72, 78 …

72 is a multiple of 6.

A number is a **factor** of a second number if it divides exactly into it, with no remainder. The second number is a **multiple** of the first one.

Example   Is 4 a factor of 20?

Solution   Turn the question round: is 20 a multiple of 4?
Looking along the multiplication square in the '4' row we can see that 20 is a multiple of 4.

Therefore 4 is a factor of 20.

Example   Find all the factors of 20.

Solution   From the multiplication square, $2 \times 10 = 20$ and $4 \times 5 = 20$.
You can also make 20 using $1 \times 20 = 20$.

Therefore the factors of 20 are 1, 2, 4, 5, 10 and 20.

Exercise 2.2
Write down:

1 The first three multiples of 5.   **2** The first five multiples of 3.
3 ✔ The first four multiples of 9   **4** The first three multiples of 8.
5 The first six multiples of 7.   **6** Is 72 a multiple of 9?
7 Is 87 a multiple of 7?   **8** Is 42 a multiple of 3?
9 ✔ Is 38 a multiple of 6?   **10** Is 75 a multiple of 5?
11 Is 6 a factor of 18?   **12** Is 3 a factor of 23 ?
13 Is 5 a factor of 52?   **14** ✔ Is 7 a factor of 42?
15 Is 8 a factor of 52?

Find all the factors of:

16 12   **17** 15   **18** ✔ 16   **19** 18   **20** 30

2.3 Prime numbers

The number 7 is a **prime** number because it only has two factors, itself and 1
$1 \times 7 = 7$.

The number 8 is not a prime number.
$1 \times 8 = 8$
and $2 \times 4 = 8$.

so 8 has four factors: 1, 2, 4 and 8.

8 is a **composite** number; it has more than two factors.

The number 1 has only one factor: $1 \times 1 = 1$, so it is neither a prime number
nor a composite number.

Here are some facts about prime numbers:

■ The first few primes are 2, 3, 5, 7, 11, 13, 17
■ Apart from 2, all prime numbers are **odd.**
■ The prime numbers do not appear inside the multiplication square,
except under the $1 \times$ heading.
■ There are infinitely many prime numbers, but mathematicians have
not yet discovered an easy way of detecting the very large ones.

Example   Find all the prime numbers between 30 and 40.

Solution   Since all the primes (apart from the first one) are odd, we need to consider the numbers 31, 33, 35, 37, 39.

33 is a multiple of 3, because $3 \times 11 = 33$.
35 is a multiple of 5, because $5 \times 7 = 35$.
39 is a multiple of 3, because $3 \times 13 = 39$.

It is not possible to find factors of 31 or 37.

$\therefore$ Prime numbers between 30 and 40 are 31 and 37.

Exercise 2.3

1 Find the next prime number after 17.

2 Find all the prime numbers between 20 and 30.

3 Decide whether 15 is prime or composite.

4 Decide whether 41 is prime or composite.

5 ✔ Decide whether 73 is prime or composite.

6 ✔ Find the next prime number after 53.

7 ✔ Find all the prime numbers between 40 and 50.

8 ✔ Decide whether 27 is prime or composite.

9 Decide whether 79 is prime or composite.

10 Decide whether 81 is prime or composite.

2.4 Number patterns

Number patterns follow a rule. Once you have worked out the rule you can find more numbers to continue the pattern.

Example   Explain the rule that is being used to make this number pattern, and find the next two numbers:

3   6   9   12   15   __   __

Solution   The numbers start at 3 and go up 3 at a time.

The next two numbers are 18 and 21.

Example   Describe the rule that makes this number pattern, and find the next two numbers:

3   8   7   12   11   __   __

Solution   Starting at 3, the pattern goes up 5, down 1, up 5, down 1.

Continuing this way, the next two numbers will be 16 and 15.

Example   The diagrams show **square** numbers.

Draw the next two diagrams, and find the next two square numbers in the pattern.

• 1   • • 4   • • • 9
             • •   • • •
                            • • •

Solution   The next two patterns are  and

The next two square numbers are 16 and 25.

Exercise 2.4

For each of these number patterns, describe in words the rule that is being used. Then find the next two numbers in the pattern.

1 4, 8, 12, 16, __, __   **2** 10, 12, 14, 16, 18, __, __

3 ✔ 6, 11, 16, 21, __, __   **4** 60, 55, 50, 45, 40, __, __

5 ✔ 100, 97, 94, 91, 88 __, __   **6** 1, 4, 9, 16, 25 __, __

7 1, 10, 11, 20, 21, __, __   **8** ✔ 1, 2, 4, 8, 16, __, __

9 1, 2, 4, 7, 11, __, __

10 Triangular numbers can be found by using patterns like these:

Continue this sequence of diagrams to find the next four triangular numbers:

1   3   6   __   __   __   __

Summary

In this Unit you have learnt the multiplication tables up to 10×10. You have found factors and multiples of simple numbers.

You have learnt to recognise a prime number as one which has only two factors; itself and 1. 1 is not a prime number. The first few primes are 2, 3, 5, 7, 11 …

You have learnt to describe and extend number patterns. It is often helpful to look at the size of the jump as you move from one number to the next.

Review Exercise 2

Write down the answers to these multiplications:

1 9×2	**2** 6×9	**3** 8×8	**4** 3×7
5 4×8	**6** 7×5	**7** 4×4	**8** 5×7
9 6×8	**10** 8×5	**11** 7×4	**12** 9×9

13 Is 32 a multiple of 6?   **14** Is 7 a factor of 54?

15 Is 39 a prime number?   **16** Find all the factors of 14.

17 Is 84 a multiple of 7?   **18** Is 9 a factor of 57?

19 Is 69 a prime number?   **20** Find all the factors of 32.

Describe in words the rule for each of these number patterns, and find the next number in each:

21 10, 13, 16, 19, 22, __   **22** 10, 13, 17, 22, 28, __   **23** 90, 81, 72, 63, 54, __

24 1, 9, 8, 16, 15, __   **25** 1, 3, 9, 27, 81, __

26*Gerald says 'I have written down a two-digit prime number. The number is between 30 and 50 and the two digits add up to 7'. What number did Gerald write down?

27*Jayne says 'I have written down a two-digit prime number. The units digit is larger than the tens digit, and the number lies between 60 and 70'. What number did Jayne write down?

28*(Activity) A classic method for finding prime numbers is the *Sieve of Eratosthenes*. This is how it works.

Start with a number grid – for example all the numbers from 1 to 100.

1	2	3	4	5	6	7	8	9	10
11	12	13	14	15	16	17	18	19	20
21	22	23	24	25	26	27	28	29	30

- Cross out the number 1.
- Put a ring around the lowest number which is not yet crossed out (it should be 2).
- Cross out all the multiples of 2.
- Put a ring around the lowest number which is not yet crossed out (it should be 3).
- Cross out all the multiples of 3.
- Put a ring around the lowest number which is not yet crossed out (it should be 5).
- Cross out all the multiples of 5.
- Put a ring around the lowest number which is not yet crossed out (it should be 7).

- Cross out all the multiples of 7.
- Now stop, and put a ring around every number which has not yet been crossed out.
- Finally, make a list of the ringed numbers. You should obtain all the primes up to 100.

[Note: You can find all the primes up to 200 by using a larger grid. In this case you need to strike out all the multiples of 2, 3, 5, 7, 11 and 13 before ringing the remaining numbers.]

Unit 3
Fractions and percentages

In this Unit you will learn how to:
- recognise approximate fractions of a whole;
- use simple percentages;
- work with equivalent fractions.

A calculator should not be used in this Unit, except perhaps for checking.

3.1 Fractions of a whole

A fraction contains two whole numbers, one over the other.

The bottom number is the **denominator** – it tells you how many equal parts the whole amount is divided into.

The top number is the **numerator** – it tells you how many of these parts to count.

Example   What fraction of this circle is coloured?

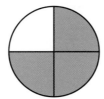

Solution   There are 4 equal parts. 3 of them are coloured.
Therefore $\frac{3}{4}$ of the circle is coloured.

Example   What fraction of this rectangle is coloured?

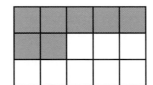

Solution   There are 15 equal parts. 7 of them are coloured.
Therefore $\frac{7}{15}$ of the rectangle is coloured.

Exercise 3.1

Write down fractions to describe the coloured portion in each of these diagrams:

1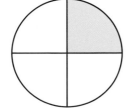

2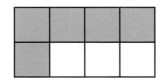

3 ✔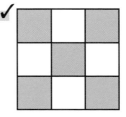

4

5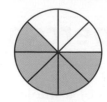

6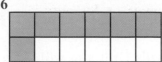

7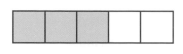

8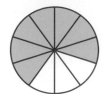

9

10 ✓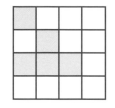

3.2 Equivalent fractions

Look at these diagrams:

 $\frac{3}{4}$ $\frac{6}{8}$

The coloured portion is exactly the same in both, so $\frac{3}{4}$ is the same as $\frac{6}{8}$.

Fractions like $\frac{3}{4}$ and $\frac{6}{8}$ are called **equivalent fractions.**

You can use simple arithmetic to find equivalent fractions, as in these three examples.

Example Find two other fractions which are equivalent to $\frac{3}{5}$

Solution Start with $\frac{3}{5}$ and multiply both numbers by 2:

$\frac{3 \times 2}{5 \times 2} = \frac{6}{10}$

Start with $\frac{3}{5}$ and multiply both numbers by 3:

$\frac{3 \times 3}{5 \times 3} = \frac{9}{15}$

$\frac{3}{5}$ is equivalent to $\frac{6}{10}$ and $\frac{9}{15}$.

There are also many others.

Example Find the missing number if $\frac{5}{8} = \frac{20}{\ast}$.

Solution 5 has been multiplied by 4 to make 20.
Doing the same on the bottom, $8 \times 4 = 32$.
The missing number is 32.
$\frac{5}{8} = \frac{20}{32}$

Example   Simplify $\frac{10}{12}$.

> Here 'simplify' means that you should reduce the fraction down to its simplest possible form.

Solution   10 and 12 can both be divided by 2 to obtain 5 and 6 respectively.

Therefore $\frac{10}{12} = \frac{5}{6}$.

Exercise 3.2

1 Find two other fractions which are equivalent to $\frac{1}{3}$.

2 Find two other fractions which are equivalent to $\frac{3}{7}$.

3 ✔ Find three other fractions which are equivalent to $\frac{4}{9}$.

4 Find the missing number if $\frac{3}{4} = \frac{30}{\ast}$.

5 Find the missing number if $\frac{7}{8} = \frac{\ast}{24}$.

6 ✔ Find the missing number if $\frac{2}{11} = \frac{8}{\ast}$

7 Simplify $\frac{2}{8}$.   **8** Simplify $\frac{10}{15}$.   **9** Simplify $\frac{30}{40}$.   **10** ✔ Simplify $\frac{24}{28}$.

3.3 Percentages

> 'Per cent' means 'out of 100'. The symbol for 'per cent' is %.
>
> 100% represents a complete whole.

Example   What percentage of this circle is coloured?

Solution   There are four equal parts.
$100\% \div 4 = 25\%$

So 25% is coloured.

Example   What percentage is coloured in this diagram?

Solution   There are five equal parts.
$100\% \div 5 = 20\%$

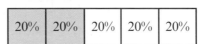

Two parts are coloured.
$2 \times 20\% = 40$

So 40 % is shaded.

Exercise 3.3
Find the percentage that has been shaded in each of these diagrams:

1

2 ✔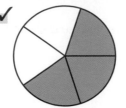

3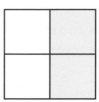

4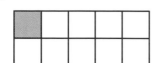

5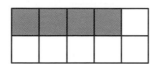

6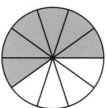

Summary

In this Unit you have learnt how to recognise fractions and percentages of a whole shape.

You have also learnt how to find equivalent fractions, and you have simplified fractions by rewriting them using the lowest possible numbers.

Review Exercise 3
Write down the fraction that is coloured in each of these diagrams:

1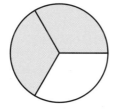

2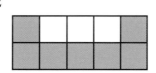

3

4

5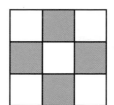

6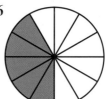

Copy these diagrams and shade the given fraction:

7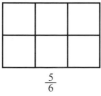
$\frac{5}{6}$

8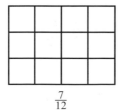
$\frac{7}{12}$

9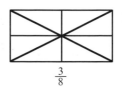
$\frac{3}{8}$

10
$\frac{1}{6}$

Simplify these fractions:

11 $\frac{21}{24}$ **12** $\frac{35}{45}$ **13** $\frac{18}{30}$ **14** $\frac{27}{63}$

Find the missing number in each list of equivalent fractions:

15 $\frac{3}{8}, \frac{6}{16}, \frac{9}{24}, \frac{12}{\ast}, \frac{30}{80}$ **16** $\frac{2}{5}, \frac{4}{10}, \frac{6}{15}, \frac{\ast}{25}$

Find the odd one out in each list:

17 $\frac{1}{4}, \frac{2}{8}, \frac{3}{12}, \frac{5}{16}, \frac{10}{40}, \frac{12}{48}$ **18** $\frac{2}{3}, \frac{7}{10}, \frac{14}{20}, \frac{35}{50}$

Write down the percentage that is coloured in each of these diagrams:

19  **20**  **21**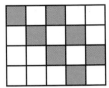

22*Nazim got 16 out of 20 questions right in a spelling test. What fraction of the questions did Nazim get right?

23*Annya scored 17 out of 20 in a mathematics test. What percentage is this?

24*Martin and Natalie are looking at a shape:

20% of the shape is shaded

$\frac{1}{5}$ of the shape is shaded

Could they **both** be right? Why?

25*Usha and Ramon are looking at a shape:

40% of the shape is shaded

$\frac{4}{9}$ of the shape is shaded

Could they **both** be right? Why?

Select the fraction that best describes this amount:

26*  $\frac{1}{2}, \frac{2}{3}, \frac{9}{10}$

Select the percentage that best describes this amount:

27*  3%, 30%, 50%, 70%

Unit 4
Working with decimals

In this Unit you will learn how to:
- recognise the relationship between simple fractions and decimals;
- add and subtract numbers given to two places of decimals;
- order decimals to three places;
- solve problems using decimals.

 A calculator should not be used in this Unit, except perhaps for checking.

4.1 Introducing decimal notation

> Fractions expressed in tenths can also be written using **decimal notation**.
> For example, one-tenth is the same as 0.1.
> Similarly, seven-tenths is the same as 0.7.
> The number after the decimal point tells you how many tenths there are.

Example   Write these numbers as decimals:

a) three-tenths; **b)** nine-tenths   **c)** six and seven-tenths.

Solution   a) Three-tenths = 0.3

b) Nine-tenths = 0.9

c) Six and seven-tenths = 6.7

Example   Write these decimals as fractions:

a) 0.9   **b)** 2.1   **c)** 3.7

Solution   a) $0.9 = \frac{9}{10}$

b) $2.1 = 2\frac{1}{10}$

c) $3.7 = 3\frac{7}{10}$

If there are two places of decimals then the two places represent tenths and hundredths respectively.

Example   Write four and thirteen-hundredths:

a) as a fraction, using figures;

b) as a decimal.

Solution   a) $4\frac{13}{100}$

b) 4.13

Exercise 4.1

Write these as decimals:

1 Seven-tenths

2 Six and one-tenth

3 ✔ One and nine-tenths

4 Four and seven-tenths

5 Two and three-tenths

6 Ten and seven-tenths.

Write these as decimals:

7 $2\frac{9}{10}$

8 $1\frac{1}{10}$

9 $6\frac{7}{10}$

10 ✔ $4\frac{3}{10}$

11 $5\frac{7}{10}$

12 $12\frac{9}{10}$

Write these as decimals:

13 Eleven-hundredths

14 One and seven-hundredths

15 ✔ Six and thirty-nine-hundredths

16 Twenty and forty-nine-hundredths.

Write these as decimals:

17 ✔ $5\frac{67}{100}$

18 $8\frac{91}{100}$

19 $3\frac{19}{100}$

20 $5\frac{7}{100}$

4.2 Using decimals

Decimals arise naturally when working with metric units, since these units are related by factors of 10. For example, 10 millimetres (mm) make 1 centimetre (cm), so if you change millimetres into centimetres then you may encounter decimals.

Example   Tomi has measured the length of a leaf as 142 mm. She wants to write this in centimetres. What should Tomi write?

Solution   Think of 142 mm as 140 mm + 2 mm.
140 mm can be written as 14 cm.
2 millimetres can be written as $\frac{2}{10}$ or 0.2 cm.

So 142 mm = 14.2 cm

Example   Adam measures the diameter of his wrist as 108 mm. Write this in centimetres.

Note the quick way of doing this question. Insert a decimal point, but keep the figures 1, 0, 8 in the same order as before.

Solution   108 mm = 10.8 cm

Example   Anne measures the length of a table as 213 cm. Write this in metres.

Solution   213 cm = 2.13 m

Again, keep the figures 2, 1, 3 in order. 200 cm would be 2 m, so it is easy to see that 213 cm is 2.13 m.

Exercise 4.2

1 ✔ Write 325 mm in centimetres. 2 Write 208 mm in centimetres.

3 Write 144 mm in centimetres. 4 Write 91 mm in centimetres.

5 Write 256 cm in metres. 6 Write 155 cm in metres.

7 Write 310 cm in metres. 8 ✔ Write 13 cm in metres.

9 Katya's hockey stick is 133 cm long. Rewrite this measurement in metres.

10 Leroy has measured the length and breadth of a rectangle as 45 mm and 27 mm. Rewrite these measurements so that they are in centimetres.

4.3 Adding and subtracting decimals

Decimals are added and subtracted in the same way as whole numbers. Make sure that you line up the decimal points in all the numbers.

Example   Add 16.3 and 7.2.

Solution   Write out an addition, lining up the decimal points:

10	1		$\frac{1}{10}$
1	6	.	3
+	7	.	2

Then add up just as if these were whole numbers:

10	1		$\frac{1}{10}$
1	6	.	3
+	7	.	2
2	3	.	5

$16.3 + 7.2 = \underline{23.5}$

Sometimes you need to insert an extra zero to make sure the numbers line up at the decimal point.

Example   Work out 32.5 – 19.14.

Solution   Write 32.5 as 32.50 so that both numbers have two decimal places.

10	1		$\frac{1}{10}$	$\frac{1}{100}$
3	2	.	5	0
– 1	9	.	1	4
1	3	.	3	6

$32.5 + 19.14 = \underline{13.36}$

Example   Alex has £34.77. He spends £16.83. How much money does he have left?

Solution

10	1		$\frac{1}{10}$	$\frac{1}{100}$
3	4	.	7	7
− 1	6	.	8	3
1	7	.	9	4

> Remember to include the £ sign when you write the final answer to a question about money.

He has £17.94 left

Exercise 4.3

Work out these sums. Do not use a calculator:

1 14.1 + 3.8   **2** 25.6 + 19.7   **3** 1.3 + 0.8

4 ✔ 44.2 + 18.6   **5** ✔ 12.8 − 9.3   **6** 45.2 − 17.3

7 16.1 − 9.2   **8** 142.8 − 29.1   **9** 12.63 + 9.48

10 67.2 + 13.89   **11** 14.81 − 1.49   **12** 66.27 − 14.98

13 ✔ 63.6 − 9.41   **14** ✔ 14.82 + 18.42   **15** 77.06 − 67.6

16 Add together £10.99 and £13.99.

17 Add together £11.61 and £6.40.

18 Take £2.44 from £5.28.

19 Jim has £46.25. He spends £13.76. How much money does he have left?

20 ✔ Tessa has £55.30. She buys a hat, and then finds she has £38.31 left. How much did she pay for the hat?

4.4 Ordering decimals

Sometimes you need to arrange a list of decimals in order of size. Compare the figures in the higher place value positions first, that is those towards the left of the number.

Example   Arrange in increasing order of size: 2.512, 2.205, 2.56, 2.7, 2.562

Solution   Writing the numbers so the place values line up:

$$\begin{array}{ccccc} 1 & & \frac{1}{10} & \frac{1}{100} & \frac{1}{1000} \\ 2 & . & 5 & 1 & 2 \\ 2 & . & 2 & 0 & 5 \\ 2 & . & 5 & 6 & \\ 2 & . & 7 & & \\ 2 & . & 5 & 6 & 2 \end{array}$$

| These figures in the units column are all equal … | … so you look at the figures in the $\frac{1}{10}$ column next … | … and so on across the place values. |

The sorted list becomes:

$$\begin{array}{ccccc} 2 & . & 2 & 0 & 5 \\ 2 & . & 5 & 1 & 2 \\ 2 & . & 5 & 6 & \\ 2 & . & 5 & 6 & 2 \\ 2 & . & 7 & & \end{array}$$

In increasing order of size the decimals are: <u>2.205, 2.512, 2.56, 2.562, 2.7</u>

Exercise 4.4

Arrange each of these lists of decimals in order of size, smallest first.

1 5.202, 5.221, 5.51, 5.251, 5.502

2 ✓ 3.21, 3.003, 3.209, 3.3, 3.01

3 0.725, 0.527, 0.75, 0.57, 0.572

4 1.55, 1.402, 1.541, 1.45, 1.425

5 10.66, 10.655, 10.665, 10.656, 10.555

Arrange each of these lists of decimals in order of size, largest first.

6 ✓ 0.365, 0.42, 0.37, 0.415, 0.4

7 0.084, 0.07, 0.091, 0.019, 0.08

8 12.5, 12.44, 12.477, 12.407, 12.4

9 1.55, 1.485, 1.5, 1.49, 1.51

10 0.772, 0.727, 0.277, 0.707

Summary

In this Unit you have learnt how to write decimals using one or two decimal places. The first decimal place tells you the number of tenths, the second the number of hundredths.

You have also learnt to add and subtract decimals, taking care to line up the two numbers at the decimal points. Arithmetic with two decimal places often occurs in questions about money.

You have learnt how to order decimals to three places, by looking at the digits in the units column, then the tenths, and so on across the numbers.

Review Exercise 4

1 Write as decimals:
   a) three and one-tenth;   **b)** four and sixty-one-hundredths;
   c) five and four-hundredths.

2 Write as decimals:
   a) $1\frac{1}{10}$ **b)** $1\frac{1}{100}$ **c)** $1\frac{11}{100}$ **d)** $4\frac{17}{100}$ **e)** $2\frac{71}{100}$

3 Write in centimetres:
   a) 164 mm   **b)** 91 mm   **c)** 1.21 m   **d)** 0.77 m   **e)** 0.02 m

Work out these additions and subtractions:

4 $16.3 + 8.9$ **5** $71.6 - 52.4$ **6** $12.35 + 7.28$
7 $96.11 - 47.83$ **8** $12.1 - 9.09$ **9** $63.8 - 38.6$
10 $12.9 + 1.09$

11 Arrange these four numbers in order of size, smallest first.
   0.799, 0.77, 0.701, 0.797

12 Arrange these six numbers in order of size, largest first.
   3.566, 3.503, 3.53, 3.536, 3.635, 3.6

13 The table shows some results from a school athletics day:

100 Metres		Triple Jump	
Joel	15.23 secs	Courtney	6.251 metres
Marcel	14.77 secs	Damini	6.521 metres
Norman	15.08 secs	Mercedes	6.35 metres
Tony	14.91 secs	Stacey	6.509 metres
Vinay	15.03 secs	Virginia	6.348 metres

a) Who came first in the 100 metres?

b) Who came third in the triple jump?

c) Who came next after Vinay in the 100 metres?

d) Who won the triple jump?

e) Homan was injured and so could not take part in the 100 metres. He can usually run this event in 15.15 seconds. In what position do you think Homan would have finished if he had been fit enough to take part?

14* Melissa is driving a taxi. When she sets off on a journey the distance meter on the instrument panel looks like this:

| 1 | 8 | 6 | 2 | 4 | 3 |

This means that the taxi has travelled 18 624.3 kilometres.

At the end of her journey the meter looks like this:

| 1 | 8 | 6 | 5 | 9 | 5 |

How far did Melissa travel during this journey?

15* Martin goes shopping with a £50 note. He spends £13.21 on clothes, £15.48 on food and £13.87 on stationery.

a) How much does Martin spend altogether?

b) How much money does Martin have after the shopping trip?

16* Three friends share out their winnings after a day at the races. One receives £7.27, another receives £4.87 and the third one receives £3.66.

a) How much did the three friends win in total?

b) How much would each have received if the winnings had been shared equally?

17* Charlene has a piece of wood which is 2.4 m long. She cuts off one piece which is half a metre long, another which is 0.45 m long and another which is 75 cm long.

a) Find the total length, in metres, of the three pieces.

b) Find the length, in centimetres, of the wood left over.

18* Mike goes on a walking trip in the Lake District. He walks 11.4 km on the first day, 18.5 km on the second day, 17.6 km on the third day and 9.3 km on the last day.

a) Find the total distance that Mike walks in the four days.

b) Mike could have covered the same total distance by walking equal distances each day. How far would he then have walked each day?

Unit 5
Coordinates

In this Unit you will learn how to:
- ■ use number pairs to describe the positions of points in a plane;
- ■ use and interpret (x, y) coordinates in the first quadrant.

A calculator is not needed in this Unit.

5.1 Number pairs

Number pairs can be used to describe the position of points on a plane (a flat 2-D surface).

A grid system on a map is a common example of the use of number pairs.

Example   The map of Treasure Island shows a Pirate Camp at (30, 40).

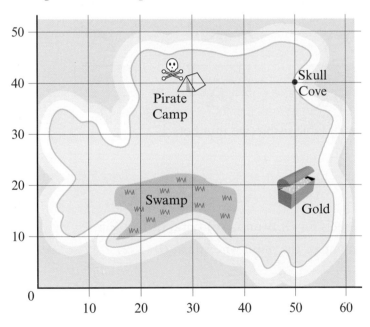

The 30 means go 30 across. The 40 means go 40 up.

Remember: always give the across number first … … then the up number.

a) What can be found at (50, 20)?

b) Why would it be dangerous for the pirates to visit (30, 20)?

c) The pirates need to meet their ship at Skull Cove. Write down the coordinates of Skull Cove.

Solution   a) At (50, 20) there is <u>gold</u>.

b) (30, 20) is in the <u>swamp</u>, so it would be dangerous to visit there.

c) Skull Cove is at <u>(50, 40)</u>

Example   The diagram shows a seating plan for class 4E's end of year mathematics test:

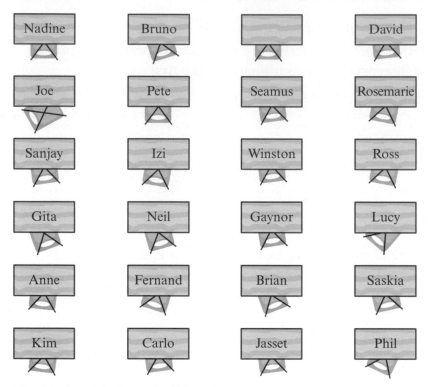

The teacher labels each table using two numbers.

Kim is at (1, 1)

Carlo is at (2, 1)

David is at (4, 6)

a) Write down the labels for **(i)** Bruno; **(ii)** Gita; **(iii)** Saskia.

b) Write down the name of the pupil who sits at **(i)** (2, 2); **(ii)** (4, 1); **(iii)** (4, 3).

c) On the day of the test a new pupil, Samir, joins the class. Write down the label for the table which Samir can use.

Solution

a)   **(i)** Bruno sits at (2, 6)

   (ii) Gita sits at (1, 3)

   (iii) Saskia sits at (4, 2)

b)   **(i)** Fernand sits at (2, 2)

   (ii) Phil sits at (4, 1)

   (iii) Lucy sits at (4, 3)

c) Samir can sit at (3, 6)

Exercise 5.1

1 ✔ The diagram shows the positions of the staff mail boxes in a staff room.

Each mail box is described by a number pair.

Mr Castro is at (1, 1).

Miss West is at (4, 2).

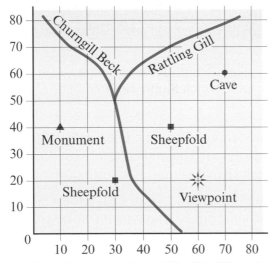

a) Mr Vincent is at the box immediately above Miss West. Write down the number pair for Mr Vincent's mail box.

b) Miss Patel is immediately to the left of Miss West. Write down the number pair for Miss Patel's mail box.

c) Mr Forsyth's mail box is at (2, 5) and Miss Hamilton's is at (2, 3). Mrs Grimes has a mail box which lies between Mr Forsyth's and Miss Hamilton's. Write down the number pair for Mrs Grimes' mail box.

2 The diagram below shows a map of the countryside. Alan is going on a walk in the area covered by this map.

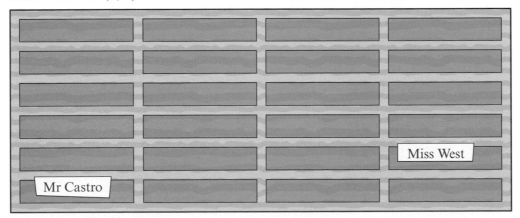

a) Alan visits the place (70, 60). What does he find there?

b) Write down a number pair to describe where the Monument is found.

c) Write down a number pair to describe the place where Rattling Gill and Churngill Beck meet.

d) Alan is told to meet another walker at a sheepfold. Write down number pairs to describe the two possible places where this meeting could be.

3   The diagram shows a small car park. Each parking space is labelled using a number pair.

The Porsche is parked in space (2, 1).

The Mini is parked in space (3, 3).

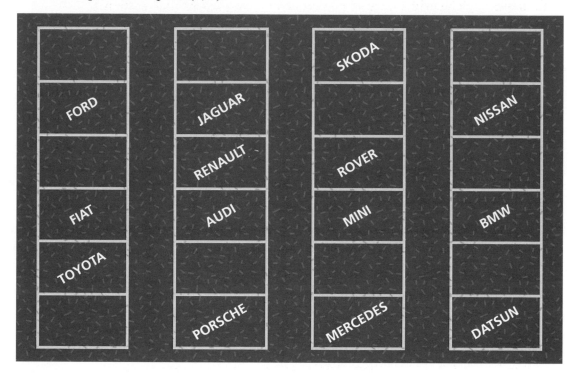

a) Which car is parked in space (2, 4)?

b) Which car is parked in (4, 3)?

c) Write down the labels for all the empty parking spaces.

4 (Activity) Draw a seating plan for your classroom. Write the names of the pupils in the correct places, and write number pairs to describe them. Is it easy to do this, or is there anything about your own classroom which makes this difficult to do?

5 (Activity) Make up a map of a desert island, similar to Treasure Island earlier in this Unit. Draw it on squared paper, and label a numbered grid. Write down some number pairs to describe certain places on your island, and see if your neighbour can find them on the map.

5.2 *x*- and *y*- coordinates

The **x-axis** is a straight line which runs from left to right.

The **y-axis** is a straight line which runs from bottom to top.

The *x*-axis and the *y*-axis cross at the **origin**, O.

Points are described by two numbers: *x*, then *y*.

For example (2, 3) means $x = 2$ and $y = 3$.

Example The grid shows some points on an *x-y* coordinate system.
A is at (2, 3).

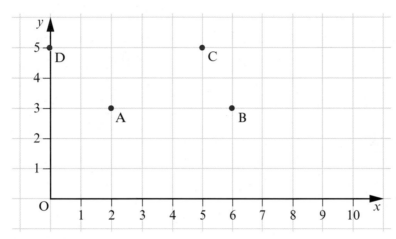

a) Write down the coordinates of B, C and D.

b) Mark the point E so that it is halfway between A and B.

c) Write down the coordinates of E.

Solution a) B is at (6, 3), C is at (5, 5) and D is at (0, 5).

b)

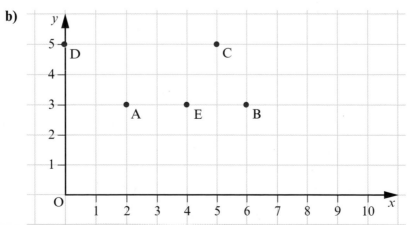

c) E is at (4, 3).

Exercise 5.2

1 ✔ Plot the points A (1, 1), B (4, 1), C (4, 4) and D (1, 4). What shape is formed by the four points?

2 Plot the points P (1, 1), Q (7, 1), R (7, 3) and S (1, 3). What shape is formed by the four points? The point M is exactly halfway between P and R. Plot the point M, and write down its coordinates.

3 Plot the points U (1, 3), V (3, 5) and W (5, 3). Add point X to your diagram so that the four points form a square. Write down the coordinates of X.

4 ✔ The four points A, B, C, D all lie in a straight line. They are A (2, 3), B (3, 4), C (✦) and D (5, 6). (The coordinates of C have accidentally been smudged.)

   a) Plot the points A, B and D.   **b)** Suggest coordinates for point C.

5 Draw a pair of coordinate axes in which x and y can each range from 0 to 10. A scale of 1 centimetre to 1 unit will work well for this question.

   Plot each of these four shapes on your coordinate axes:

   a) Join (2, 4) to (3, 2), then to (7, 2), then to (8, 4), then back to (2, 4).

   b) Join (4, 4) to (4, 9).

   c) Join (2, 5) to (4, 5), then to (4, 9), then back to (2, 5).

   d) Join (4, 5) to (7, 5), then to (4, 8), then back to (4, 5).

When you have finished you should have a picture. What do you think it is?

Summary

In this Unit you have practised describing the positions of points using number pairs, or coordinates.

Remember that in an *x-y* coordinate system the *x* (across) value is given first, then the *y* (up) value.

Review Exercise 5

1 A builder has been called out to replace some broken windows in a factory after a hurricane. The diagram shows which windows need to be replaced. The builder writes (2, 1) to describe Window A and (5, 4) to describe Window B.

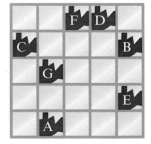

   a) Write down number pairs to describe Windows C, D and E.

   b) The window at (2, 3) is to be fitted with special toughened glass.
   Write down the letter corresponding to the position of this window.

2 Draw up a coordinate grid so that both the *x*-axis and the *y*-axis can run from 0 to 10. Follow these instructions:

a) Draw a line from (2, 4) to (2, 7).

b) Draw a line from (1, 7) to (3, 7).

c) Draw a line from (5, 4) to (5, 7).

d) Draw a line from (7, 4) to (7, 7), then (8, 6), then (9, 7), then (9, 4).

What name is spelt out?

3 Draw up a coordinate grid so that the *x*-axis can run from 0 to 12 and the *y*-axis can run from 0 to 8. Follow these instructions:

a) Draw a line from (1, 6) to (3, 2), then to (5, 6).

b) Draw a line from (4, 2) to (6, 6), then to (8, 2).

c) Draw a line from (5, 4) to (7, 4).

d) Draw a line from (9, 6) to (9, 2), then (11, 2).

What name is spelt out?

4* Draw up a coordinate grid so that the *x*-axis can run from 0 to 12 and the *y*-axis can run from 0 to 10. Follow these instructions:

a) Draw a line from (1, 5) to (2, 9), then to (3, 5).

b) Draw a line from $(1\frac{1}{2}, 7)$ to $(2\frac{1}{2}, 7)$.

c) Draw a line from (4, 8) to (4, 4), then to (6, 4).

d) Draw a line from (9, 7) to (7, 7), then to (7, 3), then (9, 3).

e) Draw a line from (7, 5) to (8, 5).

f) Draw a line from (10, 2) to (12, 6).

g) Draw a line from (12, 2) to (10, 6).

What name is spelt out?

5* Draw up a coordinate grid so that *x* and *y* can each run from 0 to 100. A scale of 1 cm to 10 units will work well. Then follow these instructions to create a map of a Desert Island:

■ The coastline passes through the points (10, 40), (20, 20), (30, 10), (50, 10), (80, 20), (70, 50), (80, 70), (65, 80), (50, 90), (40, 80), (30, 80), (20, 70) and (20, 50). Plot these points and join them up (with a wobbly line) to create the coastline.

■ Draw a small lake, Blue Lake, at (60, 20).

■ Draw a tree at the top of One Tree Hill at (40, 30).

■ Add cliffs along the coast from (20, 70) to (20, 50).

■ Add 'Misty Mountains' around (60, 70).

■ Mark a Shipwreck at (85, 40).

Unit 6
2-D shapes

In this Unit you will learn how to:
■ use mirror lines on shapes with reflection symmetry;
■ draw shapes in different orientations on grids.

A calculator will be not be required for this Unit.

6.1 Reflection symmetry

Reflection symmetry occurs when a shape has a **mirror line** or a line **of symmetry.**

The shape is made up of two halves, one of which is a reflection of the other.

The mirror line is where you would put the mirror in order to see the reflection.

Example   Draw the mirror line on this shape:

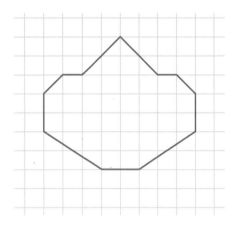

Solution

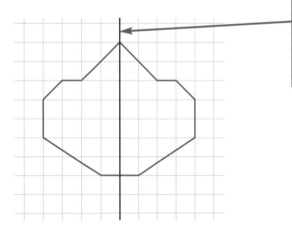

This is the mirror line. It is where you would place a mirror to see the required shape.

Example   Complete this drawing so that the red line is a line of symmetry.

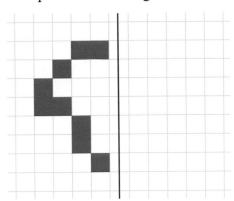

Solution

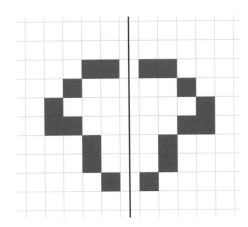

Exercise 6.1

Copy each of these diagrams on to squared paper. Complete the diagram
so that the red line is a line of symmetry (mirror line).

1 ✔

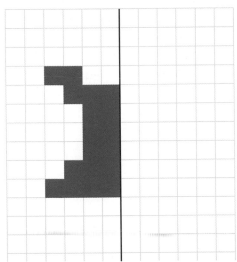

2

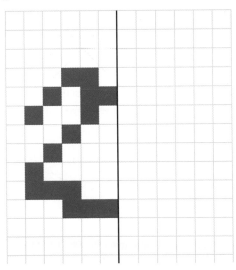

3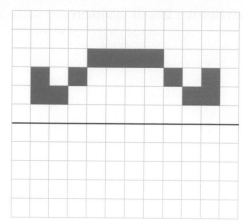

4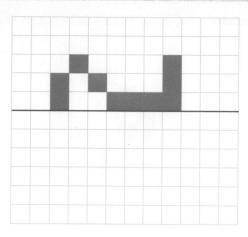

5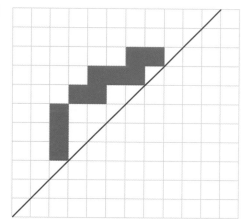

6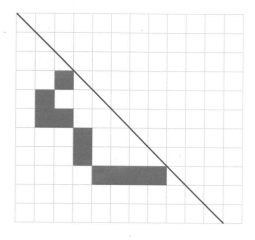

6.2 2-D shapes and grids

Sometimes you will need to take a 2-D shape drawn on a grid and move it to a different orientation. The shape might need to be translated (moved) or rotated (turned), or it could be reflected in a mirror line.

Example The diagram shows a complete 2-D shape, labelled with a letter **A**. An incomplete copy of it has been made elsewhere on the grid, labelled **B**.

a) Finish off the incomplete copy.

b) Explain how the shape **A** has been moved to **B**.

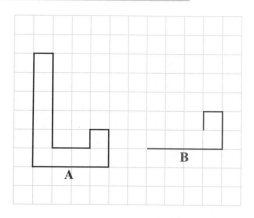

Solution   **a)**

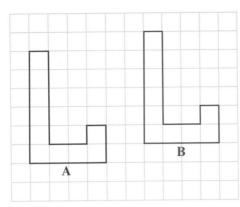

b) The shape **A** has been
translated to produce
shape B.

Example   The diagram shows a 2-D shape **P** and an incomplete copy of it, **Q**.
Finish the drawing for **Q**, and explain how **P** and **Q** are related.

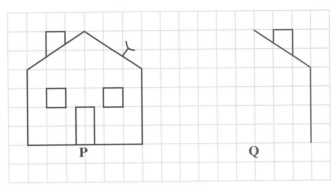

Solution

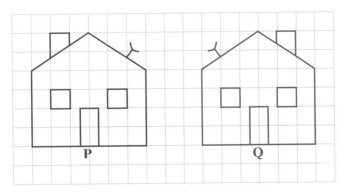

The shapes **P**
and **Q** are
mirror images, or
reflections, of
each other.

Example   The diagram shows a complete
pattern in the shape of a letter H.
This is to be redrawn using the
small 'registration marks' on the
right-hand side of the grid.

a) Complete the drawing.

b) Describe how the new shape is related to
the original one.

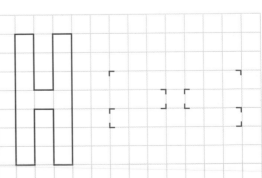

Solution **a)**

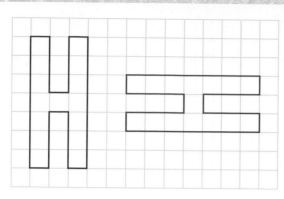

b) The original shape has been <u>rotated</u> <u>through 90°</u> to form the new one.

Exercise 6.2

Copy each of these diagrams onto squared paper, and complete the new pattern. Describe how each new pattern is related to the original one.

1

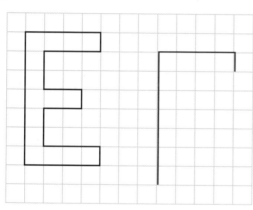

2 ✓

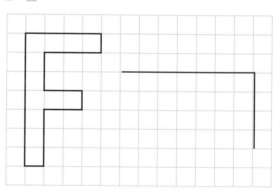

3

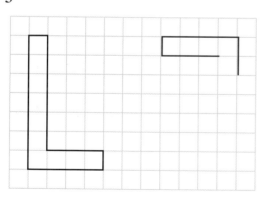

4

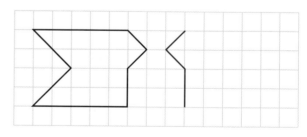

5

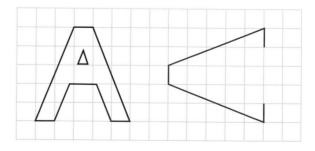

Summary

In this Unit you have learnt how to draw lines of symmetry on shapes that have reflection symmetry. You have also practised drawing 2-D shapes in different orientations on grids.

Review Exercise 6

1   Copy this shape onto squared paper. Complete the pattern so that the red line is a line of symmetry.

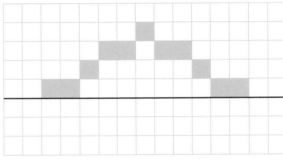

2   Copy this shape onto squared paper. Complete the pattern so that the red line is a line of symmetry.

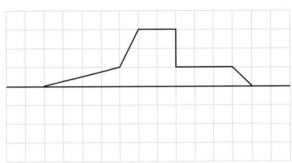

3   Look at these letters of the alphabet.

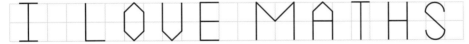

Using squared paper, make a copy of each letter that has reflection symmetry. Add the mirror lines to your drawings.

Make copies of these diagrams on squared paper. Alongside each one you should draw a new diagram, to show the result of the change described.

4   Translate (move) ten squares to the right.

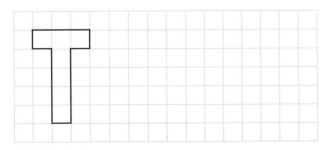

5 Reflect using the given mirror line.

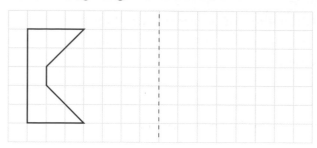

6 Rotate through 90° clockwise.

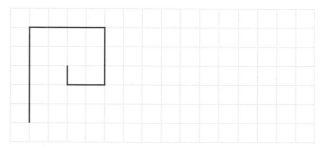

7* The shape labelled **P** has been drawn using isometric dotty paper. The shape labelled **Q** is the result of rotating **P** through 180°. The drawing of **Q** is incomplete.

a) Copy the diagram onto isometric dotty paper.

b) Finish the drawing, so that the shape **Q** is complete.

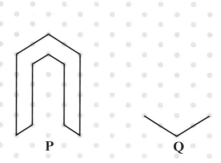

Unit 7
3-D models

In this Unit you will learn how to:

■ construct 3-D models from 2-D shapes.

7.1 3-D models

You can make 3-D models by putting several 2-D shapes together.
This can be done either by:

■ using plastic shapes such as *Polydron*; or

■ drawing a pattern (called a **net**) on card and cutting it out.

A word ending in -gon describes a flat 2-D shape.

A word ending in -hedron describes a 3-D solid.

Here are some of the 2-D shapes which can be used to build up 3-D models:

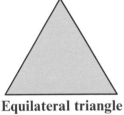

Equilateral triangle
Three equal sides

Isosceles triangle
Two equal sides

Right-angled triangle
One angle of 90°

Square
All four sides equal
All four angles equal

Regular pentagon
All five sides equal
All five angles equal

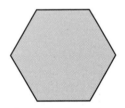

Regular hexagon
All six sides equal
All six angles equal

Example Describe carefully the 2-D shapes needed to make this solid,
called an **octahedron**. All the edges are the same length.

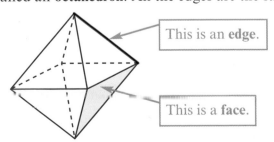

This is an **edge**.

This is a **face**.

Solution By counting, the number of faces is 8.

Each face is a triangle with 3 equal sides.

Therefore <u>8 equilateral triangles</u> are needed, to make an octahedron.

Exercise 7.1

Describe carefully the 2-D shapes needed to make these solids:

1 ✔ **2** ✔ **3** ✔

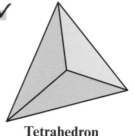

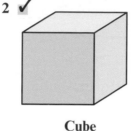

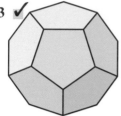

Tetrahedron **Cube** **Dodecahedron**

4 Look at this drawing of a square-based pyramid.

a) How many faces does it have?

b) Describe the shape of each face.

c) How many edges does it have?

5 Look at this drawing of a triangular prism.

a) How many faces does it have?

b) Describe the shape of each face.

c) How many edges does it have?

6 Aorja and Lisa have been using a set of plastic 2-D shapes.
You can click the shapes together to build up 3-D models.

Aorja says: Lisa says:

> I have eight identical equilateral triangles.
>
> I can build a 3-D model using all eight of my pieces.

> I have four identical squares.
>
> I need some more pieces so I can build a 3-D model.

a) Write down the name of a 3-D model which Aorja could make with his triangles.

b) Explain what extra shapes Lisa needs in order to make a 3-D model, and write down the name of her model.

7.2 Making 3-D models from nets

A **net** is a flat 2-D pattern which can be folded up to make a solid 3-D model.

The nets in this section have been drawn without any tabs, so you would need to use sticky tape to hold them together. Alternatively you could build them from plastic kits such as *Polydron*.

Example Look at the two nets below. They are intended to fold up to make a regular tetrahedron (a pyramid with a triangular base). Decide whether each one will work or not.

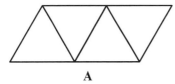

A   B

Solution Net A will fold up to make a tetrahedron:

Net B will not:

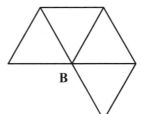

If you find it difficult to visualise these diagrams then try making a model using paper or card.

Exercise 7.2

Using squared paper, design a net for each of these 3-D models. Then cut out your net, and fold it up to check that it works.

1 A cube measuring 3 cm by 3 cm by 3cm.

2 A cuboid measuring 3 cm by 5 cm by 6 cm.

3 A square-based pyramid. The square base should be 6 cm by 6cm. Each of the four triangles should have sides of lengths 6cm, 10 cm, 10 cm.

Copy these nets onto card or stiff paper, and cut them out to make the given 3-D solid.

4 Octahedron

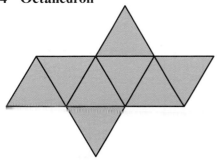

5 Triangular prism

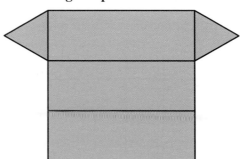

Summary

In this Unit you have practised making 3-D models from 2-D shapes. You have also used designed nets which can be folded up to make given 3-D models.

Review Exercise 7

1 Look at this drawing of a pentagonal prism.

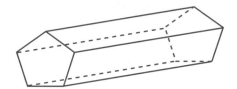

   a) Why do you think it is called pentagonal?

   b) Describe the shape of each face.

   c) How many faces does it have?

   d) How many edges does it have?

2 Gene is making models with a plastic kit. Here are all the pieces he should have:

Name of piece	Number supplied
Equilateral triangle	15
Square	18
Regular pentagon	24
Regular hexagon	16

Unfortunately two squares and one hexagon are missing.

   a) How many cubes can Gene make?

   b) How many octahedrons can he make?

   c) How many dodecahedrons can he make?

   [You may find it helpful to refer to the diagrams of an octahedron (page 43) and dodecahedron (page 44) earlier in this unit.]

3 Here is a sketch of a net for a triangular prism. The triangles on the ends are scalene, in other words the three sides might all be different lengths. These lengths are marked x, y and z.

Decide what lengths x, y and z must be in order for the net to fold up properly.

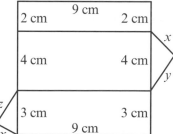

4* Look at these patterns. Which ones are nets for a cube?

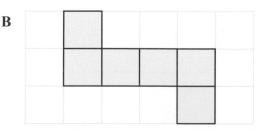

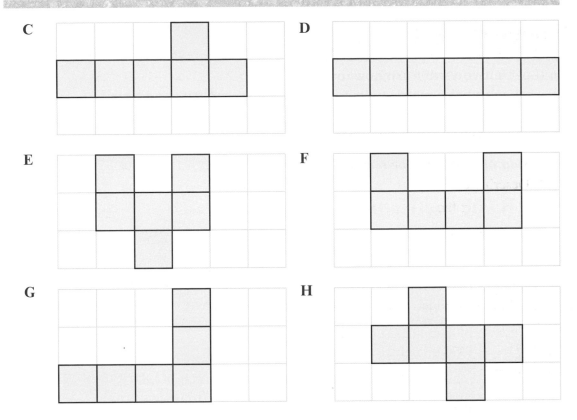

C   D   E   F   G   H

5* A pop-up dodecahedron.

Here is a method to make a 3-D model of a
dodecahedron. You will need scissors, card and a rubber
band; you do not need glue or sellotape.

Make two large copies of this diagram on card. Cut out
the two shapes.

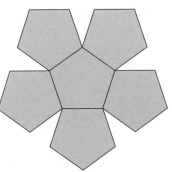

Score along the five sides of the inner pentagon to form
a shape with five floppy leaves. Do this to both shapes.

Now place one of your shapes on top of the other,
like this:

Finally, lace a rubber band around the outside of the
model, so it goes over one point, under the next, over
the next and so on. The rubber band should be large
enough to fit round the shapes only slightly stretched.

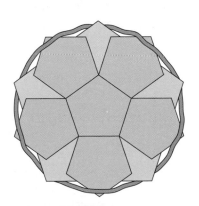

When you have finished let go, and your model
should pop up to form
a regular dodecahedron.

Unit 8
Units and scales

In this Unit you will learn how to:
- work with basic metric units for length, mass, capacity and time;
- choose appropriate metric units;
- read measurements from scales.

A calculator will be not be required for this Unit.

8.1 Basic metric units

You are already familiar with these metric units for length, mass and capacity:

Length
10 millimetres (mm) = 1 centimetre (cm)
100 centimetres = 1 metre (m)
1000 metres = 1 kilometre (km)

Mass
1000 grams (g) = 1 kilogram (kg)
1000 kilograms = 1 tonne (t)

Capacity
1 cubic centimetre (cm³) is the same as 1 millilitre (ml).
1000 cubic centimetres = 1000 millilitres = 1 litre (*l*)

Time
60 seconds (s) = 1 minute (min)
60 minutes = 1 hour (h)
24 hours = 1 day
365 days = 1 calendar year

Example   Write 123 mm in centimetres and millimetres.

Solution   123 mm = 120 mm + 3 mm
                      = 12 cm + 3 mm

<u>123 mm = 12 cm and 3 mm</u>

Example   Write 55 hours in days and hours.

Solution   2 days is 2 × 24 = 48 hours.
55 hours = 48 hours + 7 hours
                = 2 days + 7 hours

<u>55 hours = 2 days and 7 hours</u>

Example   Write 7 kg 250 g in grams.

Solution   7 kg = 7000 g
So 7 kg 250 g   = 7000 g + 250 g
                           = <u>7250 g</u>

Exercise 8.1

1 ✔ Write 155 mm in centimetres and millimetres.
2 Write 31 h in days and hours.
3 Write 1350 g in kilograms and grams.
4 Write 288 cm in metres and centimetres.
5 Write 320 sec in minutes and seconds.

8.2 Choosing and using metric units

Example What metric unit would you use to measure the mass of an egg?

Solution An egg weighs about 70 g, or 0.070 kg. It is better to avoid the use of long decimals, so a suitable unit is <u>grams</u>.

Example Suggest, in metric units, the height of an oak tree.

Solution An oak tree might be <u>20 metres</u> high.

Exercise 8.2

1 Write down a suitable metric unit for measuring each of the given objects (e.g. grams).

  a) The length of an athletics track   **b)** The mass of a sparrow
  c) ✔ The diameter of a tennis ball   **d)** The amount of paint in a large can
  e) The total running time of a pop CD   **f)** The mass of a railway carriage
  g) The volume of a coffee cup   **h)** The width of a pencil
  i) The mass of a turkey   **j)** ✔ The length of a motorway

2 Suggest a metric measurement for each object (e.g. 20 metres).

  a) The height of a table above the floor   **b)** The mass of a blue whale
  c) The mass of a new-born baby   **d)** The thickness of a slice of bread
  e) The amount of liquid in a milk shake   **f)** ✔ The mass of a coin
  g) The diameter of a hamburger   **h)** The capacity of a rucksack
  i) The length of a carrot   **j)** The volume of a thermos flask

8.3 Reading measurements from scales

Example Read the measurement indicated on this scale:

Solution The value is between 3 and 4.
There are ten intervals, so each unit is 0.1.
The marked value is midway between 3.7 and 3.8.
The scale indicates <u>3.75</u>

Exercise 8.3

Read the values given on each of these scales, giving your answer to a sensible degree of accuracy.

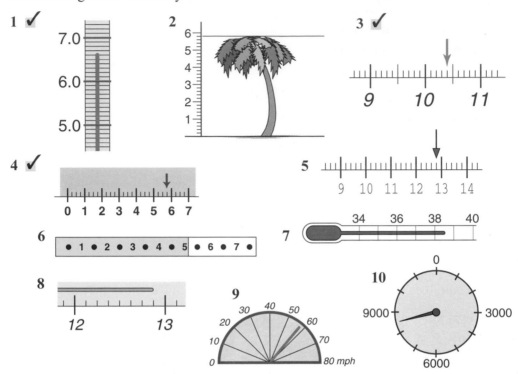

Summary

In this Unit you have practised converting quantities from one metric unit to another. Remember that there are 100 centimetres in a metre but 1000 grams in a kilogram.

You have chosen suitable metric units for measurement, and practised reading amounts shown on scales. Look for opportunities to practise in the world around you – the supermarket, or car dashboard, for example.

Review Exercise 8

1 Write 25 mm in centimetres and millimetres.

2 Write 1200 g in kilograms and grams.

3 Write 170 min in hours and minutes.

4 Write 480 cm in metres and centimetres.

5 Write two and a half hours in minutes.

6 Write 5 min 30 s in seconds.

7 Write 6 kg 300 g in grams.

8 Write 10 m 4 cm in centimetres.

9 Write 5 days and 6 hours in hours.

10 Write 11 *l* 50 ml in millilitres.

Write down a suitable metric unit for measuring each of these quantities.

11 The width of a classroom.

12 The thickness of a magazine.

13 The mass of a key ring.

14 The capacity of a car's petrol tank.

15 The time it takes to bake a pizza.

Estimate the following measurements in metric units.

16 The length of a swimming pool.

17 The volume of water in a full washing-up bowl.

18 The mass of a large Christmas cake.

19 The time it takes to walk 4 km.

20 The thickness of a computer floppy disk.

Read the values on each of these scales, giving your answer to a sensible level of accuracy.

21

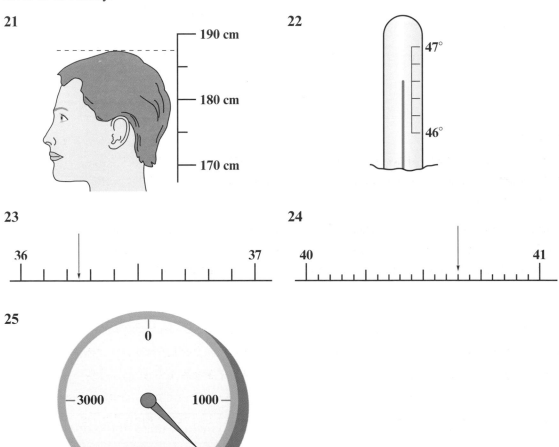

22

23

24

25

Unit 9
Perimeter and area

In this Unit you will learn how to:
- find perimeters by counting and by measuring;
- find areas by counting;
- find the approximate area of an irregular shape.

A calculator should not be used in this Unit, except perhaps for checking.

9.1 Perimeter

> Perimeter is the distance all the way around the outside of an object.
> It can be found by counting or by measuring.

Example Find the perimeter of this T shape. Each square represents one centimetre.

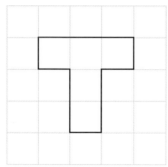

Solution Since the shape is drawn on a grid there is no need to measure. The length of each side can be found by counting:

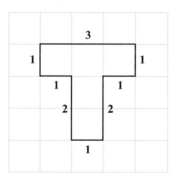

Perimeter of T-shape = 3 + 1 + 1 + 2 + 1 + 2 + 1 + 1
= 12 cm

Remember to include units in the final answer.

Example   Find the perimeter of this triangle. Give your answer in centimetres, working to one place of decimals.

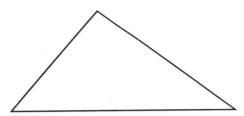

Solution   Using a ruler, the sides can be measured:

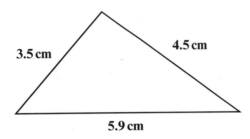

Perimeter of triangle $= 3.5 + 4.5 + 5.9$

$= \underline{13.9\,cm}$

Exercise 9.1

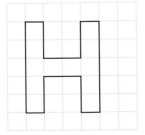

Find the perimeter of each of these shapes, by counting. The side of each grid square represents 1 cm.

1

2

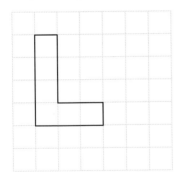

3 ✔

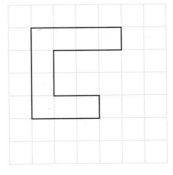

4

5

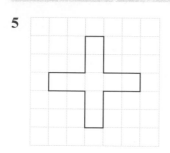

6

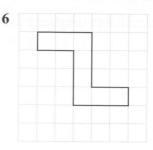

Find the perimeters of these shapes by measuring. Give your answers in centimetres, to one decimal place.

7

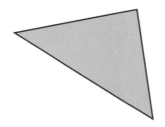

8

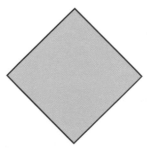

9 ✓

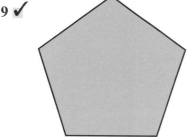

10

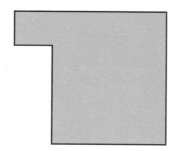

9.2 Area

Area is a measure of the amount of surface a shape covers. It can be found by counting unit squares.

Areas should always be given in square units, e.g. square centimetres.

Example   Find the area of this T shape.
Each square represents
one square centimetre.

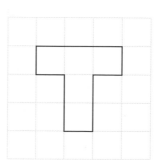

Solution   Count the unit squares inside the shape:

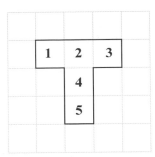

Area of T shape = 5 cm²

This is a short way of writing 'square centimetres'.

Exercise 9.2

Find the area of each shape drawn in Exercise 8.1, questions **1** to **6** (3 ✔).

9.3   Areas of irregular shapes

The area of an irregular shape can be estimated by drawing a grid over it. Grid squares count as 1 if they are at least half full, otherwise they are ignored.

Example   Estimate the area of this leaf shape. Each grid square is one square centimetre.

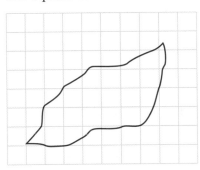

Solution   Those squares which are at least half full are marked with a spot:

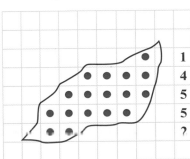

Area of leaf   = 1 + 4 + 5 + 5 + 2
              = 17 cm²

rcise 9.3

nate the area of these shapes. Each square is one square centimetre.

1 ✔

2

3

4

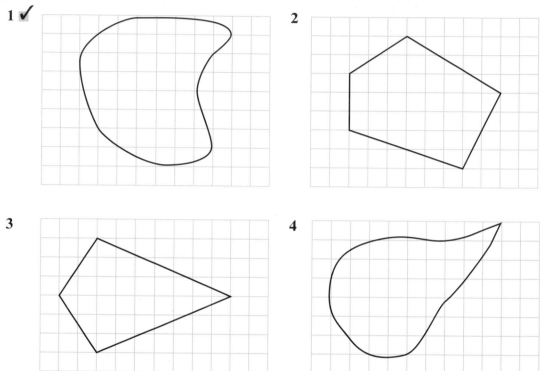

Summary

In this Unit you have practised finding perimeters by counting and by measurement. You have also found areas by counting unit squares. Areas of irregular shapes are found by drawing a grid, and counting all the squares which are more than half full.

Remember that areas should always be given in square units – often square centimetres (cm²).

Review Exercise 9

Find the perimeter and area of each of these shapes. Each square represents one square centimetre.

1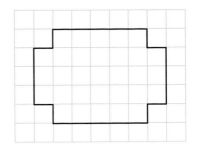

2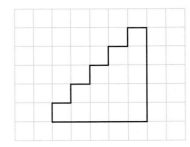

3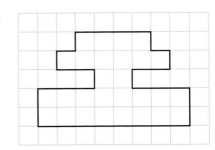

4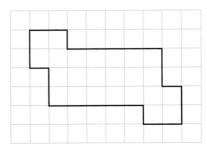

5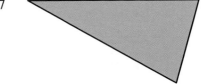

6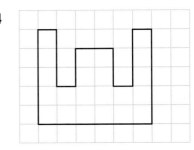

Use your ruler to measure the length of each side in these shapes, and hence find the perimeter. Give your answer in centimetres, working to one decimal place.

7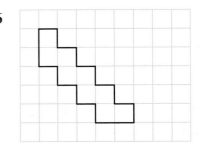

8

9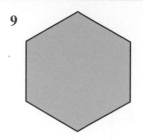

10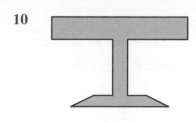

These diagrams show some mathematical shapes drawn on grids. By counting squares, estimate the area of each shape. Each square represents one square centimetre.

11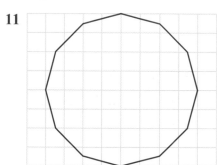

12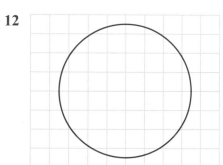

13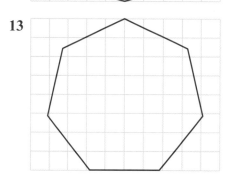

14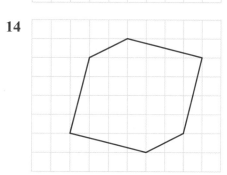

In these two diagrams each small cube is of side one centimetre. Find the total area of the **outside surface** of each solid. (Remember to count the faces that you cannot see.)

15*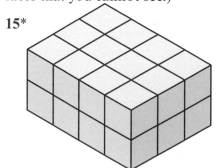

16*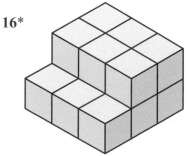

Unit 10
Looking at data

In this Unit you will learn how to:

- find the mode and range of a set of numbers;
- collect data and record them using a frequency table;
- group data where appropriate;
- use and interpret graphs of frequency tables.

A calculator will not be required for this unit.

10.1 Mode and range

In a list of numbers:

the **mode** is the number which occurs most often;
the **range** is the difference between the highest and lowest numbers in the list.

The **mode** is one way of finding what an **average** or **typical** number in the list is like.

The **range** is one way of measuring how much variety there is in the list.

Example   Here are the ages of seven children:

6, 9, 10, 13, 14, 14, 17.

Find the mode and the range.

Solution   The mode is <u>14</u>.

6, 9, 10, 13, 14, 14, 17.

The range is 17 − 6 = <u>11</u>.

> 14 occurs more often than any of the other numbers.

> 17 is the highest number in the list and 6 is the lowest.

Example   Find the mode and the range of these nine test scores:

38, 15, 24, 40, 29, 27, 35, 38, 39

Solution   First, arrange the scores in order of size:

15, 24, 27, 29, 35, 38, 38, 39, 40

The mode is <u>38</u>.
The range is 40 − 15 = <u>25</u>.

Exercise 10.1

1 ✔ Here are the ages of five friends: 23, 23, 27, 29, 32. Find the mode and the range.

2 Here are the numbers of sweets in nine packets: 17, 18, 19, 20, 22, 24, 24, 24, 25.
Find the mode and the range.

3 I went fishing every day last week, and caught 1, 6, 7, 0, 2, 5 and 2 fish on each day respectively. Find the range of the number of fish caught.

4 On my fifteen favourite music CDs there are 12, 10, 11, 8, 12, 15, 12, 11, 10, 13, 12, 12, 13, 11 and 16 tracks respectively. Find the mode and the range.

5 In a cricket match the eleven batsmen obtained scores of 51, 3, 28, 22, 47, 11, 1, 0, 1, 16 and 1. Find the range of these eleven scores.

10.2 Frequency tables

When there are a lot of data points it is a good idea to use a **frequency table**. The table tells you how many times each value occurs.

Example　The ages of thirty children are:

6 9 10 10 7　7 8 9 9 8　7 10 9 9 8

6 10 8 8 6　7 7 8 7 9　9 10 9 9 10

a) Draw up a frequency table.

b) State the value of the mode.

c) Display the data in a suitable graph.

Solution　**a)**

Age	Tally	Frequency
6	|	
7	|	
8		
9	|	
10	||	

Here are the tallies for the first five values: 6, 9, 10, 10, 7.

Age	Tally	Frequency
6	|||	3
7	⊬⊦ |	6
8	⊬⊦ |	6
9	⊬⊦ ||||	9
10	⊬⊦ |	6

This is the finished frequency table. Note how bundles of five sticks are tied together.

b) The mode is <u>9</u>.

c) The data is illustrated in this frequency diagram:

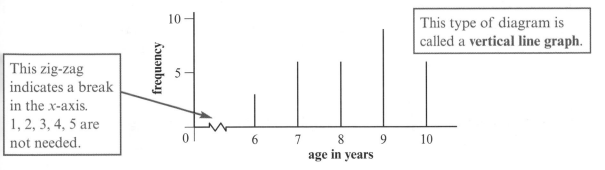

This type of diagram is called a **vertical line graph**.

This zig-zag indicates a break in the *x*-axis. 1, 2, 3, 4, 5 are not needed.

Exercise 10.2

1 ✔ Every week Veronica tries to save some of her pocket money: 50 pence, 20 pence, 10 pence or nothing. Over a seventeen-week period she saves these amounts:

10 50 20 0 10 0 20 50 20 10 10 10 20 0 50 20 10

a) Draw up a frequency table for these values.

b) Illustrate the data with a vertical line graph.

2 The 30 pupils in Mr Laing's class took a spelling test. Their scores out of ten were:

3 7 10 9 9 4 8 5 5 6 3 9 10 9 8 9 8 9 9 9 6 7 8 7 7 9 6 7 8 8

a) Draw up a frequency table for the thirty scores.

b) State the value of the mode.

c) Display the data in a vertical line graph.

3 An ordinary dice is thrown 24 times. The scores obtained are:

6 1 4 4 5 2 6 4 1 3 5 3 3 6 1 3 5 3 2 6 2 5 3 1

a) Draw up a frequency table for these 24 scores.

b) Illustrate the data with a vertical line graph.

c) Write down the value of the mode.

4 A company claims to produce matchboxes which contain, on average, 50 matches. Jenny examines 40 boxes, and finds the following data:

Number of matches	Frequency
48	3
49	6
50	11
51	12
52	8

a) State the value of the mode.

b) Display the data in a vertical line graph.

c) Explain briefly whether you think the company's claim is a reasonable one.

5 In a survey 50 teenagers are asked how many times a week they eat take-away food. The replies for 40 of them are summarised in this frequency table:

Number of times take-away food is eaten	Frequency
0	8
1	12
2	13
3	2
4	5
5	0

The replies from the other 10 teenagers are 1, 1, 2, 0, 3, 1, 2, 1, 0 and 3.

a) Draw up a new frequency table to show the results for all 50 teenagers.

b) State the mode based on all 50 replies.

c) Display the data for the 50 replies, using a vertical line graph.

10.3 Grouped data

Sometimes there are a great many different values in the data set. It is then better to arrange the data into **classes**, or **groups**, as you draw up the frequency table.

Example The noon temperature (in °C) at a certain town is recorded on twenty randomly chosen days throughout the year. The values are:

11 15 3 7 25   18 9 6 29 18   20 21 16 14 12   13 23 16 13 11

a) Draw up a frequency table, using groups of 1–5, 6–10 and so on.

b) Illustrate with a suitable graph.

c) State the modal class.

Solution **a)**

Temperature	Tally	Frequency
1 to 5		
6 to 10		
11 to 15	||	
16 to 20		
21 to 25		
26 to 30		

Here are the tallies for the first five values: 11, 15, 3, 7, 25.

Temperature	Tally	Frequency
1 to 5	|	1
6 to 10	|||	3
11 to 15	|||| ||	7
16 to 20	||||	5
21 to 25	|||	3
26 to 30	|	1

This is the finished frequency table. Note how bundles of five sticks are tied together.

b)

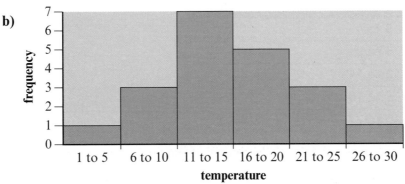

c) The modal class is <u>11 to 15</u>.

As the values have been arranged into groups there is a **modal class** instead of the ordinary mode. This is the class with the highest frequency.

Exercise 10.3

1 A weather forecaster is looking at data for a recent month from 25 different places around the world. The number of rainy days during the month is recorded at each place:

8 9 2 1 2   16 21 19 4 5   5 11 9 15 3   0 29 21 12 6   23 23 7 11 14

a) Draw up a frequency table, using groups of 0–4, 5–9 and so on.

b) Illustrate with a suitable graph.

c) State the modal group.

2 ✔ This table shows the marks scored by 50 candidates in an exam:

90	70	48	43	42	45	69	88	74	59
51	36	59	53	69	55	53	59	38	52
45	31	13	18	31	41	36	43	64	52
54	58	74	75	59	53	52	60	53	56
74	75	80	72	66	37	45	75	49	43

a) Draw up a frequency table, using groups of 0–9, 10–19 and so on.

b) Illustrate with a suitable graph.

c) State the modal group.

d) The pass mark was set at 55. How many candidates passed the exam?

3 The table shows information about the number of telephone calls received per hour by the secretary's office at Greenview school. The data has been collected into groups.

Number of calls during one hour	Frequency
0 to 4	0
5 to 9	11
10 to 14	14
15 to 19	3
20 to 24	1

a) Draw a graph to illustrate this information.

b) State the modal class.

c) How many hours does the data represent?

d) What was the smallest possible number of calls that might have been received during one hour?

Summary

In this Unit you have learnt how to find the mode (most frequent value) and the range (difference between the highest and lowest values) of a set of data.

You have used simple frequency tables to summarise data, and have used groups where appropriate. Remember that the mode becomes the modal class for grouped data, and is simply the group (or class) which has the highest frequency.

Ungrouped data should be displayed using a vertical line graph, with gaps between the vertical lines. Where data has been grouped it is more usual to use a bar chart in which the bars can touch each other.

Review Exercise 10

1   Find the range of these sets of numbers:

   a) 4, 5, 7, 8, 11

   b) 2, 2, 3, 6, 7, 7, 7

   c) 1, 2, 5, 1, 5, 2, 5, 2, 1, 2, 2

2   Find the mode of each set of numbers in question **1**.

3   During the first seven months of the year I recorded the following numbers
   of television programmes: 5, 1, 2, 1, 6, 1, 5.

   a) Find the mode of the number of programmes I recorded each month.

   b) Find the range.

4   There are five queues in a bank with 6, 4, 3, 4 and 5 people in them respectively.

   a) Find the modal length of a queue.

   b) Find the range.

5   A café owner makes a note of the numbers of complaints received each week
   for 13 weeks. The numbers are:

   2   1   0   0   2   1   2   0   0   1   0   2   1

   Find the modal number of complaints.

6   When I travel to school on the bus I sometimes see other members of my class on the
   same bus. Last month I recorded the number of members of my class (including me)
   on the bus as shown in this table:

Number of members of my class	Frequency
0	0
1	5
2	6
3	5
4	3
5	0
6	1

   a) Illustrate the data with a vertical line graph.

   b) Write down the mode.

   c) On how many occasions did I see no other member of my class?

7 After a business lecture the audience divides up into nine small discussion groups. The numbers of people in each group are:

8 8 7 8 9 7 8 8 7

a) Illustrate the data with a vertical line graph.

b) Write down the mode.

c) How many people were at the lecture altogether?

8 In a school survey Cass has asked twenty boys and twenty girls how many CD albums they owned. The results for the boys have been processed:

Boys' Ownership of CD Albums	
Smallest number	1
Largest number	7
Mode	3
Range	6

Here is the raw data which Cass collected for the girls:

1 4 5 4 4   3 5 6 2 2

2 1 4 5 5   3 3 3 5 7

a) Draw up a table for the girls' results, similar to the boys' one above.

b) What similarity do you notice between the two tables?

c) What difference do you notice between the two tables?

d) Which group, boys or girls, seems to own more CD albums?

9* Gabi writes down seven numbers. Here are some clues about the numbers.

The middle number is 8.

The number 2 occurs twice.

The mode is 9.

The numbers all add up to 44.

Work out the seven numbers in Gabi's list.

10* I asked nine friends to tell me how many pets they have. The replies were:

1 0 2 5 0 0 1 2 7

a) Find the modal number of pets.

b) Explain why the mode is not very helpful in describing the average number of pets owned by the nine friends.

Level 4 Review

Exercise 1

Do this exercise as mental arithmetic – do not write down any working.

1 Write six thousand, seven hundred and five in figures.

2 Write seventy thousand, two hundred and forty-one in figures.

3 Write 2 107 in words.

4 Write 34 060 in words.

5 Find 352×10.

6 Find 5600×100.

7 Find $43\,000 \div 10$

8 Find $108\,000 \div 100$

9 Write down the first five multiples of 9.

10 Is 45 a multiple of 7?

11 Write down all the factors of 20.

12 Is 6 a factor of 44?

13 Write down one example of a prime number between 20 and 30.

14 Is 47 a prime number?

15 Write two and nine-tenths as a decimal.

16 Write $6\frac{49}{100}$ as a decimal.

17 Write 2.7 as a fraction.

18 Write the fraction $\frac{24}{40}$ in its simplest form.

19 Find the mode of these numbers: 1 3 4 5 5 6 10

20 What fraction of this diagram has been coloured?

Exercise 2

Do this exercise as mental arithmetic – do not write down any working.

1 Lara buys nine bags of chocolate animals. Each bag contain six animals. How many chocolate animals does she buy altogether?

2 Abdul has 24 sweets and shares them out amongst 8 people. How many sweets does each person receive?

3 Write 45 mm in centimetres and millimetres.

4 Write 6 kg 45 grams in grams.

5 What metric unit would you use to measure the mass of a pen?

6 What metric unit would you use to measure the height of a building?

7 Alice has to cycle 10 km to school. She cycles 3.4 km and then stops for a rest.
   a) How much further does she have to cycle?
   b) Sarfraz says 'Alice stopped roughly half-way through her journey.'
   Petra says 'Alice stopped roughly one-third of the way through her journey.'

   Which one of them is right?

8 Miss Andrews takes 28 exercise books home to mark. She marks one-quarter of them before tea. How many does she need to mark after tea?

9 '51 is a prime number.' True or false?

10 What reading is shown on this scale?

Exercise 3

You should show all necessary working in this exercise.

1 Work out 156 + 747.

2 Work out 1248 + 31 240.

3 Work out 656 – 294.

4 Work out 1244 – 1152.

5 Amy spends £14.50 on a CD and £3.65 on a book. How much does she spend altogether?

6 Joe spends £6.20 on a shirt. How much change does he get from a £10 note?

7 Find the next two numbers in each of these number patterns:

   a) 16   19   22   25   28   *   *
   b) 44   43   41   38   34   *   *
   c) 10   20   40   80   *   *

8 The lengths of three sticks are 10.4 cm, 12.2 cm and 11.9 cm.

   a) Find the total length of the three sticks, in centimetres.

   b) Write your answer to **a)** in millimetres.

9 A film begins at 5:40 p.m. and lasts until 8:55 p.m. How long is the film:

   a) in hours and minutes?   **b)** in minutes?

10 Dionne has been drawing spots on a coordinate grid:

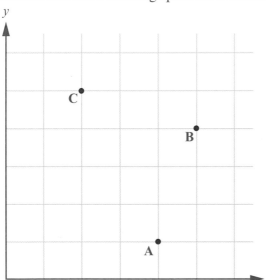

She has marked A at (4, 1) and B at (5, 4).

   a) Write down the coordinates of C.

   b) Dionne wants to add a point D so that A, B, C and D form a square. Write down the coordinates of D.

11 How many lines of symmetry does a square have?

12 Six children measured the height of a postage stamp using a selection of different instruments. Here are their measurements:

Paul	Hannah	Jo	Carlo	Indira	Lowell
2.6 cm	2.511 cm	2.55 cm	25.22 mm	2.531 cm	2.507 cm

Rewrite the table to show the measurements in order of size, smallest first, making sure they are all in centimetres.

13 Twelve children were asked how many letters they received last week. Their replies were: 0 3 6 2 3 2 3 1 2 3 0 3

   a) Write the numbers in order of size, smallest first.

   b) Find the mode.

   c) Find the range.

14 Jatin counts the number of spelling mistakes on each page of a newspaper. The results are: 0 2 1 2 0 4 2 3 3 1 2 3 2 3 4 3 1 0 3 4

   a) How many pages are there in the newspaper?

   b) What is the mode of the number of spelling mistakes?

15 What is the name of this 2-D shape?

16 What is the name of this 2-D shape?

17 What is the name of this 3-D solid?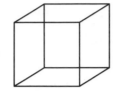

18 What is the name of this 3-D solid?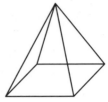

19 The diagram shows a sketch of part of Mr Jones' garden. There is a pond and a patio. Each square represents a length of 1 metre, or an area of 1 square metre.

a) Find the perimeter of the patio, in metres.

b) Find the area of the patio, in square metres.

c) Use a counting method to estimate the area of the pond.

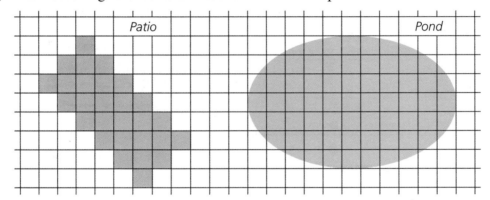

20 Class 11B did a survey to find out about how often people listen to the radio. One of the questions was: 'How many radios are there in your home?' The replies are shown in this table:

Number of radios	0	1	2	3	4	more than 4
Replies	3	10	11	2	1	0

Unfortunately two of the children were absent at the time of the survey. After they returned, they both said that there was one radio in their home.

a) Redraw the table to include the results of the two absent pupils

b) Write down the mode and the range of the replies.

LEVEL 5 Unit 11
Decimals and negative numbers

In this Unit you will learn how to:

■ recognise place value in decimal notation;

■ add and subtract numbers written as decimals;

■ multiply and divide numbers written as decimals;

■ order, add and subtract negative numbers;

■ solve problems using negative numbers and decimals.

A calculator may be used for harder multiplication and division problems.

11.1 Adding and subtracting with decimals

When a number is written in decimals each figure to the left of the decimal point has a place value – units, tens, hundreds etc.

The figures to the right of the decimal point have place values too – tenths, hundredths, thousandths etc.

Example   Doris looks at the number 62.359.
Doris wants to read the number out loud. What should she say?

Solution

1000	100	10	1		$\frac{1}{10}$	$\frac{1}{100}$	$\frac{1}{1000}$
		6	2	.	3	5	9

These are the place values.

The 6 means six tens or sixty.
The 2 means two units.
The 3 means three-tenths.
The 5 means five-hundredths.
The 9 means nine-thousandths.

Doris should say 'sixty-two point three five nine.'

Note – you **never** say sixty-two point three hundred and fifty-nine. Just name the figures after the decimal point.

Example   Add together 153.27 and 76.6.

Solution   Begin by drawing up a set of place value headings:

100	10	1		$\frac{1}{10}$	$\frac{1}{100}$
1	5	3	.	2	7
	7	6	.	6	0

Line the numbers up at the decimal point.

In this example it is helpful to insert an extra zero.

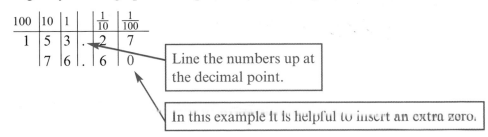

100	10	1		$\frac{1}{10}$	$\frac{1}{100}$
1	5	3	.	2	7
	7	6	.	6	0
2	2	9	.	8	7

So $153.27 + 76.6 = \underline{229.87}$

Decimals are subtracted in the same way.

Line the two numbers up at the decimal point, insert extra zeroes at the right-hand end if necessary, then subtract as normal. Remember to put a decimal point in the answer.

Exercise 11.1

1 Write in figures:
  a) Sixteen point seven four two.   b) One hundred and five point two.
  c) ✔ Ten point nought nought six.

2 Write in words:
  a) ✔ 69.25   b) 184.06   c) 21.060

Work out these additions and subtractions:

3 $21.44 + 19.8$ 4 $366.7 + 29.53$ 5 $409.46 + 27.8$

6 $355.202 + 28.49$ 7 ✔ $142.26 - 78.63$ 8 $166.27 - 84.5$

9 $245.2 - 62.17$ 10 $143.4 - 76.88$ 11 $29.295 + 83.4$

12 $735.68 - 153.75$ 13 $10.04 - 0.2$ 14 ✔ $399.99 + 24.2$

15 $16.3 + 7.277$ 16 $0.35 - 0.07$

11.2 Multiplying and dividing with decimals

Multiplying or dividing a decimal by a simple whole number is easily done without a calculator.

Example   Multiply 17.452 by 20.

Solution   First, set up the place values:

100	10	1		$\frac{1}{10}$	$\frac{1}{100}$	$\frac{1}{1000}$
	1	7	.	4	5	2

Next multiply by 2:

100	10	1		$\frac{1}{10}$	$\frac{1}{100}$	$\frac{1}{1000}$
	3	4	.	9	0	4

Then multiply by 10:

100	10	1		$\frac{1}{10}$	$\frac{1}{100}$	$\frac{1}{1000}$
3	4	9	.	0	4	

To multiply by 10 move all the digits one column to the left.

So $17.452 \times 20 = \underline{349}.04$

Harder questions are best done using a calculator.

Example   Divide 2504.32 by 17.2

Solution   By calculator, ◄————— | If you use a calculator then say so –
your teacher or examiner needs to know.

$$2504.32 \div 17.2 = \underline{145.6}$$

Exercise 11.2
Work out these without using a calculator.

1 75.34×2 **2** 231.02×3 **3** $144.68 \div 2$

4 $636.256 \div 2$ **5** ✓ 24.225×20 **6** 17.55×200

7 ✓ $45.035 \div 5$ **8** 63.224×200 **9** $196.28 \div 20$

Work out these with a calculator.

10 125.4×6.25 **11** 4.25×5.24 **12** $37.376 \div 14.6$

13 ✓ $97.0225 \div 9.85$ **14** 44.05×1.36 **15** $379.68 \div 135.6$

16 $80.936 \div 30.2$ **17** ✓ 104.22×16.5 **18** $3.9128 \div 2.5$

11.3 Adding and subtracting with negative numbers

You have probably seen a number line set out like this:

The larger numbers are to the right, smaller ones to the left.

We write $7 > 5$ to mean '7 is greater than 5'.
Similarly $-8 < -5$ means '–8 is less than –5'.

Example   Arrange these in order of size: 6.22, –7.5, –5.3

Solution   Consider their positions on the number line:

So $-7.5 < -5.3 < 6.22$

When you: **add** a **positive** number – the result is a number further to the **right**;
              add a **negative** number – the result is a number further to the **left**.

For subtraction, these rules are reversed:

> When you: **subtract** a **positive** number the result is a number further to the **left**;
> **subtract** a **negative** number the result is a number further to the **right**.

Example   Work out: $-6 + 4$; $7 + (-2)$; $12 - 9$; $6 - 11$; $5 - (-14)$; $-4 - (-10)$.

Solution   Using the number line and the rules above,

$$-6 + 4 = \underline{-2}$$
$$7 + (-2) = \underline{5}$$
$$12 - 9 = \underline{3}$$
$$6 - 11 = \underline{-5}$$
$$5 - (-14) = \underline{19}$$
$$-4 - (-10) = \underline{6}$$

> This is 'five take away negative fourteen'.
> It is the same as 'five take away minus fourteen'.

> This is 'negative four take away negative ten'.
> It is the same as 'minus four take away minus ten'.

Exercise 11.3

Arrange these numbers in order of size, smallest first:

1 $-4, 6, -3$ **2** $10, -3, -7$ **3** $-3.5, 3.5, 1.4$

4 ✔ $14.66, -7.5, -7.33, 14.05$ **5** $0.05, -0.32, -0.310, 0.6$

Work out these:

6 $-7 + 3$ **7** ✔ $-5 - 6$ **8** $6 + (-3)$

9 ✔ $-2 + (-5)$ **10** $5 - 7$ **11** $4 - (-7)$

12 $-7 - (-8)$ **13** $2.4 - 3.6$ **14** $-5.5 + 7.5$

15 ✔ $12.4 - (-3.6)$ **16** $-1.4 + (-1.5)$ **17** $-2.8 - 2.8$

18 $6.37 - 2.5 - (-1.5)$

19 On the moon the daytime temperature reaches 105°C, but at night falls to –155°C. Find the difference between day and night temperatures on the moon.

20 During Christmas week last year I recorded the temperature as 3°C on Monday, –4°C on Tuesday and –2°C on Wednesday.
   a) Which day was the warmest?
   b) Which day was the coldest?
   c) Which was the warmer out of Tuesday and Wednesday, and by how much?

11.4 Problems involving money

Sums of money are often written in pounds, using decimals for the pence.
Remember that you should always write two decimal places in pounds and pence.

Example   Anwar buys a magazine for £1.25 and a milk shake for £1.45.
How much change does he receive from a £5 note?

Solution   He spends 1.25 + 1.45 = 2.70
His change is 5.00 – 2.70 = 2.30
Answer: He receives £2.30 change.

> Note the use of two decimal places throughout.

Exercise 11.4

Add up these amounts of money:

1 £1.27, £2.99 and £3.50

2 ✔ £4.25, £1.63 and £2.04

3 £4.99, £1.44 and £0.27

4 £7.21, £0.99 and £1.05

5 £10.99, £15.50 and £8.56

6 £101.68, £62.41 and £103.75

Add up the following amounts:

7 ✔ £4.65, £0.99, £0.20

8 £3.99, 50p, £1.87

9 26p, 47p, 95p

10 83p, £4.75, £2.95

Summary

In this Unit you have learnt how to recognise place value within decimals.
You have practised adding and subtracting decimals without a calculator,
making sure that the decimal points line up. You have practised
multiplication and division of decimals, using a calculator.

You have used a number line to help visualise addition and subtraction with
negative numbers. Remember that add means move right, subtract means move
left. Subtracting a negative number is the same as adding a positive one.

You have solved problems on money (decimals) and temperature
(negative numbers).

Review Exercise 11

Without using a calculator, work out these additions and subtractions:

1 25.28 + 47.63

2 104.74 + 63.27

3 48.29 – 9.05

4 29.25 + 111.8

5 23.46 – 1.99

6 123.28 – 97.65

7 109.27 + 63.13

8 665.3 – 24.18

9 121.66 – 43.27

Use your calculator to find the answer to these:

10 24.3×73.02

11 0.0026×356

12 $170.9724 \div 98.26$

13 $33.84 \div 4.5$

14 $824.41 \div 9.5$

15 0.25×0.36

16 $0.68 \div 0.016$

17 $1.92 \div 1.6$

18 45.3×0.065

Without using a calculator, work out the value of these:

19 $-5 + 12$

20 $-12 + 5$

21 $17 - (-3)$

22 $-6 + (-5)$

23 $21 + (-5)$

24 $-7 - (-7)$

25 $0 - (-4)$

26 $5 - (-6)$

27 $-7 + (-8)$

Solve these problems, without using a calculator.

28* Over six weeks Susan saves £1.26, £4.25, £1.55, £2.48, £1.33 and 50 pence. Find the total amount that she saves.

29* A camera costs £64. I have £10 towards this already, and I am able to save £4.50 each week. How many weeks will it take until I can afford the camera?

30* Three rods measure 1.65 m, 2.21 m and 3.4 m. Find the total length if all three rods are laid out end to end.

The table shows some information about the weather during a particular 24-hour period in five French ski resorts:

Resort	Tignes	Val Thorens	Les Arcs	Valmorel	Pra Loup
Temperature (maximum) °C	12°	11°	11°	14°	15°
Temperature (minimum) °C	–5°	–9°	–4°	–3°	–1°
Sunshine (hours)	4.2	3.9	4.4	4.1	8.4

31* In one of these resorts the maximum temperature was 15° higher than the minimum temperature. Which resort?

32* Find the difference between the maximum and minimum temperatures in Valmorel.

33* Find:
   a) the highest temperature in the table
   b) the lowest temperature in the table
   c) the difference between the highest and the lowest temperatures.

34* One of these resorts is the highest ski resort in Europe, and so it tends to experience colder temperatures than the others. Which one do you think it might be?

Another resort is much further south than the rest, and so it tends to have more sunshine. Which one do you think it might be?

35* Find the average number of hours of sunshine for the five resorts.

36* Terri has £25.66 in her bank account. She writes out three cheques, for £10.43, £16.25 and £21.44. The bank honours these three cheques, but then writes to Terri telling her that her account is overdrawn. They charge her £15 for writing the letter. Find the size of Terri's overdraft, including the charge for the letter.

37* Desmond visits the United States of America. He has $20.00 in his pocket, but then he buys a burger for $2.45 and a postcard for 35 cents. He finds a quarter and a dime. How much money has he now?
($1 is 100 cents, a quarter is 25 cents and a dime is 10 cents.)

Unit 12
Multiplication and division without a calculator

In this Unit you will learn how to:
- multiply larger numbers using long multiplication;
- divide two numbers using tables in reverse;
- you will also practise multiplication and division using tables.

A calculator should not be used in this Unit, except perhaps for checking.

12.1 Long multiplication

To multiply a 3-digit number by a 2-digit number without a calculator long multiplication is used. The larger number is written in the first line, with the smaller number underneath. Multiplications then follow, one line at a time:

Example   Multiply 269 by 32.

Solution

```
    2 6 9
×   3 2
```
Copy out the question, with the larger number – 269 – above the smaller one – 32.

```
    2 6 9
×   3 ②
    5 3 8
```
Multiply by the units digit, 2. The answer to 269 times 2 is 538.

```
    2 6 9
×   ③ 2
    5 3 8
        0
```
Now for the 30, represented by this 3. Enter a zero – 0 – underneath the 538.

```
    2 6 9
×   3 2
    5 3 8
  8 0 7 0
```
... then multiply 269 by 3. The answer, 807, is written alongside the zero.

```
    2 6 9
×   3 2
    5 3 8
  8 0 7 0
  8 6 0 8
```
Finally, add up 538 and 8070, to obtain the grand total of 8608.

So 269 × 32 = 8608

Check: 269 × 32 is about 300 × 30 = 9000 so 8608 looks about right.

The same method can be used for longer problems, with more lines of working. The next example shows all the stages completed:

Example   Multiply 1876 by 274.

Solution

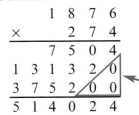

```
      1  8  7  6
  ×      2  7  4
      7  5  0  4
   1  3  1  3  2  0
   3  7  5  2  0  0
   5  1  4  0  2  4
```

The 1876 has been multiplied by 4, then by 70, and finally by 200.

This triangular pattern of 0s always occurs in this type of problem.

So 1876 × 274 = <u>514 024</u>

Check: 1876 × 274 is about 2000 × 300 = 600 000 so 514 024 looks about right.

Exercise 12.1

1 175 × 19   **2** ✔ 324 × 47   **3** 822 × 13   **4** 453 × 33

5 775 × 26   **6** 47 × 74   **7** 309 × 23   **8** ✔ 512 × 62

9 936 × 79   **10** 308 × 81   **11** 327 × 121   **12** 985 × 39

13 505 × 120   **14** 51 × 729   **15** 405 × 90   **16** 3522 × 23

17 ✔ 4977 × 49   **18** 532 × 619   **19** ✔ 225 × 225   **20** 57 × 924

12.2 Long division

Harder problems are solved using long division. The two numbers are written in the same line, separated by a bracket. Working is done underneath, and the answer appears on the top.

Example   Divide 6071 by 13.

Solution

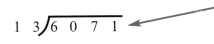

Set out the division, taking care to space out the figures; place value is very important! Do not cramp up your work.

13, 26, 39, 52, 65, 78, 91, 104, 117

Make a list of the multiples of 13, going up from 1 × 13 to 9 × 13 – this saves time later.

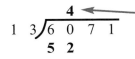

13 into 6 won't go, so try 13 into 60. The best you can do is 4 × 13 = 52.

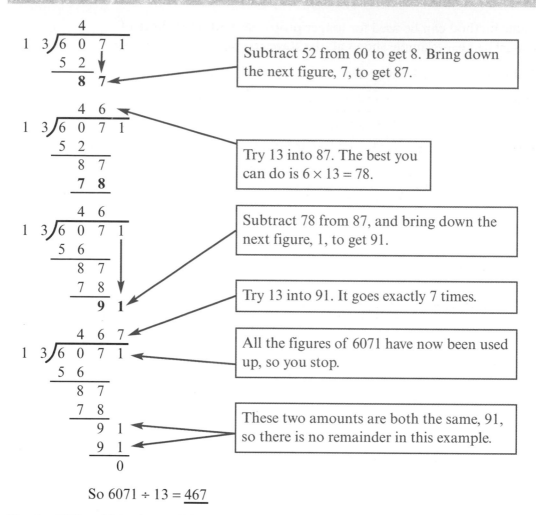

Subtract 52 from 60 to get 8. Bring down the next figure, 7, to get 87.

Try 13 into 87. The best you can do is $6 \times 13 = 78$.

Subtract 78 from 87, and bring down the next figure, 1, to get 91.

Try 13 into 91. It goes exactly 7 times.

All the figures of 6071 have now been used up, so you stop.

These two amounts are both the same, 91, so there is no remainder in this example.

So $6071 \div 13 = \underline{467}$

Check: $6071 \div 13$ is about $6000 \div 10 = 600$ so 467 looks about right.

The same method can be used for longer problems, with more lines of working. The next example shows all the stages completed. This time there is a remainder.

Example   Divide 91 481 by 17.

Solution

```
        5 3 8 1
  1 7 )9 1 4 8 1
      8 5
        6 4
        5 1
        1 3 8
        1 3 6
            2 1
            1 7
              4
```

This can be written as $5381\frac{4}{17}$ if you want to give the remainder as a fraction.

So: $91\,481 \div 17 = \underline{5381 \text{ remainder } 4}$.

Check: $91\,481 \div 17$ is about $90\,000 \div 20 = 4500$ so 5381 looks about right.

Exercise 12.2

Work out the answers to these long divisions. State the value of any remainder.

1 $33\,278 \div 14$ **2** ✔ $110\,964 \div 21$ **3** $4931 \div 19$

4 $71\,855 \div 22$ **5** $101\,664 \div 32$ **6** $119\,940 \div 28$

7 $33\,891 \div 43$ **8** $764\,332 \div 31$ **9** ✔ $22\,275 \div 81$

Work out the answers to these long divisions. Give the remainder as a fraction.

10 $9266 \div 41$ **11** $11\,062 \div 29$ **12** $7861 \div 53$

13 $20\,020 \div 82$ **14** $29\,703 \div 77$ **15** $53\,487 \div 31$

16 $22\,999 \div 24$ **17** $23\,396 \div 62$ **18** ✔ $98\,901 \div 99$

Summary

In this Unit you have learnt to multiply a 3-digit number by a 2-digit number without using a calculator. You have also learnt how to divide one number by another using long division, giving the remainder either as a whole number or as a fraction.

Long multiplication and long division without a calculator are skills which may be tested in the Key Stage 3 exam and at GCSE.

Review Exercise 12

Write down the answers to the following multiplication and division problems:

1 7×5 **2** 4×10 **3** 9×2 **4** 8×9

5 8×4 **6** $48 \div 4$ **7** $18 \div 3$ **8** $22 \div 2$

9 $24 \div 3$ **10** $49 \div 7$ **11** 11×4 **12** 7×7

13 $35 \div 5$ **14** $84 \div 7$ **15** 4×9 **16** $121 \div 11$

17 12×12 **18** $64 \div 8$ **19** $48 \div 6$ **20** 11×12

Use long multiplication to work out these:

21 127×15 **22** 34×160 **23** 418×24

24 318×53 **25** 1251×42 **26** 713×731

Use long division to work out these:

27 $945 \div 21$ **28** $9683 \div 23$ **29** $23\,901 \div 31$

30 $30\,233 \div 49$ **31** $8701 \div 27$ **32** $84\,121 \div 19$

33 In an international soccer tournament there are twenty-four teams, and each team has a squad of sixteen players. How many players are there in the tournament?

34 Thirteen coaches leave an airport, with forty-seven passengers on board each coach. Another coach carries 32 passengers. Find the total number of passengers on all fourteen coaches.

35* A school tuck shop buys 144 pencils at 19p each, and 64 pens at 93p each.
    a) Find the cost of all the pencils.
    b) Find the cost of all the pens.
    c) Find the total cost of all the pencils and pens together.

36* On a visit to my local pet shop I buy seven tins of dog meat at 49p for each tin, three toys at 67p each toy, and a bottle of flea shampoo costing £1.67.
    a) Calculate the total amount spent on all these items.
    b) Calculate the change I should receive from a £10 note.

37* Work out the exact value of $1 \times 2 \times 3 \times 4 \times 5 \times 6 \times 7 \times 8 \times 9 \times 10 \times 11 \times 12$.

38* At Silvertub School there are 27 classes. This year there are 521 pupils, and the Head Teacher wants to arrange that the classes are all as near to the same size as possible. How many pupils should the Head place in each class?

39* At Greyhall School there are 31 classes, all containing the same number of pupils. There are 744 pupils altogether. Find the number of pupils in each class.

40* **a)** Make a list of the first twenty multiples of 17 (i.e. 17, 34, 51 etc.)
    b) Make a list of the first twenty multiples of 19.
    c) Find a number which both 17 and 19 divide into exactly.

Unit 13
Fractions and percentages

In this Unit you will learn how to:
- ■ reduce a fraction to its simplest form by cancelling;
- ■ find a fraction of a given amount;
- ■ find a percentage of a given amount;
- ■ recognise the relationship between fractions and percentages;
- ■ solve problems using fractions and percentages.

13.1 Cancelling fractions

Look at the diagrams below:

They illustrate that the fractions $\frac{1}{2}$, $\frac{2}{4}$ and $\frac{3}{6}$ are really all the same. We say that these are **equivalent fractions**.

The fraction $\frac{1}{2}$ is said to be in its **lowest terms** because it cannot be written using simpler numbers.

The fractions $\frac{2}{4}$ and $\frac{3}{6}$ can be **cancelled down** to give an answer of $\frac{1}{2}$.

Example   Write these fractions in their lowest terms:

a) $\frac{6}{10}$ b) $\frac{15}{55}$ c) $\frac{36}{84}$

Solution   a)

The 6 and the 10 can each be divided by 2.

b)

The 15 and the 55 can each be divided by 5.

c)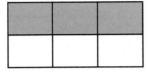

The 36 and the 84 can each be divided by 2, then by 2 again, then by 3.

Exercise 13.1
Write these fractions in their lowest terms. Show each step of the cancelling process.

1 $\frac{4}{10}$ 2 ✓ $\frac{6}{9}$ 3 $\frac{20}{70}$ 4 $\frac{18}{30}$

5 $\frac{4}{12}$ 6 $\frac{11}{33}$ 7 $\frac{16}{24}$ 8 $\frac{15}{25}$

9 $\frac{30}{45}$ 10 ✓ $\frac{16}{80}$ 11 $\frac{18}{27}$ 12 $\frac{42}{70}$

13.2 Finding fractions of a given amount

Example   Find three-quarters of 1244.

Solution $1244 \div 4 = 311$ | Divide by 4 to find **one**-quarter … |

$311 \times 3 = 933$ | … then multiply by 3 to find **three**-quarters. |

$\frac{3}{4}$ of 1244 is $\underline{933}$.

Exercise 13.2
Find:

1 One-fifth of 75

2 Three-eighths of 352

3 $\frac{2}{7}$ of 133

4 $\frac{5}{12}$ of 192

5 Two-thirds of 5841

6 Five-ninths of 126

7 $\frac{4}{9}$ of 5607

8 $\frac{2}{13}$ of 52

9 ✓ Three-quarters of 124

10 Three-tenths of 3560

11 $\frac{2}{11}$ of 1936

12 ✓ $\frac{5}{7}$ of 427

13 Seven-tenths of 1250

14 Four-fifths of 905

15 $\frac{1}{12}$ of 1320

16 $\frac{3}{16}$ of 256

17 Two-sevenths of 161

18 Five-eighths of 232

19 $\frac{7}{8}$ of 296

20 $\frac{8}{9}$ of 216.

13.3 Finding a percentage of a given amount

To find **1%** of a quantity, divide by **100**.
Other percentages can then be found easily.

Example   Find 27% of £160.

Solution   1% of 160 is 160 ÷ 100 = 1.6

⟵ Divide by 100 to find 1% …

27% is 27 × 1.6 = 43.2

⟵ … then multiply by 27 to find 27%.

So 27% of £160 is £43.20

Some percentage questions can be shortcut by using simple fractions.
Examples include:

$10\% = \frac{1}{10}$ $25\% = \frac{1}{4}$ $50\% = \frac{1}{2}$ $75\% = \frac{3}{4}$

Example   Last Sunday there were 124 people in the congregation for the morning service at St Mary's Church. The vicar is expecting an increase of 25% next week. How many people does he expect?

Solution   25% is the same as $\frac{1}{4}$.

124 ÷ 4 = 31.   ⟵ Find $\frac{1}{4}$ of 124 …

124 + 31 = 155.   ⟵ … then add it on.

The vicar expects 155 people next week.

Exercise 13.3

1 ✓ Find 18% of 3500.

2 Find 3% of 600.

3 Find 75% of 240.

4 Find 8% of 220.

5 Find 50% of 60.

6 Find 60% of 80.

7 ✓ Find 21% of $2000.

8 Find 18% of £150.

9 Find 10% of £12 500.

10 Find 6% of 45 000 people.

11 ✓ Increase 240 by 35%.

12 Increase $600 by 13%.

13 Decrease 800 by 25%.

14 Find 6% of 1800.

15 Decrease £3000 by 4%.

16 Find 12.5% of £400.

17 Increase 580 by 25%.

18 ✓ Decrease 360 by 70%.

19 Find 12% of 80.

20 Find 80% of 12.

13.4 Changing fractions into percentages

To change a fraction into a percentage, multiply it by **100%**.

Example   Write $\frac{4}{5}$ as a percentage.

Solution   We need to find $\frac{4}{5} \times 100\%$.

$\frac{1}{5}$ of 100% is 20%.

$\therefore \frac{4}{5}$ of 100% is $4 \times 20\% = 80\%$.

So $\frac{4}{5} = 80\%$.

Example   Write $\frac{5}{7}$ as a percentage.

Solution   We need to find $\frac{5}{7} \times 100\%$.

By calculator, $\frac{5}{7} \times 100\% = 71.42857\ldots\%$

So $\frac{5}{7} = \underline{71.4}\%$ (to one decimal place).

Exercise 13.4

Change these fractions into percentages. If any are not exact then give the answer correct to one decimal place.

1 $\frac{3}{8}$ 2 $\frac{2}{3}$ 3 $\frac{9}{10}$ 4 $\frac{3}{20}$

5 $\frac{7}{10}$ 6 ✔ $\frac{5}{8}$ 7 $\frac{3}{40}$ 8 ✔ $\frac{4}{11}$

9 $\frac{1}{20}$ 10 ✔ $\frac{5}{7}$ 11 $\frac{9}{11}$ 12 $\frac{7}{9}$

13 $\frac{7}{25}$ 14 $\frac{5}{12}$ 15 $\frac{2}{15}$ 16 $\frac{11}{50}$

17 ✔ $\frac{7}{50}$ 18 $\frac{19}{25}$ 19 $\frac{24}{25}$ 20 $\frac{14}{15}$

13.5 Changing percentages into fractions

To change a percentage into a fraction, divide it by **100%** and cancel the fraction if possible.

Example   Write 24% as a fraction.

Solution   24% is the same as $\frac{\overset{12}{\cancel{24}}}{\underset{50}{\cancel{100}}} = \frac{\overset{6}{\cancel{12}}}{\underset{25}{\cancel{50}}} = \frac{6}{25}$

So 24% = $\underline{\frac{6}{25}}$

> Remember to cancel down the fraction as far as possible.

An alternative method is to enter the fraction as 24 ⌟ 100 using the fraction key $\boxed{a^{b}\!/_{c}}$ on your calculator. The calculator will then automatically cancel the fraction for you.

If the percentage is not a whole number you may need to multiply the top and bottom of the fraction before cancelling, as in this next example.

Example   Write $37\frac{1}{2}\%$ as a fraction.

> Multiply top and bottom by 2.

Solution $\dfrac{37\frac{1}{2}}{100} = \dfrac{75}{200} = \dfrac{15}{40} = \dfrac{3}{8}$

So $37\frac{1}{2}\%$ is the same as $\underline{\frac{3}{8}}$.

Exercise 13.5

Change these percentages into fractions. You may use the cancelling method shown in the example, or your calculator's fraction key, to give the fraction in its simplest form.

1 32% **2** 4% **3** 44% **4** 16% **5** 14%

6 18% **7** ✔ $2\frac{1}{2}\%$ **8** 61% **9** 99% **10** 80%

11 5% **12** $17\frac{1}{2}\%$ **13** 50% **14** ✔ 15% **15** 55%

16 86% **17** ✔ 26% **18** 19% **19** ✔ $16\frac{2}{3}\%$ **20** 12.5%

Summary

In this Unit you learnt how to cancel down fractions into their lowest terms. You have practised finding fractions and percentages of quantities, and you have increased or decreased amounts by a given percentage. You have learnt how to change a fraction into a percentage by multiplying by 100%, and how to change a percentage into a fraction by dividing by 100%.

Percentage problems are often set in the context of money; further practice of percentage problems will be found in the following Review section. Remember that answers to money problems should always be written using two decimal places.

Review Exercise 13

Cancel these fractions down so that they are in their lowest possible terms:

1 $\frac{5}{15}$ **2** $\frac{13}{26}$

3 $\frac{60}{80}$ **4** $\frac{12}{20}$

5 $\frac{44}{77}$ **6** $\frac{24}{42}$

7 $\frac{105}{140}$ **8** $\frac{144}{360}$

Find:

9 Three-fifths of 750   **10** Seven-eighths of 1024

11 $\frac{4}{9}$ of 81 million   **12** $\frac{4}{15}$ of 180

13 Nine-tenths of 120

14 Five-elevenths of 121

15 $\frac{3}{10}$ of 360

16 $\frac{6}{7}$ of 98.

Calculate:

17 12% of $250

18 $17\frac{1}{2}$% of £450

19 25% of £640

20 3% of 2500 people

21 82% of 5000 m

22 $33\frac{1}{3}$% of 900 *l*.

23 Increase £250 by 12%.

24 Increase 650 kg by 4%.

25 Decrease $45 by 9%.

26 Increase 300 cm by 90%.

27 Decrease 7000 m by 15%.

28 Decrease 56 000 lire by 4%.

29 Find the smallest and the largest quantity in each list:
    a) two-fifths,   20%,   one-third,   35%
    b) 50%,   four-ninths,   43%,   nine-twentieths
    c) five-sevenths,   71%,   two-thirds,   65%

30 Last year I spent £260 on rail fares, and this year I expect to spend 6% more. Calculate how much I expect to spend on rail fares this year.

31 One mile is 1760 yards. How many yards are there in three-quarters of a mile?

32 A certain type of radio is supposed to be sold for £35. Three shops offer different sale prices:

Cheapskate Sounds
One-third off all purchases

Cost Less Music
Everything slashed by 35%

Bargain Audio
£10 off all purchases

Find the actual cost of the radio at each of the three shops. State which is offering the best deal.

33 One ton is 2240 pounds. How many pounds are there in two and three-eighths tons?

34 Annabel scored 38 out of 40 in a mathematics test and 11 out of 16 in an English test. In which subject did she achieve the higher percentage?

35 One acre is 4840 square yards. How many square yards are there in two-elevenths of an acre?

36 Of the items stocked in a shop 12% are made in Britain. The shop stocks 350 items altogether. How many of these are made in Britain?

37* There are 630 pupils on the roll at Westbury School. Two-sevenths of them wear glasses and 10% wear contact lenses. How many pupils wear neither?

38* Of the 120 people at a theatre performance, 24 are senior citizens. What percentage of the audience is this? What fraction is it?

39* Half of the children at my school are boys, and 10% of them are 16 or over. There are 135 boys under 16. How many children altogether are there at my school?

40* A holiday apartment costs 8960 French francs to hire, but a 10% discount is offered for early booking. A deposit of one-quarter of the total bill has to be sent at the time of booking.
Calculate the size of deposit required when an early booking is made.

41* On a double-decker bus there are 9 passengers on the upper deck and 15 passengers on the lower deck. What percentage of the passengers are on the upper deck?

42* A ship is carrying 540 passengers. Half of them are English and one-third are American; the rest are Australian.
a) How many Australian passengers are there?
b) What fraction of all the passengers are Australian?

43* I have just had my car serviced. The bill is in two parts. Part 1 of the bill is for £165.00 plus VAT (a tax) at $17\frac{1}{2}$%; Part 2 of the bill is for £140.00 but does not attract VAT. Find the total amount that I have to pay for my car service.

44* A certain plant grows by 5% of its height each day. At midday on Monday it was 400 mm high.
a) How tall was it at midday on Tuesday?
b) How tall was it at midday on Wednesday?

45* Jim invests £100 in a building society. At the end of each year interest of 6% is added to the value of his investment.
a) Find the total amount that Jim has after one year.
b) Find the total amount he has after two years (i.e. increase the answer to part a) by 6%)
c) Find the total amount after three years.
d) How long will it take until Jim's investment has reached £200?

46* Here is some information about my computer:
- The hard disk can hold 2 gigabytes of data
- 1 gigabyte is 1024 megabytes
- One-eighth of the hard disk is free space
a) Calculate the number of megabytes of free space.
After deleting some files I find that I have 410 megabytes of free space.
b) Calculate the percentage of my hard disk which is now free.

Unit 14
Ratio and direct proportion

In this Unit you will learn how to:

■ reduce a ratio to its simplest form by cancelling;

■ divide an amount into a given ratio;

■ use direct proportion;

■ solve problems using ratios and proportions.

14.1 Introducing ratio

> A **ratio** is a set of two (or more) numbers showing how something is divided up into portions. Sometimes ratios may be written in their lowest terms, rather like fractions.

Example In class 5B at Greenview School there are 14 boys and 18 girls. Write the ratio of boys to girls in its simplest terms.

Solution The ratio is $14:18$

$= 7:9$

> The symbol $14:18$ is read as '14 to 18'. Since both 14 and 18 are multiples of 2 you can cancel these numbers down to 7 and 9.

On other occasions ratios are written in the form $1:n$ or $n:1$.

Example An office photocopier can make copies which are larger or smaller than the original. Fiona enlarges a diagram which was 12 cm long; it is now 18 cm long. Write this as a ratio
a) in its simplest form using whole numbers;
b) in the form $1:n$ where n is a decimal fraction.

Solution The ratio is $12:18$

$= 2:3$

Now divide both numbers by 2, to get a ratio of $1:$ something.

So $2:3 = 1:1.5$

Exercise 14.1

Write these as ratios in their simplest form, using whole numbers.

1 $6:8$ **2** $16:20$ **3** $12:30$ **4** $25:35$

5 $25:75$ **6** $28:35$ **7** $32:40$ **8** ✓ $34:51$

Write these ratios in the form $1:n$, where n is a decimal number greater than one.

  9 $4:5$ **10** $2:7$ **11** $10:17$ **12** $5:9$

Write these ratios in the form $n:1$, where n is a decimal number greater than one.

13 $7:4$ **14** $11:5$ **15** $21:10$ **16** $5:2$

14.2 Dividing an amount into a given ratio

Sometimes we need to divide up an amount according to a given ratio. The method is to add up all the parts of the ratio first, and find the value of one 'share'. Then multiply this up to solve the problem.

Example   Josh is 13 years old and Sam is 12. They are given 100 stamps for their collection, and they decide to share them out in the ratio of their ages. How many stamps does each of them receive?

Solution   The ratio is 13:12

$13 + 12 = 25$

Divide 100 up into 25 'shares':

$100 \div 25 = 4$

and so 1 share is equal to 4 stamps.

Therefore Josh gets $13 \times 4 = \underline{52}$ stamps.

Sam gets $12 \times 4 = \underline{48}$ stamps.

> The key step is to take the ratio $13:12$ and work out $13 + 12 = 25$.
>
> Then divide 25 into the total of 100 stamps, to get 4 stamps.
>
> Finally multiply 4 stamps by the age of each boy to find out how many stamps each gets.

Exercise 14.2

1 £18 is to be divided in the ratio $5:4$. Work out the size of each part.

2 ✔ A cake weighing 450 grams is to be divided into two parts in the ratio $7:8$. Work out the weight of each part.

3 253 marbles are to be divided in the ratio $7:4$. Work out the size of each part.

4 A photographer examines 108 pictures taken at a wedding. The ratio of good pictures to failures is $7:2$. Work out how many pictures were good, and how many were failures.

5 A factory makes red cars and blue cars in the ratio $3:5$. Last week it produced a total of 96 cars in these two colours. Calculate the number of cars of each colour which were made last week.

6 Two girls share 60 sweets in the ratio $5:7$. Work out how many sweets each girl gets.

7 ✔ A stick 1 m long is to be cut into two parts so that their lengths are in the ratio 3:7. Find the length of the shorter part.

8 Gregory wants to mix three chemicals, A, B, C, in the ratio $2:3:5$. He wants to make 400 grams of the mixture altogether. How much of chemical A does he need?

9 A box of fireworks contains bangers and rockets in the ratio of $5:2$. If there are 21 fireworks altogether, how many of them are bangers?

10 The books in Greenview School Library are classed either as fiction or non-fiction. The librarian calculates that there are 10 fiction books for every 22 non-fiction.
  a) Write this ratio in its simplest form.
  b) Calculate the number of each type of book, if the library has 2400 books altogether.

14.3 Direct proportion

If two quantities are always in the same ratio then we say they are in **direct proportion**.

The rule $y = 2x$ is an example of direct proportion, since y is always twice the size of x. In this case the number 2 is called the **constant of proportionality**.

Example   The cost of a school trip is directly proportional to the number of pupils who go. If 50 pupils go then the cost is £80. Find the cost if 90 pupils go.

This problem can be solved either by a ratio method or by using algebra.

Here is the solution using ratios:

Solution   The ratio of pupils: cost is $50 : 80 = 5 : 8$.

We want this to become 90 : something if 90 pupils go.

Ratio	5	8
×18	90	?

5 must be multiplied by 18 to turn into 90 (that is $90 \div 5 = 18$).

So 8 must be multiplied by 18 as well.

The cost is $8 \times 18 = \underline{£144}$.

Alternatively, here is the solution using algebra:

Solution   Let the cost be c, for a number of pupils n.

Then $c = kn$

When $n = 50$, $c = 80$.

Therefore $80 = k \times 50$,
so $k = 80 \div 50 = 1.6$

Since the constant of proportionality
is 1.6 we can now write

$c = 1.6n$

Thus for 90 pupils, $n = 90$, giving

$c = 1.6 \times 90$

$= \underline{£144}$

> The first step is to describe the relationship between c and n using a formula, $c = kn$
>
> Next, use the given numbers to find the value of k.
>
> Finally, now you know the formula, use it to solve the problem.

Exercise 14.3

Solve these problems about direct proportion. You may choose to use either a method based on ratios or an algebraic method.

1 The mass of a piece of steel pipe is directly proportional to its length. A piece 80 cm long has a mass of 5 kg. Find the mass of a piece of pipe 200 cm long.

2 ✔ The cost of placing an advertisement in a magazine is directly proportional to the number of lines it takes up. An advertisement of 5 lines will cost 80 pence. Find the cost of an advertisement of 12 lines.

3 A tank is being filled with water. The depth of the water is directly proportional to the time for which the tap has been running. Ten minutes after the start the water is 30 cm deep. How deep will it be 25 minutes after the start?

4 A minibus is driving along a stretch of motorway. The distance it travels is proportional to the time for which it has been travelling. In 20 minutes it travels 30 kilometres. How far will it travel in 30 minutes?

5 My video player has a counter. The number of counts showing is proportional to the time for which the tape has been running. After 30 minutes the counter reads 2400. What will be the reading on the counter after 75 minutes?

6 The cost of fitting a new floor to a room is directly proportional to the area of the floor. An area of 10 square metres would cost £250. Find the cost of fitting a new floor to a room whose area is: **a)** 35 square metres **b)** 8 square metres.

7 A photographer copies a photograph measuring 6 inches by 4 inches, and enlarges it until the short side has become 10 inches. Find the length of the long side in the enlargement.

8 Peter claims that the time it takes to do his paper round is directly proportional to the number of papers he has to deliver. Here is some data about his paper round last week:

	Monday to Friday	Saturday
Time taken	2 hours	3 hours
Number of papers delivered	80	120

a) Explain how the data in the table supports Peter's claim.

b) On Sunday Peter has to deliver 70 papers. Calculate the time taken, assuming his claim remains true.

Summary

In this Unit **you have learnt how to simplify ratios so that they are in their simplest form using whole numbers, and you have also written them in the form $1:n$ or $n:1$. You have found how to divide an amount according to a given ratio.**

You have solved problems about direct proportion, using methods based on ratio or algebra.

Review Exercise 14

Write these ratios in their simplest form, using whole numbers:

1 $14:18$	**2** $44:33$	**3** $12:30$	**4** $14:21$
5 $20:25$	**6** $18:21$	**7** $38:57$	**8** $95:90$

Write these ratios in the form $1:n$ or $n:1$, where n is a decimal number bigger than 1:

9 $5:8$	**10** $2:3$	**11** $4:9$	**12** $13:10$
13 $11:4$	**14** $11:5$	**15** $10:19$	**16** $17:2$

17 A piece of string 200 cm long is to be divided into two pieces in the ratio 2 : 3. Find the length of each piece.

18 A mathematics exam paper is to be divided into two sections, A and B. The marks available in each section should be in the ratio $4:5$ and the exam should be out of 45 marks altogether. How many marks should be available for section A?

19 The ratio of boys to girls in a school is $8:5$. There are 496 boys.
a) Calculate the number of girls in the school.
b) Hence calculate the total number of children in the school.

20 Each day Caspar reckons the ratio of the time he spends asleep to the time awake is 3 : 5. If he is right, how much time does Caspar spend asleep each day?

21 An old cookery book says that the time for which I cook a turkey should be directly proportional to its weight. A turkey weighing 6 pounds should be cooked for 2 hours. How long should I cook a turkey weighing 14 pounds?

22 The time it takes a teacher to mark a pile of exam papers is directly proportional to the number of papers. On Wednesday she marks 25 papers in $2\frac{1}{2}$ hours.
a) How long does it take her to mark 42 papers on Thursday?
b) On Friday she marks for $3\frac{1}{2}$ hours. How many papers does she mark?

23 The cost of buying a necklace with your name on it is directly proportional to the number of letters in your name. Sarah buys such a necklace and has to pay £2.40. How much does her sister Rosalind have to pay for one?

24 A cereal manufacturer decides that the cost of a packet of cereal should be directly proportional to the amount of cereal inside. A 375 g box costs £1.99. Calculate the price you think they should charge for a 500 g box.

25* On an orange squash bottle it says 'add 1 part of squash to 7 parts of water'. How much water would I need to make up 400 ml of drink?

26* My television can be set to display a picture in a *widescreen* 16 : 9 format, when the width and height are in the ratio of 16 : 9. If the programme being broadcast is not suitable for widescreen viewing then I select a *standard* 4 : 3 format instead. In either format the height of the picture is unchanged at 36 cm.
Calculate the width of the picture when I am watching:
a) in *widescreen* format; b) in *standard* format.
c) Calculate the ratio of the *standard* width to the *widescreen* width, giving your answer as a ratio of whole numbers in its simplest form.

27* In a certain country the voting system is based on proportional representation. This means that the number of seats for any given political party is proportional to the number of votes they gained in the last election. There are 110 seats available in total.

	People's Party	Democratic Party	New Socialist Party	Raving Monster Party
Number of votes	12 250	16 000	9 500	395
Number of seats				

a) Copy and complete the table, showing how many seats each party should get.
b) Do your answers add up to 110?

Unit 15
Rounding and estimation

In this Unit you will learn how to:
- round off quantities to one or two significant figures;
- use approximations to estimate the answer to a calculation;
- use approximations to check the reasonableness of an answer.

 A calculator may be used to compare an estimate with the exact answer.

15.1 Significant figures

> Count significant figures from the left-hand side of a number.

In the number 34 679

> the 3 is the first significant figure;
> the 4 is the second significant figure;
> the 6 is the third significant figure;
> and so on.

Sometimes you need to round a number to one or two significant figures. The other figures are set to zero, and it is important to make sure that the place value is not disturbed (e.g. the 3 remains the 10 000 column). Rounding up occurs if the first of these other figures is a 5 or more, but not if it is 4 or less.

Example In one day 34 679 people visited a supermarket.
Write this number correct to: **a)** two significant figures
b) one significant figure.

Solution **a)** 34 679

These three figures will be set to zero.

These are the two significant figures.

If this figure is 4 or less then the 34 stays as 34
... if it is 5 or more the 34 rounds up to 35.

34 679 correct to two significant figures is 35 000.

b) 34 679

This is the one significant figure.

As this is a 4 you do not round up.

34 679 correct to one significant figure is 30 000.

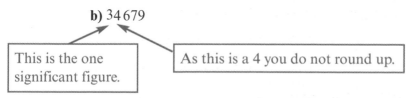

Exercise 15.1

Round these correct to two significant figures:

1 ✔ 157   **2** 24 677   **3** 599   **4** 176 206

5 450   **6** 32 144   **7** 1 450 877   **8** ✔ 207 000

Round these correct to one significant figures:

9 ✔ 41 207   **10** 259   **11** 1094   **12** 108

13 70 020   **14** ✔ 65 700   **15** 2 099 999   **16** 3579

15.2 Estimation

To obtain an estimate of the answer to a calculation:

> Round off all the numbers to one significant figure; then do the calculation using these approximate numbers.

Example   There are 33 coaches on a cross-channel ferry. Each coach carries 49 passengers. Estimate the total number of passengers on the coaches.

Solution   The exact calculation is 33×49.

Rounding each of these to one significant figure, the estimate is

$$30 \times 50 = 1500.$$

The coaches carry approximately <u>1500 people</u>.

> Give the final estimate to 1 or 2 significant figures.

Exercise 15.2

Round the numbers to one significant figure, and use the result to estimate the answer to each of these calculations.

1 ✔ 58×21 **2** 399×31 **3** 47×22

4 360×87 **5** $4899 \div 46$ **6** $377 \div 19$

7 ✔ $5877 \div 32$ **8** 774×773 **9** $1906 \div 44$

Round the numbers to one significant figure, and hence make estimates of the answers to these problems.

10 ✔ A confectionery bar weighs 65 grams. Find the total weight of 19 bars.

11 In a lottery 23 people each win £2800. Find the total amount they win.

12 If 354 sweets are shared out between 11 friends how many does each receive?

13 Some wedding guests travel by taxi to the reception. Each taxi can carry 4 people. How many taxis are needed for 77 guests?

14 A star cluster contains about 200 stars. Find the total number of stars in 27 clusters.

15 In a lottery 31 friends win a total of £576 229. How much does each receive?

16 Films cost £ 4.99 each to process, and I have 11 films. Find the cost of processing all 11 films.

17 A ream (500 sheets) of paper is shared out between 18 students. How many sheets does each receive?

18 If 37 803 letters are sorted into piles of 200 how many piles will there be?

19 ✔ It takes me one hour to mark 17 exam scripts. Altogether I mark for 31 hours. How many exam scripts do I mark in this time?

15.3 Checking the reasonableness of an answer

In this section you will be given some calculations followed by a suggested answer. The answer is either exactly right or else it is very wrong. Use the method of estimation to detect the wrong answers, and then correct them by calculator.

Example   Check the calculation $377 \times 244 = 91\,988$

Solution   An estimate is $400 \times 200 = \underline{80\,000.}$
Since this is fairly close to 91 988 the answer looks reasonable.

Example   Check the calculation $3780 \div 18 = 21$

Solution   An estimate is $4000 \div 20 = \underline{200}$
Since this is nowhere near 21 the answer looks wrong.
Checking on a calculator shows that the answer is $\underline{210.}$

Exercise 15.3

Some of these calculations are wrong. Use the method of estimating to check the reasonableness of the answers. If you find any that are badly wrong then use a calculator to obtain the correct exact answer.

1 $87 \times 14 = 1218$ **2** $33 \times 11 = 863$

3 $16 \times 702 = 1123$ **4** $117 \times 82 = 9594$

5 $365 \times 98 = 35\,770$ **6** ✔ $4020 \div 15 = 268$

7 ✔ $10\,570 \div 14 = 155$ **8** $2891 \div 49 = 259$

9 $23 \times 79 = 1817$ **10** $27\,783 \div 63 = 4411$

Summary

In this Unit you have practised rounding off numbers to one or two significant figures. You have made estimates of the answers to arithmetic problems by working with rounded numbers, and you have detected errors when checking the reasonableness of an answer.

At Key Stage 3 and GCSE you may be asked to 'estimate the value of …'. You must remember to set out a calculation based on rounded numbers – do not just guess!

Review Exercise 15

Round these correct to two significant figures:

1 54 206	**2** 1997	**3** 207	**4** 2 539 200
5 7006	**6** 4502	**7** 561	**8** 7777
9 3333	**10** 9999		

Round these correct to the stated number of significant figures:

11 64 256 (3 s.f.)	**12** 386 (1 s.f.)	**13** 60 801 (1 s.f.)
14 2996 (3 s.f.)	**15** 106 277 (3 s.f.)	**16** 4502 (1 s.f.)
17 11 451 (4 s.f.)	**18** 186 000 (2 s.f.)	**19** 13 million (1 s.f.)

Obtain estimates for the answers to these calculations. Then use your calculator to find the exact answer.

20 552×21	**21** $552 \div 23$	**22** $3102 \div 47$
23 144×244	**24** 1.96×615	**25** 28.1×42.5
26 $33.28 \div 25.6$	**27** $266.7 \div 3.5$	**28** 21.05×54.2

Do questions **29** to **37** using rounded numbers.
Do not work out exact answers.

29* In a clothes shop I buy three items costing £11.99, £13.60 and £25.30. The bill comes to £ 60.89. Does this seem reasonable?

30* In a Year 7 end of term test I score 57 in English, 63 in mathematics, 22 in technology and 51 in science. My teacher says I scored 260 altogether. By rounding all the marks to one significant figure show that my teacher is wrong.

31* Five anglers compare their catches for the month of February: they are 23, 61, 11, 22 and 48 fish respectively. Estimate the total number of fish caught by all five of them.

32* I have a box file which can hold 800 pages. I wish to store six sets of work in the box file; these contain 210, 35, 79, 112, 21 and 29 pages respectively.

Estimate the total number of pages, and hence say whether the box file is large enough to hold them all.

33* A pack of butter weighs 225 grams. Estimate the total weight of 18 packs of butter.

34* A rock band plays a world tour of 39 concerts. They reckon that on average 7900 people watch each concert. Calculate an estimate of the total number of people who watch the concerts. Is this figure more than a million, or less?

35* One bag of rabbit food lasts my rabbit, Patch, for 12 days. Roughly how many bags would Patch need for a whole year?

36* A newspaper once claimed that the president of the world's largest computer software company becomes $20 million richer each day. Assuming this claim to be correct, calculate an estimate of how much richer he becomes over a period of three months.

37* Mrs Green's classroom contains 28 tables, 1 teacher's desk and 29 chairs. There are 26 pupils in class 5B. Estimate the total number of legs in the room when Mrs Green is teaching class 5B.

38* The number of seconds in a year can be calculated like this:

$$365 \times 24 \times 60 \times 60$$

a) Explain where these numbers come from.
b) Calculate an estimate of the answer, using values rounded to one significant figure.
c) Obtain the exact answer, using your calculator.

Unit 16
Algebra

In this Unit you will learn how to:
- ■ use brackets in arithmetic and algebra;
- ■ substitute numbers into algebraic formulae;
- ■ use root and power keys on a calculator;
- ■ construct and use simple formulae;
- ■ multiply out simple expressions involving brackets.

A calculator will be required for the substitution exercises.

16.1 Introducing brackets

You should already be aware that dividing and muliplying take priority over adding and subtracting when you do ordinary arithmetic.

Example   Work out the value of $3 + 5 \times 2$.

Solution $3 + (5 \times 2)$

$= 3 + 10$

$= \underline{13}$

> There are two processes: + and ×
> The × has to be done first, even though it occurs later in the expression.

If you want the processes to be done in the opposite order, then brackets should be used. (Some TV game shows appear not to know this!)

> If you have to work out the value of a numerical expression containing **brackets** …
>
> …then the part written **inside** brackets should be worked out before the rest.

> Division and Multiplication come next …
>
> …and finally Addition and Subtraction.

These rules are sometimes remembered by the 'word' BODMAS – which will be used in the next section.

Example   Work out the value of $(3 + 5) \times 2$.

Solution $(3 + 5) \times 2$

$= 8 \times 2$

$= \underline{16}$

> This time there are **brackets**, so work that part out first.

Sometimes there can be more than one set of brackets. The principle is the same – find the value of the insides of the brackets first.

Example Work out the value of $(3 + 8) \times 2 + 18 \div (7 - 4)$.

Solution
$$(3 + 8) \times 2 + 18 \div (7 - 4)$$
$$= 11 \times 2 + 18 \div (7 - 4)$$
$$= 11 \times 2 + 18 \div 3$$
$$= 22 + 6$$
$$= \underline{28}$$

> There are two sets of **brackets**, so clear them first.
> $3 + 8 = 11$ and $7 - 4 = 3$.

> Now do the $\times$ and $\div$ stages, leaving the $+$ until the very end.

Exercise 16.1

Find the values of each of these. Do them one step at a time, and do not use a calculator.

1 $3 \times 4 + 2$ **2** $3 + 4 \times 2$ **3** $4 + (5 - 3)$

4 $(4 + 5) - 3$ **5** $6 + 9 \div 3$ **6** $3 \times (12 + 3)$

7 $2 \times (6 - 3) + 1$ **8** $(15 - 3) \div 4$ **9** $6 + 2 \times (6 + 2)$

10 $4 \times 5 + 6 \times 7$ **11** $4 \times (5 + 6) \times 7$ **12** $(13 - 2) \times (3 + 4)$

13 $13 - 2 \times 3 + 4$ **14** $25 \times (5 - 1) - 99$ **15** $(10 + 1) \times (10 - 1)$

Work out the values of each of these. You will find a calculator helpful.

16 $2.4 + 5 \times (3.6 + 6.3)$ **17** $2.2 + 3.3 \times 4.4 - 5.5$

18 $9.6 \div (2.1 - 0.7) + 3.5 \times 3$ **19** $2.2 \times 3.3 + 4.4 \times 5.5$

20 $(7.1 + 4.5) \div (0.8 + 1.7)$

16.2 Substitution

You will often need to substitute numbers in place of letters in an algebraic formula. You might need to use BODMAS:

Brackets   Brackets should be dealt with first …

Order   … then Order (squares, cubes etc.)

Division

Multiplication   Multiplying and Dividing next (in any order) …

Addition

Subtraction   … and finally Adding and Subtracting (again in any order).

Example   If $a = 5$ and $b = 4$ work out the value of $3a + b^2$.

> $3a$ means '3 times a.'
> b^2 means 'b times b.'

Solution $3a + b^2 = 3 \times 5 + (4)^2$ ← Brackets and Order done first …

$= 3 \times 5 + 16$ ← … then the Multiplication …

$= 15 + 16$ ← … and lastly the Addition.

$= \underline{31}$

Example   If $c = 1$, $d = 4$ and $e = 2$ work out the value of $2(4c + 3e)^2 - 3d$.

Solution $2(4c + 3e)^2 - 3d = 2(4 \times 1 + 3 \times 2)^2 - 3 \times 4$

$= 2(4 + 6)^2 - 3 \times 4$ ← Bracket first: $4 + 6 = 10$

$= 2(10)^2 - 3 \times 4$ ← Squaring next: $10^2 = 100$

$= 2 \times 100 - 3 \times 4$ ← Then Multiply …

$= 200 - 12$ ← … and finish with the Subtraction.

$= \underline{188}$

Exercise 16.2

If $a = 6$, $b = 2$ and $c = 3$ then work out the value of:

1 $3a - 4b$ **2** $6b + a^2$

3 ✔ $3(2a + c) + 4b$ **4** $10(a + c + 4)$

5 $5a + 4b - c^2$ **6** ✔ $4a - 3b + 2c \div 3$

7 $(a + 2b + c)^2$ **8** $3(a + b) - 2(b + c)$

If $p = 7$, $q = 2$ and $r = 3$ work out the value of:

9 $p + q + r$ **10** $2p + 3q + 4r$

11 ✔ $p^2 + q^2 + r^2$ **12** $(p + q + r)^2$

13 $2p - 3q + 4r^2$ **14** $p^2 + q \div 2 + 5r$

If $x = 8$, $y = 4$ and $z = 3$ work out the value of:

15 $4(x + y)$ **16** $2x - 3y + 4z$

17 $x - y^2$ **18** ✔ $2(x - y) - z^2$

19 $(p - r) \div q$ **20** $(p - 2r) \times (p - 2q)$

16.3 Powers and roots

On your calculator use $\boxed{x^2}$ to find the square of a number

On your calculator use $\boxed{x^y}$ then $\boxed{3}$ to find the cube of a number

On your calculator use $\boxed{\sqrt{}}$ to find the square root of a number

Example   Calculate $6.2^2 + 3.8$.

Solution   Using a calculator, press these keys:

$\boxed{6}\ \boxed{.}\ \boxed{2}\ \boxed{x^2}\ \boxed{+}\ \boxed{3}\ \boxed{.}\ \boxed{8}\ \boxed{=}$

$6.2^2 + 3.8 = \underline{42.24}$

Example   Calculate $404.2 - (5.63 + 1.4)^3$, correct to 4 significant figures.

Solution   First, work out the bracket:
$5.63 + 1.4 = 7.03$

Using a calculator, press these keys:

$\boxed{4}\ \boxed{0}\ \boxed{4}\ \boxed{.}\ \boxed{2}\ \boxed{-}\ \boxed{7}\ \boxed{.}\ \boxed{0}\ \boxed{3}\ \boxed{x^y}\ \boxed{3}\ \boxed{=}$

The full calculator display is 56.771073

> It is a good idea to write down more figures than you need…

$404.2 - (5.63 + 1.4)^3 = \underline{56.77}$
(to 4 significant figures)

> …then do the rounding off.

Example   Find $2.8 \times 3.5 - \sqrt{14.6}$,
correct to 3 significant figures.

Solution   Using a calculator, press these keys:

$\boxed{2}\ \boxed{.}\ \boxed{8}\ \boxed{\times}\ \boxed{3}\ \boxed{.}\ \boxed{5}\ \boxed{-}\ \left(\boxed{\sqrt{}}\ \boxed{1}\ \boxed{4}\ \boxed{.}\ \boxed{6}\right)\ \boxed{=}$

The full calculator display is 5.979005365

$2.8 \times 3.5 - \sqrt{14.6} = \underline{5.98}$
(to 3 significant figures)

> Some calculators need 14.6 first, then the √ key. Check how yours works.

Exercise 16.3
Find the values of these. Write down the full calculator display, and also round off your answer correct to 3 significant figures.

1 $1.3 \times 2.8 + 4.5^2$ **2** $8.7^3 - 7.8^3$

3 $(3.5 + 2 \times 1.1)^2$ **4** $5.2^2 + \sqrt{4.9}$

5 ✓ $3 \times 4.6 - 2.9^3$ **6** $120 - 7.5^2$

7 $\sqrt{289} + 3$ **8** ✓ $10 \div 2 + 5^2$

9 $4^3 + 73$ **10** $\sqrt{(8^2 + 15^2)}$

If $s = 2.4$, $t = 1.9$, $u = 1.1$, $v = 0.6$ find, correct to 4 significant figures, the values of:

11 $s^2 + t^3$ **12** $\sqrt{(s + t)}$

13 $u^2 - v^3$ **14** ✓ $(4s + 5)^3$

15 $\sqrt{s} + \sqrt{t}$ **16** $2(t + 2v) - 3u$

17 $s^2 + t^3 + u^2 + v^3$ **18** $5(s + t)^3$

19 $4s^2 - t - v$ **20** ✓ $\sqrt{(s + tv)}$

16.4 Constructing and using formulae

Example Look at this number machine:

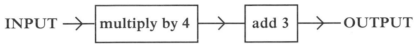

If x is the input, write a formula for the output.

Solution Work your way through the diagram:

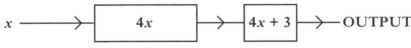

Output $= \underline{4x + 3}$

Example I start the day with a tub containing 125 Smarties. Each hour I eat 6 Smarties. How many do I have left after 4 hours? How many after n hours?

Solution In 4 hours I eat $6 \times 4 = 24$ Smarties.
I have $125 - 24 = 101$ left.

In n hours I will eat $6n$ Smarties.
I have $\underline{125 - 6n}$ left.

Exercise 16.4

Write algebraic formulae for these number machines (let the input number be x).

 1 Input; multiply by 3; add 6; output

 2 ✓ Input; multiply by 2; subtract 5; output

 3 Input; add 1; multiply by 3; output

 4 Input; subtract 2; multiply by 7; output

 5 Input; square; add 1; output

 6 Input; add 1; square; output

7 Input; square; double; add 3; output

8 Input; subtract 3; square; output

9 ✔ Input; add 3; divide by 2; output

10 Input; add 4; square root; output

Write algebraic formulae to answer these questions.

11 I have £3 in my bank account, and I save £2 every month. How much money do I have after 3 months? How much do I have after x months?

12 A reservoir is 60 feet deep at the beginning of August, but the level then goes down a foot every day. How deep is it after one week? How deep after n days?

13 A music judge awards 100 points to start with, but then takes off 2 points for each mistake. Find the score obtained by a cellist who makes 5 mistakes. Find the score obtained by a violinist who makes x mistakes.

14 ✔ Baby Georgina weighed 9 pounds at birth, and then gained 2 pounds each month. What did she weigh when she was six months old? What was her weight after x months?

15 A floppy disk can store 1440 kilobytes of data. I want to store some files of size 20 kilobytes on the floppy disk. How much space remains after I have stored 12 files? How much after I have stored n files?

16 I start a car journey with a full tank of 70 litres. Each hour I use up 8 litres. How much fuel remains after 3 hours? How much remains after x hours?

17 At the beginning of the school year the stationery room has 1200 green exercise books. If 90 books are issued each month how many are left after n months?

18 ✔ I am buying a new lounge suite on interest-free credit. I begin by owing the shop £1500, but each month this figure is reduced by £50. How much do I still owe after 8 months? How much after t months?

19 Theatre tickets cost £3 for an adult and £2 for a child. Find the total cost for 6 adults and 3 children. Find the total cost for x adults and y children.

20 A taxi firm operates cars, which can carry four passengers, and minibuses, which can carry nine passengers. Find the number of passengers who can be carried by two cars and five minibuses. How many passengers can be carried by a cars and b minibuses?

16.5 Simplifying formulae

$a + a$ is written as $2a$
$3 \times b$ is written as $3b$
$2c + 3c$ is simplified to $5c$
$2d + 3e$ cannot be simplified

Example   Simplify these expressions:

1 $4a + a$ **2** $5 \times b + 2 \times c$

3 $3 \times d - 2 \times e + 4 \times d$ **4** $9 \times f \times f$

Solution   **1** $4a + a = \underline{5a}$ **2** $5 \times b + 2 \times c = \underline{5b + 2c}$

3 $3 \times d - 2 \times e + 4 \times d$ **4** $9 \times f \times f = \underline{9f^2}$
$= 3d - 2e + 4d$
$= \underline{7d - 2e}$

Exercise 16.5
Simplify these algebraic expressions:

1 a) $a + a + a$ **2 a)** $8d - 3d$
   b) $3b + 2b - b$ **b)** $4 \times e + 5 \times e$
   c) $c + c + 3c$ **c)** $9 \times f - 3 \times f$

3 a) $5j - 2k - 2j$ **4 a)** $5 \times p \times p$
   b) $3l - 2l + 6l$ **b)** $4 \times q + 3 \times r \times r - 3 \times q$
   c) ✔ $m + 2n + 3m + 4n$ **c)** $3 \times x \times x - 2 \times x + x \times x$

5 a) $9s + 7t + 5s - 3t$ **6 a)** ✔ $7 \times y \times y \times y$
   b) $15u - 8u - 6u$ **b)** $5 \times z + 6 \times a + 7 \times z$
   c) $6x - 15x + 21x$ **c)** ✔ $4 \times b \times b + 5 \times b \times b + 7 \times b$

16.6 Multiplying out brackets

Sometimes you will need to multiply out brackets in algebra problems. You will often see the instruction 'Simplify…' in such a problem.

Example   Simplify $2(x + 3y)$.

Solution $2(x + 3y)$

$= \underline{2x + 6y}$

> The 2 outside the bracket tells you that the contents of the bracket must be multiplied by 2. x becomes $2x$, and $3y$ beomes $6y$.

Sometimes there might be two sets of brackets to multiply out. Look for opportunities to collect matching terms together afterwards.

Example   Simplify $2(x + 3) + 5(2x + 1)$.

Solution $2(x + 3) + 5(2x + 1)$

$= 2x + 6 + 5(2x + 1)$

> First multiply out each set of brackets in turn.

$2x + 6 + 10x + 5$

> Then collect together matching terms.

$= \underline{12x + 11}$

Special care needs to be taken when a question involves minus signs.

Example   Simplify $6(x + 2) + 3(2x - 3)$.

Solution $6(x + 2) + 3(2x - 3)$

$= 6x + 12 + 6x - 9$

$= \underline{12x + 3}$

> When collecting together matching terms:
> $6x + 6x$ gives $12x$
> $+ 12$ and $- 9$ gives $+3$.

Exercise 16.6

Multiply out the brackets in each of these.

1 ✔ $2(x + 4y)$ **2** $3(x + 2y)$ **3** $5(2x + y)$

4 $7(a + 5)$ **5** $10(2b + 3)$ **6** $15(2c + 1)$

7 $6(3d + 4)$ **8** $20(3e + 2)$ **9** $8(f + 7)$

10 $12(2x + 5y)$ **11** $5(8y + 3)$ **12** $11(3x + 7)$

13 $6(5x - 2)$ **14** $7(12 - 7x)$ **15** $15(2x - 5y)$

Multiply out the brackets and simplify each of these.

16 ✔ $4(x + 1) + 5(x + 2)$ **17** $4(2x + 1) + 5(3x + 2)$

18 $3(x + 2) + 2(x + 3)$ **19** $3(4x + 2) + 2(3x + 1)$

20 $3(4x + 7) + 2(3x + 2)$ **21** $12(y + 5) + 10(2y + 7)$

22 $4(5x + 2) + 3(8x + 3)$ **23** $3(7x + 2) + 7(5x + 3)$

24 $5(9x + 1) + 9(5x + 1)$ **25** $8(4x + 5y) + 3(5x + 3y)$

Simplify:

26 $4(x + 1) + 3(x - 2)$ **27** $2(3x + 2) + 5(2x - 1)$

28 ✔ $5(2x + 5y) + 6(2x - y)$ **29** $3(4x - 5) + 7(2x + 3)$

30 $12(4x + 7y) + 15(3x - 5y)$

Summary

In this Unit you have learnt how to substitute numbers into algebraic formulae. Remember to use BODMAS when there are several different stages involved. You have practised the use of a calculator in finding the values of expressions involving brackets, square roots and cube roots.

You have used algebraic formulae to describe 'number machines' (simple flow charts) and practised turning written information into algebra. You have also learnt how to multiply out and simplify algebraic expressions involving brackets.

Review Exercise 16

In questions **1–3** $a = 3$, $b = 4.2$, $c = 5$, $d = 2$, $e = 0$, $f = 4.9$ and $g = 10$.

Use your calculator to find the values of:

1 a) $5a + 3b$ **2 a)** $c^2 + d^2$ **3 a)** $(a + 2b + 3c + 4d) \times e$
   b) $10ab$ **b)** $5(3b - 2f)$ **b)** $2fg - 3d$
   c) $6c + 3d$ **c)** $(3c - g)^2$ **c)** $c - f \div g$

In questions **4–9** use the square key, power key or square root key on your calculator to find the value of the expression. Give your final answer correct to 3 significant figures.

4 2.9^3 **5** $\sqrt{15}$ **6** $5.2 \times 3.5 + 1.8^2$

7 $\sqrt{64} + 2.5 \times 3.5$ **8** $(2 + 3 \times 5)^3$ **9** $5(3^2 + 2^3)$

In questions **10–15** write down algebraic formulae for these number machines:

10 Input; multiply by 4; subtract 5; output   **11** Input; subtract 5; multiply by 4; output

12 Input; subtract 2; square; output   **13** Input; square root; add 5; output

14 Input; add 5; square root; output   **15** Input; add 5; subtract 7; output

Simplify the expressions given in questions **16–27**.

16 $5 \times p \times 3 \times p$ **17** $5x + 11x - 15x$ **18** $a + 2b + 3a - 4b$

19 $7y - 13y + 6y$ **20** $5c + 6d + 7cd$ **21** $10x - 5y - 14x + 2y$

22 $2e^2 + 3f - e^2$ **23** $15a - 13b - 14a + 14b$ **24** $7x + 3(2x + 5) + 3$

25 $5(2x + 3) + 2(x + 3) + 5$ **26** $2(3x + 4) + 3(x - 5)$ **27** $3x + 2(2x + 5) - 4x + 3(x + 1)$

28* Simplify $4a + 5a^2 + 6a$

29* Simplify $5p + 4q - 3p - 2pq + 6q$

30* The number x is used as input with this set of instructions: Input; add 1; cube; add 1; output. Write down a formula for the output.

31* A bag of sweets contains t toffees, c chocolates and e eclairs. Each toffee weighs 15 grams, each chocolate weighs 20 grams and each eclair weighs x grams.
   a)   How many sweets are there altogether?
   b)   Find the total weight of all the sweets.

32* Simplify: $7 \times y \times y + 4 \times y \times y$.

33* My money-box contains x 1p coins, y 2p coins and z 5p coins.
   a)   Write down a formula for the total number of coins, n.
   b)   Write down a formula for the total value of the coins, v.

34* Simplify $\sqrt{x^2}$.

35* A water tub contains 45 gallons of rainwater. A three-gallon watering can is filled n times from the tub. Write down a formula for the amount of water remaining in the tub. Explain briefly any restrictions on the value of the number n.

36* Use your calculator to work out the value of:

$$\sqrt{\left(\frac{3.4 \times 1.8}{2.7 + 1.4}\right)}$$

37* Look at this number machine:

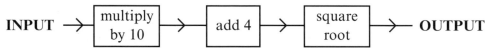

INPUT $\rightarrow$ | multiply by 10 | $\rightarrow$ | add 4 | $\rightarrow$ | square root | $\rightarrow$ OUTPUT

a) What is the output when the number 6 is input?
b) What is the output when the number x is input?

Unit 17
Coordinates in all four quadrants

In this Unit you will learn how to:
- use coordinates in all four quadrants;
- interpret the meaning of coordinates with negative signs;
- solve problems using coordinates in all four quadrants.

17.1 Introducing negative coordinates

You should already be familiar with this type of coordinate system:

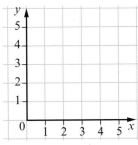

This is called the
first quadrant.

In this Section you will be working with negative x-coordinates as well:

This new region on
the left is called the
second quadrant.

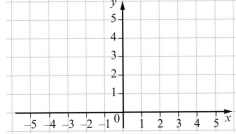

Example   Draw coordinate axes in which x can run from -10 to 10
and y from 0 to 10.

a) Plot these points and join them up to form a rectangle:
(6, 2), (−8, 2), (−8, 8), (6, 8).

b) Write down the coordinates of the centre of the rectangle.

Solution

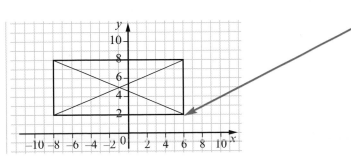

When plotting (6, 2)
remember to go 6
across first, then 2 up.

When plotting (−8, 2)
you plot −8 in the
across (x) direction
first, then 2 in the up
(y) direction

The centre of the rectangle is at (−1, 5).

Shape, space and measures

Exercise 17.1

For each question, draw up a fresh set of coordinate grids on squared paper. You should let x run from –10 to 10 and y from 0 to 10. A scale of 1 unit to 1 grid square should work well.

1 Connect up the points (3, 3), (–7, 3), (–5, 8) and (5, 8), then join back to (3, 3) again to form a closed shape. What name does this shape have?

2 ✔ Connect up the points (–5, 1), (1, 1), (1, 7) and (–5, 7), then join back to (–5, 1) again. What shape have you made?

3 ✔ Connect up the points (9, 2), (–7, 2), (–5, 6), (7, 6) then back to (9, 2) again. What name is given to the shape you have made?

4 Follow these instructions to make a drawing of Tom the cat:

a) Join (3, 6) to (4, 9), then to (2, 8).

b) Join ((–5, 6) to (–6, 9), then to (–4, 8).

c) Join (0, 3) to (–2, 3), then to (–1, 2), then back to (0, 3).

d) Join (–3, 6) to (–3, 5), then to (–2, 5), then (–2, 6), then back to (–3, 6).

e) Join (0, 5) to (1, 5), then to (1, 6), then (0,6), then back to (0, 5).

f) Join (–1, 1) to (3, 2), then to (3, 6), then (2, 8), then (–4, 8), then (–5, 6), then (–5, 2), then back to (–1, 1).

5 Follow these instructions to spell a favourite word:

a) Join (–10, 2) to (–10, 6), then to (–9, 4), then (–8, 6) then (–8, 2).

b) Join (–7, 2) to (–6, 6), then to (–5, 2). Join $(-6\frac{1}{2}, 4)$ to $(-5\frac{1}{2}, 4)$.

c) Join (–3, 2) to (–3, 6). Join (–4, 6) to (–2, 6).

d) Join (–1, 6) to (–1, 2). Join (–1, 4) to (1, 4). Join (1, 2) to (1, 6).

e) Join (4, 6) to (2, 6), then to (2, 4), then (4, 4), then (4, 2), then (2, 2).

f) Join (6, 3) to (7, 2), then to (8, 6).

17.2 Coordinates in all four quadrants

The system with negative numbers on the axes can be extended further still:

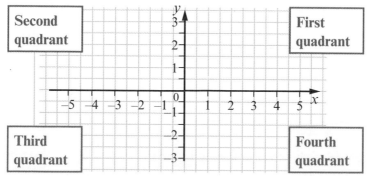

There are now many different ways in which minus signs can appear, so you need to be careful when reading or plotting points.

Example   Write down the coordinates of the points A, B, C, D, E in the diagram below.

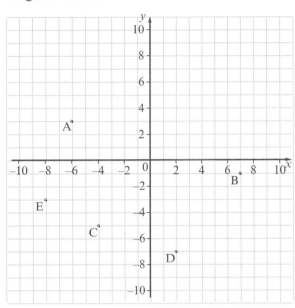

Solution   A is at (–6, 3).
B is at (7, –1).
C is at (–4, –5).
D is at (2, –7).
E is at (–8, –3).

Exercise 17.2

1 ✔ Write down the coordinates of P, Q, R, S, T and U in the diagram below.

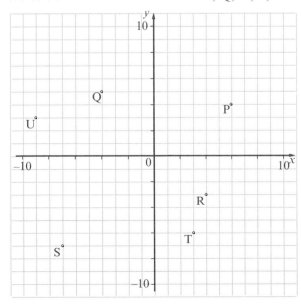

2 Look at the diagram on the right.

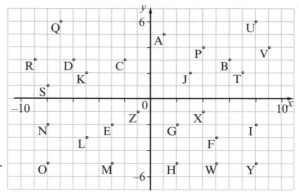

Use this diagram as a codebreaker to decode the following message:

(–8, –2) (–8, –5) (5, –5) // (8, –5) (–8, –5) (8, 6) // (–2, 3) (1, 5) (–8, –2) //
(8, 6) (–8, 1) (–3, –2) // (1, 5) (–5, –3) (–5, –3) // (5, –3) (–8, –5) (8, 6) (–9, 3) //
(–7, 6) (8, 6) (1, 5) (–6, 3) (–9, 3) (1, 5) (–8, –2) (7, 2) (–8, 1) //!

3 Draw a set of coordinate axes in which *x* and *y* can run from –10 to 10. Then construct these four shapes on your grid:

   a) Join (5, 1) to (8, 4), then to (5, 7), then (2, 4), then back to (5, 1). Label this A.

   b) Join (2, –3) to (5, –2), then to (8, –3), then (5, –4), then back to (2, –3). Label this B.

   c) Join (–3, –3) to (–7, –1), then to (–6, –3), then (–7, –5), then back to (–3, –3). Label this C.

   d) Join (–7, 1) to (–5, 3), then to (–5, 7), then (–7, 5), then back to (–7, 1). Label this D.

   e) Write down the name for each of the quadrilaterals A, B, C, D.

Summary

In this Unit you have extended your knowledge of coordinates to all four quadrants.

Remember that the across (*x*) number is plotted first, then the up (*y*) number. Minus signs indicate moving left (*x*) or down (*y*) instead.

Review Exercise 17

1 Sanjay draws this rectangle on a coordinate grid.

   a) Write down the coordinates of the four corners of Sanjay's rectangle.

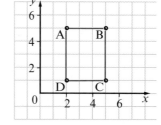

      Joanne draws a rectangle by moving Sanjay's rectangle 3 units to the left.

   b) Write down the coordinates of the four corners of Joanne's rectangle.

      Wil draws a rectangle by moving Sanjay's rectangle 3 units down and 4 units to the left.

   c) Write down the coordinates of the four corners of Wil's rectangle

2 On a sheet of A4 squared paper draw up a set of coordinate axes so that *x* can run from –18 to 15 and *y* from –15 to 20. A scale of 1 unit to one 5 mm square is recommended.

On your grid plot the following points. Join each point to the next one, in order, to reveal an animal.

(11, 3), (13, 0), (13, –3), (13, –7), (13, –9), (14, –12), (11, –13), (5, –13), (–1, –13), (–6, –13), (–10, –13), (–13, –12), (–16, –10), (–16, –9), (–16, –8), (–15, –8), (–14, –9), (–13, –10), (–10, –11), (–3, –12), (2, –11), (–1, –10), (0, –10), (0, –8), (–1, 0), (–4, 2), (–6, 4), (–7, 7), (–7, 9), (–8, 10), (–9, 9), (–10, 10), (–11, 11), (–10, 12), (–10, 14), (–8, 15), (–8, 16), (–7, 18), (–6, 17), (–5, 16), (–2, 15), (0, 11), (1, 10), (4, 9), (5, 9), (7, 8), (9, 6), (11, 3)

3 On squared paper draw up a set of coordinate axes so that x can run from –15 to 15 and y from –10, to 10. A scale of 1 unit to one 5 mm square is recommended. On your grid plot the following points. Join each point to the next one, using a smooth curve where appropriate.

(0, 6), (1, 5), (3, 7), (6, $8\frac{1}{2}$), (9, 10), (11, 10), (12, 9), $10\frac{1}{2}$, 7), (8, 4), (5, 3), (5, 2), (6, 2), (6, 1), (6, 0), (5, –1), (5, –2), (6, –4), (7, –6), (8, –8), (5, –4), (4, –5), (3, –5), (3, –4), (2, –3), (1, –3), ($\frac{1}{2}$, –1), (0, 0).

Now reflect all the points, using the y-axis as a mirror line, and join up all the new points in a similar way, to reveal the final object. You might like to add some colour to finish it off.

4* For this drawing you will need a set of coordinate axes in which x can run from –12 to 12 and y from –15 to 15.

Plot each of the following sets of points, connecting them with a smooth curve as you go.

(–3, 5), (–3, 8), (–$4\frac{1}{2}$, $9\frac{1}{2}$), (–4, $10\frac{1}{2}$), (–$4\frac{1}{2}$, $11\frac{1}{2}$), (–4, $12\frac{1}{2}$), (–3, $13\frac{1}{2}$), (–1, 14), (0, $14\frac{1}{2}$), (1, 14), (2, 14), (5, $14\frac{1}{2}$), (7, 14), (9, 13), (10, 12), (11, 11), ($11\frac{1}{2}$, 10), (11, 8), (10, 7), (9, 6), (8, 5), (6, $3\frac{1}{2}$) //

(–$2\frac{1}{2}$, $5\frac{1}{2}$), (–3, 4), (–$3\frac{1}{2}$, $2\frac{1}{2}$), ($3\frac{1}{2}$, $1\frac{1}{2}$), (–$2\frac{1}{2}$, $2\frac{1}{2}$), (–2, $3\frac{1}{2}$), (–$1\frac{1}{2}$, $4\frac{1}{2}$) //

(3, 4), (4, $3\frac{1}{2}$), ($5\frac{1}{2}$, $2\frac{1}{2}$), ($6\frac{1}{2}$, $2\frac{1}{2}$), (6, 3), (5, 4), (4, $5\frac{1}{2}$) //

(–$1\frac{1}{2}$, 3), (–1, $1\frac{1}{2}$), (0, 0), (1, –2), ($1\frac{1}{2}$, –4) (1, –$4\frac{1}{2}$), (0, –$4\frac{1}{2}$), (0, –$3\frac{1}{2}$), (–$\frac{1}{2}$, –3) (–1, –4), (–1, –5), (1, –6), (3, –5), ($3\frac{1}{2}$, –$3\frac{1}{2}$), ($3\frac{1}{2}$, –$1\frac{1}{2}$), (3, 0), (3, 2), (3, 4) //

(–3, –$13\frac{1}{2}$), (–4, –14), (–5, –14), (–7, –$13\frac{1}{2}$), (–8, –13), (–9, –$12\frac{1}{2}$), (–10, 12), (–11, $11\frac{1}{2}$), (–12, 10), (–12, 8), (–11, 6), (–8, 5), (–7, 4), (–6, $3\frac{1}{2}$), (–4, 3), (–$3\frac{1}{2}$, $2\frac{1}{2}$) //

(–6, $3\frac{1}{2}$), (–$6\frac{1}{2}$, 1), (–6, –2), (–5, –4), (–4, –6), (–$3\frac{1}{2}$, –9), (–$3\frac{1}{2}$, –12), (–$3\frac{1}{2}$, –$13\frac{1}{2}$), (–2, –$13\frac{1}{2}$), (–1, –13), (–$\frac{1}{2}$, –$12\frac{1}{2}$), (–1, –10), (–1, –7), (–$\frac{1}{2}$, –$6\frac{1}{2}$), (1, –6) //

(–5, –4), (–$5\frac{1}{2}$, –7), (–5, –9), (–$4\frac{1}{2}$, –11), (–$4\frac{1}{2}$, –$12\frac{1}{2}$), (–$3\frac{1}{2}$, –$12\frac{1}{2}$) //

(2, –6), (3, –7), (3, –9), ($2\frac{1}{2}$, –10), (2, –11), ($1\frac{1}{2}$, –12), (2, –13), (3, –$13\frac{1}{2}$), (4, –13), (5, –12), ($5\frac{1}{2}$, –$8\frac{1}{2}$), (5, –4), ($5\frac{1}{2}$, –$\frac{1}{2}$), ($5\frac{1}{2}$, $2\frac{1}{2}$) //

($\frac{1}{2}$, –7), (1, –8), ($\frac{1}{2}$, –10), ($\frac{1}{2}$, –11), (1, –12), ($1\frac{1}{2}$, –12) //

Finally, add two small circles centred at (3, 9) and (–3, 9).

Unit 18
Geometry of 2-D shapes

In this Unit you will learn how to:

- recognise acute, obtuse and reflex angles;
- measure and draw angles to the nearest degree;
- solve problems using the sum of angles at a point;
- solve problems using the sum of angles in a triangle;
- solve problems about angles in quadrilaterals or pentagons.

A protractor will be required for the measuring and drawing exercises.

18.1 Acute, obtuse and reflex angles

Acute angles are less than 90°.
Right angles are exactly 90°.
Obtuse angles are more than 90° but less than 180°.
Reflex angles are more than 180°.

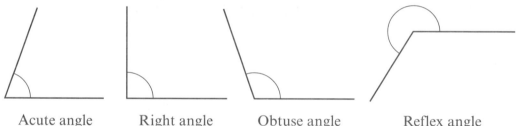

Acute angle   Right angle   Obtuse angle   Reflex angle

Example   Describe the four angles in this shape:

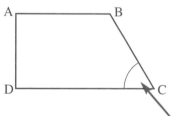

Solution   Angle DAB is a right angle.
Angle ABC is obtuse.
Angle BCD is acute.
Angle CDA is a right angle.

> Angle BCD means 'the angle at C formed by the lines BC and DC'.
> It is this angle.

Exercise 18.1
Say whether each of these angles is an acute, right, obtuse or reflex angle.

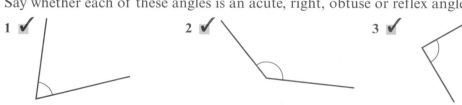

1 ✔   2 ✔   3 ✔

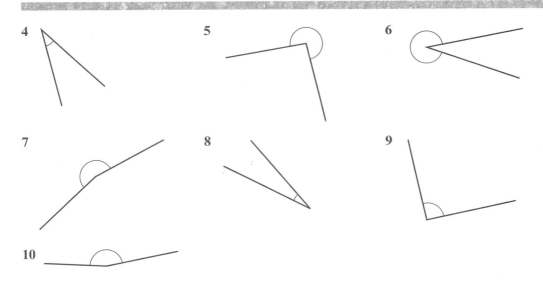

4   5   6

7   8   9

10

18.2 Drawing and measuring angles

Semicircular protractors have two scales marked on them.

One scale runs from 0 to 180° and the other runs from 180° to 0.

Estimate the size of the angle first – by judging whether it is acute or obtuse. This helps to ensure that you use the correct scale.

Example   Measure this angle to the nearest degree:

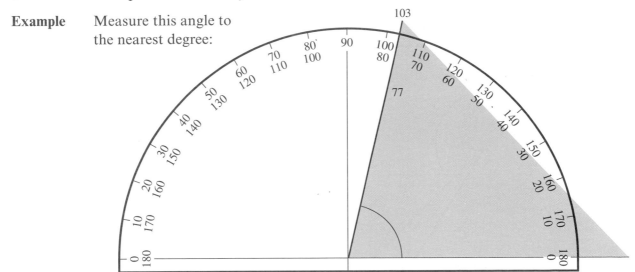

Solution   By eye, the angle is clearly acute.
Placing a protractor over the angle offers two choices: 77° or 103°.

Since the angle is acute, 103° cannot be correct.

The angle is 77° (to the nearest degree).

Exercise 18.2

For questions **1**–**6** estimate the size of each angle then measure it, and write down its value correct to the nearest degree.

1 ✔

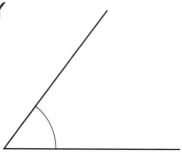

2

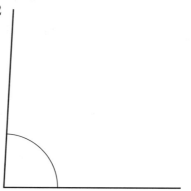

3 ✔

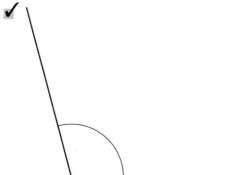

4

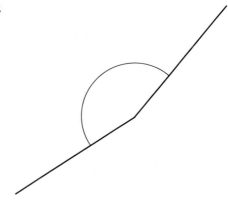

5 ✔

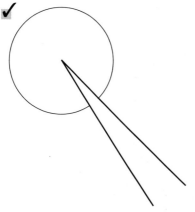

6

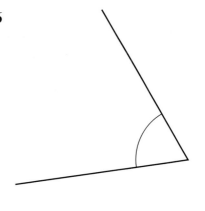

7 Use a protractor to draw these angles. Try to make your diagrams accurate to the nearest degree.

   a) 22°   **b)** 45°   **c)** 170°   **d)** 17°
   e) 80°   **f)** 127°   **g)** 225°   **h)** 190°
   i) 66°   **j)** 90°   **k)** 350°   **l)** 115°

18.3 Angles at a point

When angles meet at a point they all add up to 360°.

Example Find the missing angle *x*.

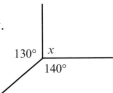

130° | *x*
140°

Solution Since the angles meet at a point they all add up to 360°.

Therefore 130 + 140 + *x* = 360
270 + *x* = 360
x = 360 − 270
= 90°

Exercise 18.3

Find the missing angles in each of these diagrams. Show your working clearly.

1 ✔

85°
a
105° 90°

2

b 127°
100° 80°

3 ✔

110°
115° *c*

4

90°
207° \ *d*

5

45° *e*
60°

6

72° *f*
135° 45°

This symbol means 90°.

7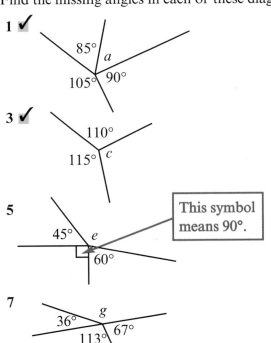

36° *g*
113° 67°

8

39°
h

9

32° *i* 73°
108° 41°

10

j
j 110°

18.4 Angles in a triangle

The three angles inside a triangle add up to 180°.

Example   Find the missing angle, marked *x*.
(*The diagram is not to scale.*)

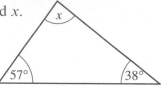

Solution   *x*, 57° and 38° add up to 180°.
$$x + 57 + 38 = 180$$
$$x + 95 = 180$$
$$x = 180 - 95$$
$$\underline{x = 85°}$$

Exercise 18.4

Find, by calculation, the missing angles marked with letters.

1 ✔

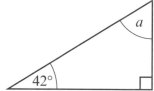

2

3

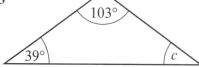

4

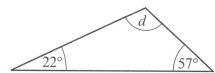

5 ✔

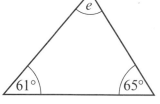

6

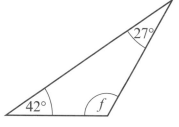

7

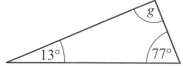

8

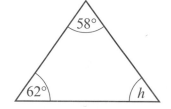

18.5 Angles in 2-D shapes

The three angles inside a triangle add up to 180°.

The four angles inside a quadrilateral add up to 360°.

The five angles inside a pentagon add up to 540°.

Example Find the missing angle x.
(The diagram is not to scale.)

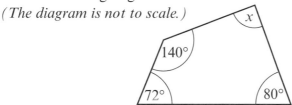

Solution Since the shape has four sides it is a quadrilateral, so the angles add up to 360°.

$$72 + 80 + 140 + x = 360$$
$$292 + x = 360$$
$$x = 360 - 292$$
$$= \underline{68°}$$

Exercise 18.5

Find, by calculation, the missing angles marked with letters. Remember to check whether each shape is a triangle (180° sum), quadrilateral (360°) or pentagon (540°). Show all your working.

(The diagrams are not drawn to scale.)

1
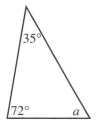

2
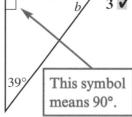
This symbol means 90°.

3 ✔
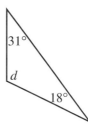

4
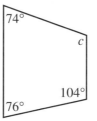

5 ✔
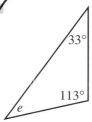

6

7
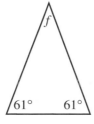

8
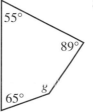
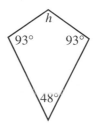

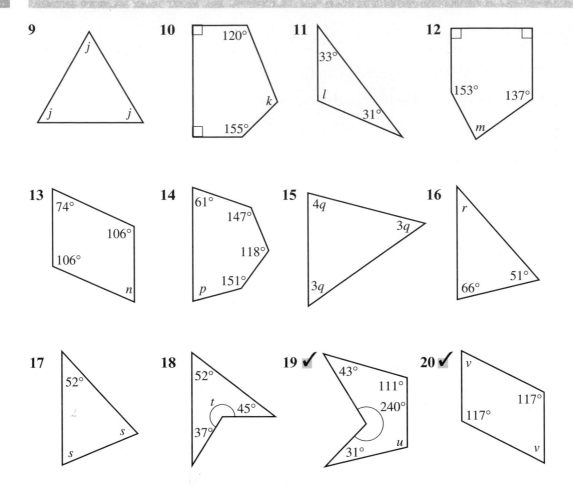

Summary

In this Unit you have practised recognising acute, right, obtuse and reflex angles. You have used a protractor to measure and construct angles to within one degree. When measuring, it is always a good idea to check whether the angle is acute or obtuse first, so that the angle is read off the correct scale.

You have found missing angles using the principle that angles meeting at a point add up to 360°. You have also found that angles in a triangle add up to 180° (or 360° for a quadrilateral, or 540° in a pentagon).

Review Exercise 18

1 Give the three-letter name of each of the angles *a* to *f* and say whether it is an acute, right or obtuse angle.

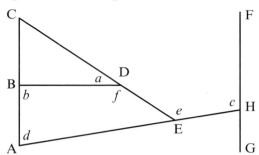

2 Measure the sizes of each of the three angles in triangle ABC. Check that they add up to 180°.

3 Measure the sizes of each of the four angles in the quadrilateral ABCD. Check that they add up to 360°.

4 Find the size of the missing angles denoted by letters.
(The diagrams are not drawn to scale.)

a)

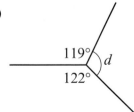

b)

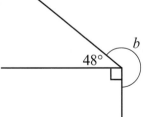

c)

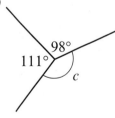

d)

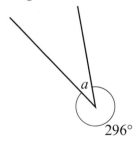

e)

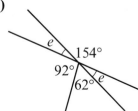

f)

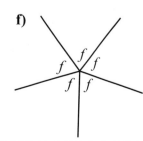

5 Find the size of the missing angles denoted by letters.

a)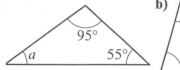

b)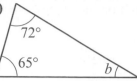

c)

d)

e)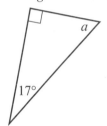

f)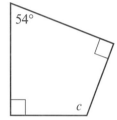

6 Find the size of the missing angles denoted by letters.
(The diagrams are not drawn to scale.)

a)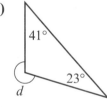

b)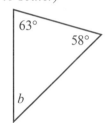

c)

d)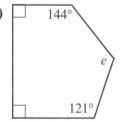

e)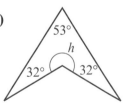

f)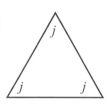

g)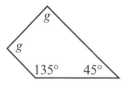

h)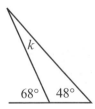

j)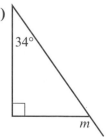

k)

l)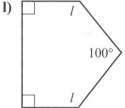

m)

7* The angles in a triangle are x, $2x$ and $3x$. Find x.

8* The angles in a pentagon are $2x$, $3x$, $5x$, $8x$ and $9x$. Find x.

Unit 19
Symmetry and congruence

In this Unit you will learn how to:
- identify orders of rotational symmetry;
- identify the symmetries of 2-D shapes;
- recognise congruent shapes.

19.1 Rotational symmetry

If a shape is rotated about its centre and at some point in the rotation it appears not to have moved, the shape has **rotational symmetry**.

Example Describe the rotational symmetry of these objects.

a)

b)

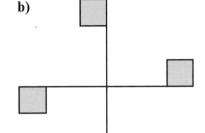

c)

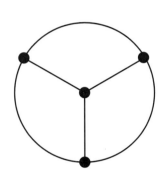

Solution   a) Rotational symmetry of <u>order 2</u>.
  b) Rotational symmetry of <u>order 4</u>.
  c) Rotational symmetry of <u>order 3</u>.

> To obtain these answers you count the number of different positions into which the shape can be rotated.

Exercise 19.1

Describe the order of rotational symmetry of each shape.

1 ✔

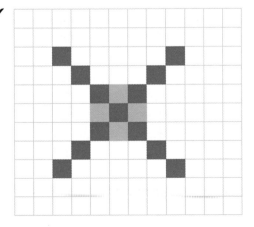

2

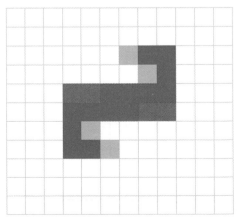

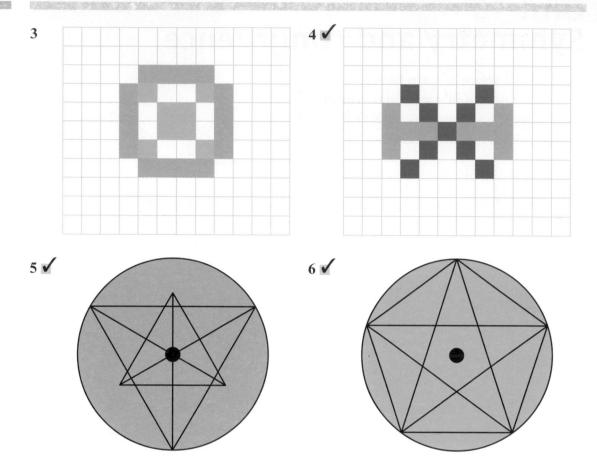

3

4 ✔

5 ✔

6 ✔

19.2 Identifying symmetries of 2-D shapes

These three objects each have a different kind of symmetry:

1 Reflection symmetry (line symmetry, or mirror symmetry)

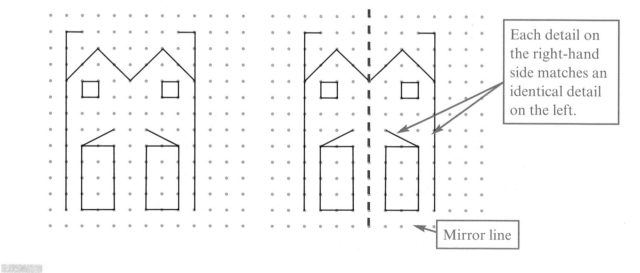

Each detail on the right-hand side matches an identical detail on the left.

Mirror line

2 Rotation symmetry (or point symmetry, or S-symmetry)

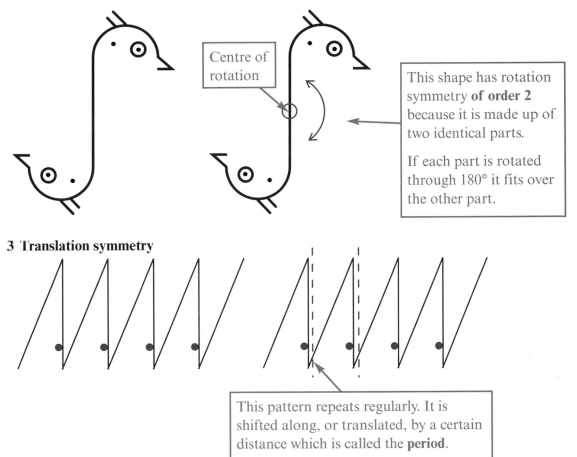

Centre of rotation

This shape has rotation symmetry **of order 2** because it is made up of two identical parts.

If each part is rotated through 180° it fits over the other part.

3 Translation symmetry

This pattern repeats regularly. It is shifted along, or translated, by a certain distance which is called the **period**.

Reflection symmetry: An object has one or more mirror lines.
Rotation symmetry: An object has a centre of rotation.
Translation symmetry: A pattern is generated by repeatedly moving along.

Example   Describe the symmetries of each of these shapes.

1

2

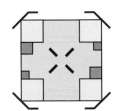

3

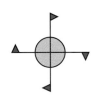

Solution   **1** Reflection symmetry (one mirror line).
2 Reflection symmetry (two mirror lines). It also has rotation symmetry of order 2.
3 Rotation symmetry of order 4.

Exercise 19.2

Look at diagrams **1**–**10** below. Some of them are symmetric, and some are not. Describe the type of symmetry as precisely as you can.

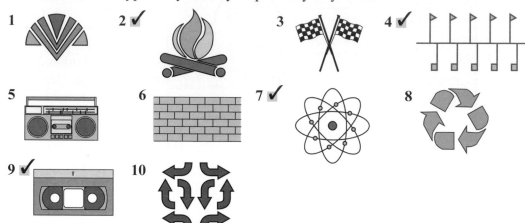

1 2 ✔ 3 4 ✔

5 6 7 ✔ 8

9 ✔ 10

In questions **11**–**20** you are given part of a drawing. Copy each one on to squared paper, and complete it so that it has the required type of symmetry. (The mirror line or the centre of rotation is marked in red.)

11

Reflection symmetry

12

Rotation symmetry, order 2

13

Rotation symmetry, order 4

14

Reflection symmetry

15

Reflection symmetry

16

Rotation symmetry, order 4

17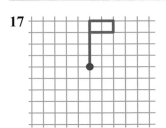

Rotation symmetry, order 3

18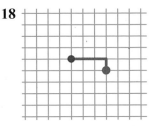

Rotation symmetry, order 8

19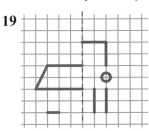

Reflection symmetry

20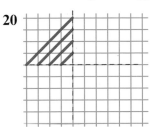

Reflection symmetry
(two mirror lines)

19.3 Congruence

Two shapes are **congruent** if they are exactly the same shape and size.

The two shapes do not have to be the same way round – one could be
a reflected version of the other.

Example Which two shapes are congruent?

A   **B**   **C**   **D**

Solution Clearly **A**, **B** and **C** are all different. **D** is a rotated version of **A**.

∴ <u>**A** and **D**</u> are congruent.

Example Which two shapes are congruent?

A   **B**   **C**    **D**

Solution Clearly **A**, **B** and **D** are all different. **C** is a rotated and reflected
version of **A**.

∴ <u>**A** and **C**</u> are congruent.

Exercise 19.3

1 ✔ Which two triangles are congruent?

 A B  C 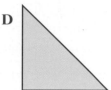 D

2 ✔ Which two shapes are congruent?

A 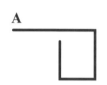 B C D E

3 Name the shape which is congruent to:

a) A **b)** F **c)** E **d)** D

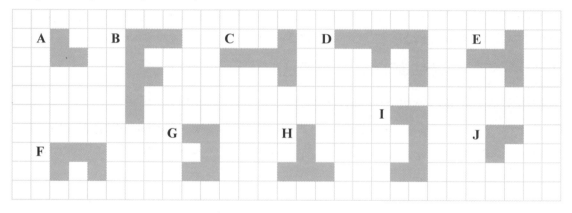

Summary

In this Unit you have learnt how to recognise the order of rotational symmetry of an object. You can classify 2-D shapes according to whether they exhibit reflection, rotation or translation symmetry.

You have also identified congruent objects, that is objects which are the same shape and size. Remember that a matching pair of left- and right-handed objects do count as congruent.

Review Exercise 19

1 Describe the symmetries, if any, of each object.

a) 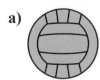 **b)** **c)** **d)** **e)** **f)**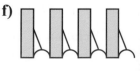

2 On squared paper draw a set of coordinate axes so that x can run from 0 to 15 and y from −15 to 15.

a) Plot the following points, and join them up in the order given:
(0, 0), (1, 1), (5, 1), (7,11), (11, 12), (10, 1), (13, 1), (14, 3), (15, 3), (14, 0).

b) Reflect all the points using the *x*-axis as a mirror line. Again, join them up in order.

c) What object is revealed when both sets of points are combined?

3 Look at these letters of the alphabet. Make a list of those which have:
a) rotation symmetry
b) reflection symmetry
c) no symmetry at all.

4 Henry draws an isosceles triangle. Madge draws an isosceles triangle.

Henry says 'Both triangles are isosceles, so they must be congruent'.

Is Henry right? Explain your reasoning.

5 (Activity) You will need to work with one or two friends for this activity. You will also need some square dotted paper, and some scissors.

On dotted paper draw two congruent shapes and cut them out.
For example, you might make these:

Now fit them together to make a single shape:

Finally, copy the outline of the combined shape onto a fresh sheet of dotted paper:

Challenge a friend to find out how to divide the complete shape into two congruent parts.

6* Make a copy of each diagram on squared paper, and shade in some extra squares so that the pattern has the required type of symmetry.
Use the smallest possible number of extra squares.

a)

b)

c)

d)

Reflection symmetry (vertical mirror line)

Reflection symmetry (horizontal mirror line)

Rotation symmetry, order 2

Rotation symmetry, order 4

Unit 20
Metric and imperial measures

In this Unit you will learn how to:

- use rough equivalents between metric and imperial units;
- convert one metric unit to another;
- make estimates in relation to everyday situations;
- read measurements from a variety of scales.

A calculator will be required for some of the exercises.

20.1 Metric and imperial units

Metric units were first used in France at the beginning of the 19th century. They are based on powers of ten, for example 10 mm = 1 cm.

Length:	Centimetres, metres, kilometres
Mass:	Grams, kilograms, tonnes
Volume:	Cubic centimetres, cubic metres, litres

Imperial units are older and tend to be based on the scale of the human body. Unlike metric units they do not usually go up in powers of ten, for example 12 inches = 1 foot.

Length:	Inches, feet, yards, miles, fathoms
Mass:	Pounds, ounces, stones, tons
Volume:	Cubic inches, cubic feet, pints, gallons

The following are not exact but they do give rough equivalents between the two systems:

Length	
	1 inch = 2.5 centimetres
	1 foot = 30 centimetres
	5 miles = 8 kilometres

Mass	
	1 kilogram = 2.2 pounds
	30 grams = 1 ounce
	1 tonne = 1 ton

Volume	
	1 gallon = 4.5 litres
	1 litre = $1\frac{3}{4}$ pints

Example   My car can hold 12 gallons of petrol. Roughly how many litres is this?

Solution $12 \times 4.5 = 54$
12 gallons is roughly <u>54 litres</u>.

Example   Crystal the dog weighs 11 pounds. Roughly how many
kilograms is this?

Solution $11 \div 2.2 = 5$
Crystal weighs roughly <u>5 kilograms</u>.

Exercise 20.1

In questions **1–10** give the approximate metric equivalent to the
imperial measure:

1 20 miles (in kilometres)   **2** 7 pints (litres)

3 6 inches (centimetres)   **4** ✔ 350 miles (kilometres)

5 10 gallons (litres)   **6** 4 feet (centimetres)

7 ✔ 4 ounces (grams)   **8** 10 ounces (grams)

9 22 pounds (kilograms)   **10** 8 inches (centimetres)

In questions **11–20** give the approximate imperial equivalent to the
metric measure:

11 48 kilometres (in miles)   **12** 150 centimetres (feet)

13 9 litres (gallons)   **14** 720 kilometres (miles)

15 20 kilograms (pounds)   **16** 12 kilograms (pounds)

17 30 centimetres (inches)   **18** 15 tonnes (tons)

19 270 grams (ounces)   **20** 10 centimetres (inches)

20.2 Converting one metric unit to another

The metric measures of length are:

> 10 millimetres (mm) = 1 centimetre (cm)
> 1000 millimetres (mm) = 100 centimetres (cm) = 1 metre (m)
> 1000 metres (m) = 1 kilometre (km)

For weight, or mass, these units are used:

> 1000 milligrams (mg) = 1 gram (g)
> 1000 grams (g) = 1 kilogram (kg)
> 1000 kilograms (kg) = 1 tonne (t)

Small volumes are usually measured in cubic centimetres or in litres;
larger ones in cubic metres:

> 1 millilitre (ml) = 1 cubic centimetre (cm³)
> 10 millilitres (ml) = 1 centilitre (cl)
> 1000 cubic centimetres (cm³) or 1000 ml = 1 litre (l)
> 1 cubic metre (m³) = 1000 litres (l)

Units of time are the same in both the metric and the imperial system:

1000 milliseconds = 1 second	24 hours = 1 day
60 seconds = 1 minute	365 days = 1 calendar year
60 minutes = 1 hour	

Example   Write 10 cm 6 mm in millimetres.

Solution   10 cm = 100 mm
So 10 cm 6 mm = 100 + 6
                       = 106 mm.

Example   How many cups, each holding 330 ml, can be filled from a jug holding 4000 cm³?

Solution   330 ml is the same as 330 cm³.
∴ the number of cups is 4000 ÷ 330 = 12.12 (by calculator)
So 12 cups can be filled.

This symbol means 'therefore'.

Exercise 20.2

In questions **1–10** change the given metric measure into the unit indicated in brackets.

1 5 kg 150 g (grams)   **2** 3500 cm³ (litres)

3 ✔ 1 m 37 cm (centimetres)   **4** 5 min 20 sec (seconds)

5 5 m 8 cm (centimetres)   **6** 36 cl (millilitres)

7 ✔ 25 cl 3 ml (millilitres)   **8** 7 kg 35 g (kilograms)

9 1 day 5 hours 17 min (minutes)   **10** 6 km 350 m (kilometres)

11 How many pieces of wood, each 15 cm long, can be cut from a piece of length 4 m?

12 An oxygen bottle lasts for 50 minutes. How many would a mountaineer need to keep him going for six and a half hours?

13 ✔ Six people get into a lift. Find the total weight, assuming that each person weighs 70 kg. The lift can take a maximum weight of half a tonne. Explain whether the lift can take these six people.

14 Add together 12 cm, 94 mm and 7 cm. Give the answer in millimetres.

15 Four bags weigh 350 g, 1.25 kg, 225 g and half a kilogram. Find the total weight of all four bags, in kilograms.

16 One day baby Rana spends 1 hour and 5 minutes feeding, 5 hours and 20 minutes pla 35 minutes being bathed, and the rest of the time asleep. For how long does she sleep?

17 A ball of string is 5 m long. I cut off three pieces, of length 2.4 m, 55 cm and 1.3 m. Find the length remaining.

18 An outdoor swimming pool contains 320 cubic metres of water. It is leaking at the rate of 800 litres per day. How long will it take to empty?

19 Wine glasses have a capacity of 90 ml. How many can I fill from a bottle containing 72 cl?

20 A set of wind chimes contains six rods of length 79 mm, 103 mm, 125 mm, 144 mm, 163 mm and 180 mm. Find the total length of the six rods, in centimetres. Is it possible to cut them all from a single rod 1 m long?

Summary

In this Unit you have learnt how to use metric and imperial units. Make sure that you memorise the approximate equivalents given on page 114.

Review Exercise 20

1 Give the approximate metric equivalent to these imperial measures.

a) 60 miles (kilometres) b) 2 gallons (litres)
c) 88 pounds (kilograms) d) 14 inches (centimetres)
e) 2 pints (litres) f) 5 ounces (grams)

2 Give the approximate imperial equivalent to these metric measures.

a) 720 kilometres (miles) b) half a kilogram (pounds)
c) 3 tonnes (tons) d) 60 centimetres (feet)
e) 30 kilograms (pounds) f) 45 litres (gallons)

3 Change these metric measures into the unit given in brackets.

a) 7 m 19 cm (millimetres) b) 25 centilitres (millilitres)
c) 7 days 11 hours (hours) d) 2400 mm (metres)
e) 12 kg 25 g (grams) f) 45 litres (cubic centimetres)
g) 420 000 cm³ (litres) h) 22 cubic metres (litres)

4 State the metric unit that you would use to measure:

a) The volume of a classroom b) The weight of a goldfish
c) The length of a cat's tail d) The time remaining in a soccer match

5 Look at this list of metric quantities:

250 grams	20 millilitres	5000 litres	7 tonnes
80 million years	500 years	300 millilitres	90 seconds
900 kilograms	2 grams	20 minutes	250 litres

From the list, select the one that you think most closely matches the following:

a) The mass of a humming bird b) The age of a fossil
c) The amount of water in a bath tub d) The length of time I can hold my breath
e) The mass of an elephant f) The amount of fizzy drink in a ring-pull can

6* How many millimetres are there in a kilometre?

7* A physics teacher says: 'There are roughly a million seconds in a fortnight'. Calculate the number of seconds in a fortnight, and comment briefly on the teacher's statement. (A fortnight is fourteen days.)

8* Use your ruler to measure the length, in millimetres, of this drawing of a car:

The real car is 70 times the size of this drawing. Calculate the length of the real car, giving your answer to a sensible level of accuracy.

9* Shah measures the weight of a sack of potatoes in kilograms; Marie measures the weight of the same sack in grams. Shah says to Marie: 'My answer will be one thousand times as big as yours'. Is Shah right or is he wrong?

10* Every second the sun becomes four million tonnes lighter (it burns up this much mass to keep on shining). How much lighter does it become:
a) in one minute
b) in one day?

11* Baby Joe was 4 kilograms at birth, and weighed 10 kilograms at age 8 months.
a) Roughly how many pounds did he weigh at birth?
b) How many grams per day does he gain in weight, on average?

12* Gravity on the moon is much lower than on earth, so that objects appear to have only about one-sixth of their normal weight. Zara weighs 198 pounds on earth.
a) What is Zara's weight in kilograms?
b) How much would Zara weigh, in kilograms, if she went to the moon?

13* A drum of cable is 100 m long. Pieces of length 35 cm are cut from it. How many pieces can be cut, and how much cable will be left over?

14* Which is heavier: a kilogram of coal or a kilogram of feathers?

15* A competition asks people to guess how many bottles of champagne it would take to fill the school swimming pool. Obi decides to work it out mathematically. He uses the following information:
- A champagne bottle contains 70 centilitres.
- 100 centilitres makes 1 litre.
- 1000 litres is 1 cubic metre.
- The volume of the school pool is about 420 cubic metres.
What answer does Obi get?

Unit 21
Areas of squares and rectangles

In this Unit you will learn how to:
- find the area of a square by calculation;
- find the area of a rectangle by calculation;
- find the area of a compound shape;
- solve problems using squares and rectangles.

A calculator will be required for this unit.

21.1 Area of a square

The area of a square can be found by multiplying its width and height (which are the same) together. For simple whole number problems this should be done by hand. Harder problems can be done by calculator, using the $\boxed{x^2}$ key.

Example   Find the area of this square.

8 cm

8 cm

Solution   Area = 8 × 8

                      = 64 cm²

Example   Find the area of this square.

7.8 cm

7.8 cm

Solution   Area = 7.8 × 7.8

                      = 60.84

                      = 60.8 cm² (3 s.f.)

On your calculator you could use the square key instead: $\boxed{7}$ $\boxed{\cdot}$ $\boxed{8}$ $\boxed{x^2}$ $\boxed{=}$

Remember to give the answer in the correct units. These examples were based on centimetres, so the area is in square centimetres. This is written cm² for short.

When using a calculator, avoid an unreasonably long string of decimals. In the second example the measurements of the square were only given to 2 significant figures, so your answer should not be given to more than 2 or 3 significant figures.

Exercise 21.1

Find the area of each of these squares, without a calculator. Give exact answers.

1 ✔ 4 cm by 4 cm	**2** 3 cm by 3 cm	**3** 5 cm by 5 cm
4 7 cm by 7 cm	**5** ✔ 9 cm by 9 cm	**6** 6 cm by 6 cm
7 10 cm by 10 cm	**8** 12 cm by 12 cm	**9** 11 cm by 11 cm

Find the area of the square whose side length is given, using a calculator.
Give answers to 3 s.f.

10 ✓ 2.8cm   **11** 3.5cm   **12** ✓ 5.1cm

13 1.9cm   **14** 0.7cm   **15** 8.3cm

16 10.2cm   **17** 7.05cm   **18** 11.5cm

19 Maurice wants to cover a square of card with glitter. The square measures 12.5 cm along each side, and he has enough glitter to cover an area of 150 cm². Work out whether he has enough glitter or not.

20 Tina wants to paint a square with an area of about 300 cm². She is not sure whether to paint one 17 by 17 cm, 17.5 by 17.5 cm or 18 by 18 cm.
  a) Work out the area of each of the three squares.
  b) Use your answers to decide which one Tina should choose.

21.2 Area of a rectangle

The area of a square can be found by multiplying its width and height together. As with squares, simple whole number problems should be done by hand, saving the calculator for harder problems.

Example   Find the area of this rectangle.

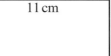

Solution   Area = 11 × 8

             = 88 cm²

Example   Find the area of this rectangle.

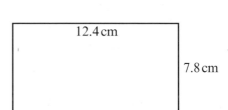

Solution   Area = 12.4 × 7.8

             = 96.72

             = 96.7 cm² (3 s.f.)

As the answer is an area, remember to give the answer in the correct units; in this case cm².

Exercise 21.2

Find the area of each of these rectangles, without using a calculator. Give exact answers.

   1 ✓ 4 cm by 5 cm   **2** 3 cm by 7 cm   **3** 5 cm by 2 cm

   4 7 cm by 4 cm   **5** ✓ 2 cm by 9 cm   **6** 4 cm by 6 cm

   7 10 cm by 7 cm   **8** 12 cm by 5 cm   **9** 8 cm by 11 cm

Find the area of each of these rectangles, using a calculator. Give answers to 3 s.f.

10 ✔ 4.6 cm by 3.8 cm **11** 15.5 cm by 25.5 cm

12 ✔ 2.9 cm by 7.7 cm **13** 3.8 cm by 5 cm

14 2.5 cm by 13.2 cm **15** 0.9 cm by 1.1 cm

16 11.2 cm by 11.9 cm **17** 22 cm by 7.75 cm

18 2.9 cm by 3.25 cm **19** 10.3 cm by 20.3 cm

20 Bradley has made a rectangle out of card. It measures 14.5 cm by 20.5 cm. Jon has made one too; his measures 12 cm by 26.6 cm.
   a) Work out the area of each of the two rectangles.
   b) Use your answers to decide whose rectangle has the larger area.

21.3 Finding the area of a compound shape

Sometimes you need to find the area of a **compound shape** made up of squares and rectangles. The method is to find each separate area, then add them up.

Example   Find the area of this shape:

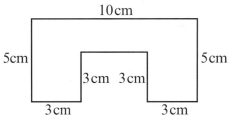

Solution   Break the shape up into three parts:

Area A (square) = 3 × 3 = 9 cm²
Area B (rectangle) = 2 × 10 = 20 cm²
Area C (square) = 3 × 3 = 9 cm²

The total area is 9 + 20 + 9 = <u>38 cm²</u>

Example   Find the area of this shape:

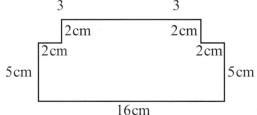

Solution   The shape is a rectangle with two corners missing:

Area of whole rectangle = 16 × 7
              = 112 cm².

Area of each corner = 2 × 2
              = 4 cm².

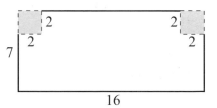

Therefore the area of the shape is 112 − 4 − 4 = <u>104 cm²</u>.

Exercise 21.3

Find the area of each of these compound shapes. Draw a sketch of each one, to show how you are breaking it into simpler pieces.

1

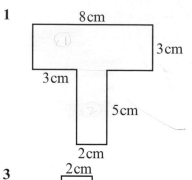

2

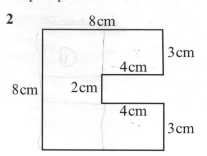

3

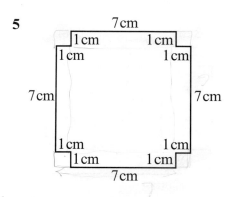

4

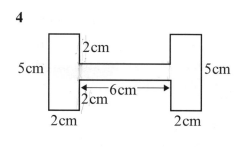

5

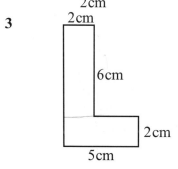

6

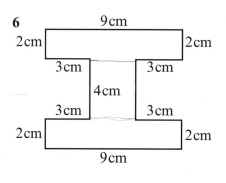

7

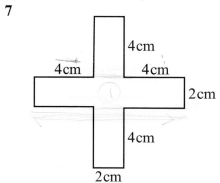

8

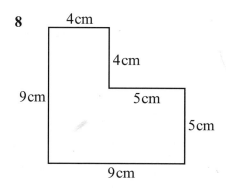

Summary

In this Unit you have practised finding the areas of squares and rectangles, with and without a calculator. You have rounded off answers containing long strings of decimals, usually to an accuracy of 3 significant figures.

You have also found the areas of compound shapes by breaking them into simpler parts. Remember to draw small sketches so you can see how the shapes are being broken up.

Review Exercise 21

Find the areas of these squares and rectangles. Do not use a calculator.

1 20 cm by 20 cm   **2** 30 cm by 30 cm

3 10 cm by 15 cm   **4** 14 cm by 3 cm

5 9 cm by 20 cm   **6** 3 cm by 13 cm

7 2 cm by 26 cm   **8** 5 cm by 25 cm

Find the areas of these squares and rectangles, using a calculator. Round your answers to 3 significant figures where appropriate.

9 4.4 cm by 4.4 cm   **10** 8.55 cm by 9.4 cm

11 8.25 cm by 6.4 cm   **12** 1.25 cm by 1.25 cm

13 9.9 cm by 11.1 cm   **14** 44.5 cm by 58.2 cm

15 4.05 cm by 6.35 cm   **16** 240 cm by 320 cm

Find the areas of these compound shapes:

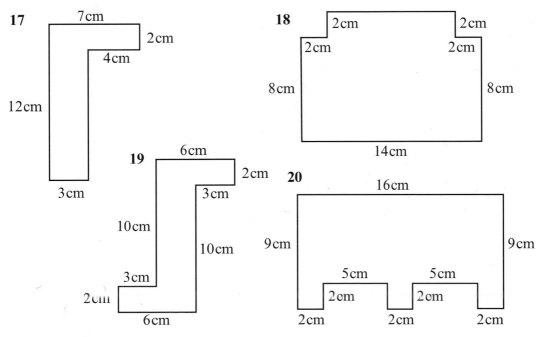

Unit 22
Averages and frequency diagrams

In this Unit you will learn how to:
- calculate the mean and the range for a set of discrete data;
- calculate the median and the mode;
- construct and interpret frequency diagrams;
- compare two distributions, using range and an average.

A calculator will be required for this Unit.

Discrete data may be recorded exactly, with no error. The number of people in a car is discrete, but the weight of a baby is not, since it can only be measured to a limited level of accuracy.

22.1 Mean and range

The mean is one way of describing the average of a set of data, while the range tells you the amount of variation within a set of data.

> The **mean** is the ordinary average of a set of numbers:
> Mean = (the total of all the values in a data set) ÷ (the number of values)
>
> The **range** is the difference between the extreme values:
> Range = (the greatest value) − (the least value)

Example   Find the mean and range of these eight numbers:
11   17   7   10   12   11   15   9

Solution   The total is $11 + 17 + 7 + 10 + 12 + 11 + 15 + 9 = 92$
There are 8 values altogether.
∴ Mean = $92 \div 8$
= 11.5

> The mean does not have to be a whole number, even if all the values in the data set are whole numbers.

The greatest value is 17, the least is 7.
∴ Range = $17 - 7$
= 10

> Don't just say 'from 7 to 17' – you **must** carry out the subtraction.

Exercise 22.1

In questions **1–16** find the mean and the range of the given values.

1 8, 3, 5, 2, 2

2 ✔ 7, 8, 4, 11, 12, 8, 7, 10

3 54, 27, 33, 46, 48

4 ✔ 5.4, 7.7, 5.9, 11.3, 9.6, 8.4

5 144, 108, 119, 97, 121

6 10, 100, 1000

7 7, 8, 9, 10, 11, 12, 13

8 2.4, 5.6, 7.2, 6.7

9 2, 3, 5, 7, 11, 13, 17, 19   **10** 1, 2, 0, 0, 2, 1, 2, 1

11 63, 11, 4, 21, 105   **12** ✔ −1, 2, 0, −2, 1, 3

13 2, 2, 2, 6, 6, 6   **14** 1103, 1245, 1381

15 3000, 4000, 7000, 10 000   **16** 0.05, 0.12, 0.005, 0.012

17 Five items in a clothes shop are priced at £10.99, £12.50, £25.10, £17.45 and £2.50. Find the mean price of the five items.

18 Four movies last for 121 minutes, 135 minutes, 141 minutes and 167 minutes. Find the mean length of the movies.

19 Eight punnets of strawberries are counted, and found to contain 16, 19, 18, 21, 15, 16, 20 and 17 fruits respectively. Find the mean number of strawberries per punnet and the range.

20 ✔ Ten confectionery bars are weighed on a digital balance. The weights, to the nearest gram, are recorded as 63, 66, 68, 65, 66, 68, 67, 70, 66 and 69 grams. Find the mean weight.
The label carries the message 'Average weight 65 grams'. Do you think the manufacturer is justified in making this claim?

22.2 Median and mode

The mean is not the only way of finding the average of a set of values. Two other common measures are the median and the mode.

The **median** is the middle value, once the values have been arranged in order of size.

The **mode** is the value which occurs most often.

Example   Find the median and mode of this set of values:
10 9 7 9 9 8 4 8 7 6 11

Solution   First, arrange the values in order of size:
4 6 7 7 8 8 9 9 9 10 11

The median is 8.

The mode is 9.

There are five numbers above it and five below.

9 occurs more often than any other value in the list.

Example   Find the median and mode of these values:

                     6   7   7   9   10   11   13   13   14   19

Solution   This time there are two middle numbers:

                     6   7   7   9   10   11   13   13   14   19

The median is 10.5 ← | This always happens when you have an **even** number of values – in this case **10**. Simply take the mean of the two middle values.

There are also two modes.
The modes are 7 and 13 (bimodal) ← | Bimodal means 'having two modes'. Sometimes there are more than two modes, and sometimes there is no mode at all.

Exercise 22.2

In questions **1–10** find the median and the mode.

1 ✔ 1, 3, 3, 5, 5, 6, 7, 7, 7   **2** 2, 2, 7, 9, 11

3 4, 11, 12, 14, 16, 16   **4** 5, 7, 7, 8, 11, 15, 15

5 1, 2, 4, 5, 7, 9, 11, 12, 17   **6** 1, 2, 1, 2, 2, 1, 2, 1, 0, 3

7 ✔ 9, 3, 6, 5, 14, 3, 12, 7   **8** 1.9, 2.6, 2.2, 2.8, 2.6, 2.1, 2.5

9 56, 63, 45, 32   **10** 2, 7, 4, 8, 7, 7, 2, 4, 9, 11, 4, 2

22.3 Tally charts and frequency diagrams

Example   Class 2B carried out a traffic survey. Fifty cars were chosen at random as they approached the traffic lights outside the school, and the number of occupants recorded. Here are the results:

         1 3 1 2 1   2 1 4 3 3   2 1 2 2 3
         1 2 2 4 3   1 2 1 2 4   4 1 1 1 2
         2 2 1 2 3   2 2 1 3 5   4 5 2 1 2
         4 3 2 1 2

    Draw up a frequency table, and display the results in a diagram.
    State the value of the mode.

Solution   We begin by preparing a tally chart:

Number of occupants	Tally	Frequency
1					
2			
3			
4		
5		

The numbers 1, 3, 1, 2, 1 are tallied like this.

This is the finished tally chart:

Number of occupants	Tally	Frequency
1	卌 卌 卌	15
2	卌 卌 卌 ||||	19
3	卌 |||	8
4	卌		6
5				2

Tallies are tied up in bundles of 5.

The data can be displayed in a bar chart or a vertical line graph:

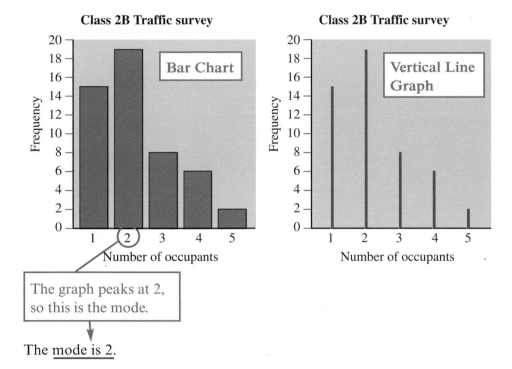

Class 2B Traffic survey — Bar Chart

Class 2B Traffic survey — Vertical Line Graph

The graph peaks at 2, so this is the mode.

The mode is 2.

Exercise 22.3

1 For each set of data, construct a tally chart, and illustrate the data with a frequency diagram.

a) 7 8 9 7 7   4 7 8 7 5   5 7 7 6 7   8 7 7 5 7

b) 1 4 5 6 2   2 2 1 4 3   1 4 5 6 6   2 2 1 3 5
    3 1 3 2 6   2 6 6 2 1   3 2 4 6 6   5 6 4 6 6

c) 0 0 1 4 1   0 1 0 1 0   0 1 1 3 2   2 3 2 3 3
    1 0 2 2 0   0 2 2 1 0

d) 16 10 11 15 15   20 16 15 11 10   16 11 16 15 16   17 14 17 16 18
    15 15 17 13 17   17 16 14 18 14   15 14 18 15 17   16 16 16 16 16

2 The diagram below illustrates the scores of 80 Year 7 pupils in a mathematics test:

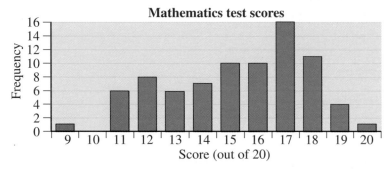

Mathematics test scores

a) Write down the value of the mode.
b) Find the range of the scores.

3 ✔ The diagram shows the scores obtained when an ordinary six-sided die is thrown repeatedly.

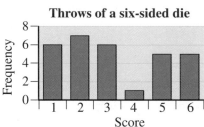

Throws of a six-sided die

a) Calculate the total number of throws.
b) Write down the value of the mode.

22.4 Comparing two distributions

Example   Here are the pulse rates of 10 boys and 12 girls:

Boys: 54 71 66 58 61 62 66 73 66 62
Girls: 61 69 76 62 64 60 69 68 77 75 75 78

> The comment should be in two parts
> ● how the **averages** compare
> ● how the **ranges** compare.

Calculate the mean and the range for each group. Comment briefly on how the two groups compare.

Solution   For the boys, 54 + 71 + … + 62 = 639
Mean = 639 ÷ 10 = <u>63.9</u> Range = 73 – 54 = <u>19</u>

For the girls, 61 + 69 + … + 78 = 834
Mean = 834 ÷ 12 = <u>69.5</u> Range = 78 – 60 = <u>18</u>

<u>Comment</u>

The boys seem to have a much lower mean value than the girls, i.e. their average pulses are slower. The ranges are almost identical however, indicating that the variation is similar within each group.

Exercise 22.4

1 ✔ The temperatures at two scientific stations are measured daily, throughout the year. The results are summarised in this table:

	Station A	Station B
Maximum temperature °C	18°	24°
Minimum temperature °C	3°	–6°
Median temperature °C	10°	11°

Comment briefly on how the two stations compare.

2 Janine has been conducting a homework survey. She asked a random sample of Year 7 and Year 11 pupils how many nights they spend doing more than 30 minutes of homework.

'How many nights per week (on average) do you spend doing at least 30 minutes homework?'

The results of Janine's survey are shown in these diagrams.

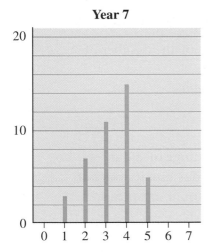

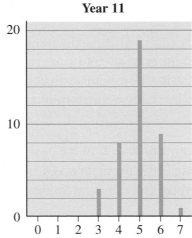

a) Suggest suitable labels for the x- and y-axes on these diagrams.

b) Find the mode and range for the Year 7 pupils.

c) Find the mode and range for the Year 11 pupils.

d) Comment briefly on how the two sets of data compare.

3 The weights, in kilograms, of thirteen girls were recorded as follows:

    55 43 45 52 41   38 47 44 43 41   51 42 45

The weights, in kilograms, of fourteen boys were similarly recorded:

    55 43 58 61 44   66 54 61 49 55   58 57 52 59

a) Find the mean and range of the girls' weights.

b) Find the mean and range of the boys' weights.

c) Comment briefly on the two sets of data.

4 ✔ The salaries of twenty accountants are to be compared. Ten of them are fully qualified, while the other ten are still trainees. The salaries, in £, are summarised in this table:

	Fully Qualified	Trainee
Least value	37 200	21 700
Median	41 100	25 250
Mean	43 200	24 700
Greatest value	45 500	29 350

Comment briefly on any similarities or differences between the two groups.

5 Greenview School's Head Teacher is analysing recent results of the school's soccer team. The number of goals scored in home and away matches are given in the tables below.

Home matches 6 0 1 3 3   4 3 4 4 5   1 3 4 1 3   1 2 5

Away matches 2 2 0 1 2   0 0 2 1 3   2 1 2 0 2   0 2 2

a) Draw up two tally charts to show the frequencies of the number of goals scored in home matches and away matches.

b) Illustrate both distributions with vertical line graphs.

c) Comment briefly on the two distributions.

Summary

In this Unit you have learnt how to find the mean and range of a data set. Remember that the mean is the usual 'average' in everyday use; it does not have to be a whole number. The range measures the amount of spread.

Two other 'averages' are the mode (most frequent) and median (middle value). Remember to arrange the values in order of size before finding the median.

It is often useful to make a tally chart, from which a frequency diagram can be drawn. The mode will correspond to the highest point of the frequency diagram, which can be drawn either as a bar chart (thick columns, not touching) or a vertical line graph (thin lines).

When comparing two data sets you should look at the average (mean, median or mode) and also the spread (measured by the range).

Review Exercise 22

1 Find the mean and range of each data set:

a) 6, 2, 6, 10, 5
b) 101, 118, 107, 121, 114
c) 6.5, 5.8, 7.2, 7.0, 6.8, 6.1, 8.0, 7.7
d) 5, 11, 8, 8, 7, 3, 12, 9, 10, 11
e) 2.2, 3.5, 4.8, 7.6, 8.0
f) 3, 1, 4, 1, 6
g) 4, −1, −5, 1, −1, 5
h) 90, 88, 96, 90, 84, 92

2 Find the median and the mode of each data set:

a) 2, 9, 3, 2, 5, 3, 8, 3, 6
b) 5, 9, 4, 12, 6, 5, 8, 4
c) 1, 3, 2, 3, 1, 1, 3, 2, 1, 3
d) 61, 27, 43, 41, 29, 55, 48
e) 8, 3, 7, 8, 3, 2, 5, 8, 1, 8
f) 97, 98, 99, 100, 101
g) 1, 5, 10, 20, 1000
h) 74, 77, 81, 77, 75, 81, 75, 84, 77, 81

3 Draw up a tally chart to show the number of a's, b's, c's etc. in this extract of text:

On a clear night, away from city lights, try looking up and estimating the number of stars visible to the unaided eye. The answer is several thousand.

a) State the modal letter.
b) Explain why you cannot find a mean for this set of data.

4 The diagram shows the results of a survey about brothers and sisters:

	Year 7 pupils	Year 11 pupils
Number of brothers or sisters	**Frequency**	**Frequency**
0	6	3
1	21	11
2	25	26
3	8	14
4	0	4
5	0	1
6 or more	0	0
Total	60	59

a) Draw two vertical line graphs to show the two sets of data.
b) Comment briefly on any differences between the results for Year 7 pupils and Year 11 pupils.

5 The graph shows information about some cars at a used car sale.
  a) Calculate the total number of cars.
  b) State the value of the mode.
  c) Calculate the mean number of previous owners of a used car.

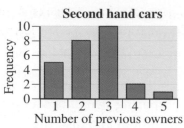

Second hand cars

6 Vinay counts the number of letters in each word of a sample of text from the eighteenth century, and another sample from the twentieth century. Here are his results:

	Eighteenth century text	Twentieth century text
Least length	2	2
Greatest length	17	11
Mean length	4.25	4.28

Vinay says 'If you look at the greatest lengths then it is clear that eighteenth century writers used much longer words than we do nowadays.'
Explain carefully whether you agree with Vinay's conclusion.

7* The table shows part of a brochure for a winter holiday:

Departure	Hotel Galli	Hotel Amerikan	Hotel Capriolo	Hotel Cassana
Dec 20	485	479	419	439
Dec 27	545	549	499	649
Jan 03	455	329	299	489
Jan 10	455	335	309	385
Jan 17	465	349	319	389
Jan 24	485	369	329	405

  a) Find the mean price for the four hotels in the week departing Jan 10.
  b) Find the mean price of a week at the Hotel Capriolo.
  c) Find the ranges of the prices in the four hotels during these six weeks.

8* The table shows the examination results of three students in four subjects.

Student	Mathematics	English	French	Science
Damian	43	58	84	48
Lois	77	55	66	51
Richard	79	11	68	60

  a) Find the mean score for each student.
  b) Find the mean score for each subject.
  c) Calculate the range of the marks.
  d) Richard was ill on the day of one of these examinations.
     Say which one you think it was.

9* Three jazz CDs have 7 tracks, 4 tracks and 13 tracks, while five folk CDs have 13 tracks, 11 tracks, 12 tracks, 15 tracks and 11 tracks.
   a) Find the mean number of tracks on the three jazz CDs.
   b) Find the mean number of tracks on the five folk CDs.
   c) Find the mean number of tracks on all eight CDs.

10* Gordon records the share prices of five companies every day for six months. The table gives some summary information about his data.

	Woofo Pet Foods	Floppidisk Software	Away-u-go Alarms	Goy-Goy Baby Toys	Volatile Chemicals
Maximum	246p	277p	299p	310p	314p
Minimum	203p	166p	277p	201p	177p
Mean	212p	214p	280p	250p	256p

   a) Identify the company whose prices show the greatest range.
   b) Comment briefly on the comparison between the figures for Floppidisk and Goy-Goy.

11* Each week I buy one national lottery ticket, and I choose the same six numbers each time. Five of the numbers are 5, 6, 11, 14 and 17, but I have forgotten the sixth number. I can remember, however, that the mean of my six numbers is 15. Calculate the value of the sixth number.

12* Class 4E are comparing the amount of pocket money they each receive. The ten boys have a mean of 80 pence per week, the least being 50 pence and the greatest £1.25. For the fifteen girls the mean is £1.00, with the least being 85 pence and the greatest £1.40.
   a) John says 'the mean for the class is 90 pence'. Explain how you think John obtained this figure, and say briefly why it is wrong.
   b) Calculate the correct mean amount of pocket money for Class 4E.
   c) Find the range for the class.

13* Catherine says 'If you look at 1, 2, 2, 4, 5 then the mean is 2.8 but the mode is only 2. This demonstrates that the mean is always greater than the mode'.
   Explain carefully whether you think Catherine's statement is correct.

14* Sonia records the amount of cloud cover in oktas during a twelve-day period. (8 oktas indicates total cloud cover, 0 oktas indicates no cloud at all.)
   Here are the results:

$$3 \ 7 \ 4 \ 7 \ 0 \ \ 0 \ 1 \ \ 5 \ 5 \ 3 \ 1$$

   Unfortunately Sonia has spilt ink over one of the readings. She can remember, however, that the mean of all twelve numbers is 3.25.

   a) Calculate the value of the reading covered by the ink blot.
   b) State the mode of the twelve readings.

Unit 23
Pie charts and line graphs

In this Unit you will learn how to:
- construct and interpret pie charts;
- construct and interpret line graphs;
- interpret other statistical diagrams.

A calculator will be required for this Unit.
A protractor is necessary for the pie chart work, and a pie chart scale (reading in percentages) is also useful.

23.1 Pie charts

A pie chart is used to display categorical (descriptive) data – i.e. the sizes of various classes, or categories. The frequencies are scaled until they add up to 360, then drawn using a protractor. Alternatively you can scale them to percentages, then use a pie chart scale.

Example   In a car park it is found that there are 11 red, 8 blue, 6 white, 3 green and 2 black cars. Display this information in a pie chart.

Solution   First we draw up a frequency table:

Colour	Frequency	Pie Chart Angle
Red	11	
Blue	8	
White	6	
Green	3	
Black	2	

The frequencies add up to $11 + 8 + 6 + 3 + 2 = 30$

$360 \div 30 = 12$, so all the frequencies are multiplied by 12.

Colour	Frequency		Pie Chart Angle
Red	11	$11 \times 12 = 132$	132°
Blue	8	$8 \times 12 = 96$	96°
White	6		72°
Green	3		36°
Black	2		24°

The resulting pie chart may now be drawn:

> When you make pie charts it is often a good idea to mark the angle in the centre of each sector.

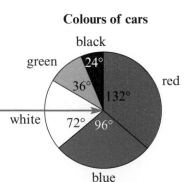

Colours of cars

Exercise 23.1

1 Martina is going to draw a pie chart to display the colours of 20 pencils. Three of them are red. What angle should she make the red sector of the pie chart?

2 Luc is drawing a pie chart to show the types of weather on different days during the year. 40% of the days are wet. What angle should he draw for this slice of the pie chart?

3 Sixty shoppers were asked to name their favourite type of fizzy drink. Twenty-four named cola, 18 lemonade, 13 orange and 5 other drinks. Display this information in a pie chart.

4 ✔ A school's mathematics department has an annual budget of £6000. £3000 is spent on books, £1600 on photocopying, £800 on classroom equipment and £250 on staff training. Display this information in a pie chart (don't forget to include a category for 'other').

5 I emptied my money-box and found that it contained exactly 90 coins. Thirty of them were 2p coins, seven 1p, twenty-one 10p, twenty-six 5p and the rest were foreign. Draw a pie chart to illustrate this information.

6 Tim is a concert violinist. He reckons that he practises for 5 hours a day, teaches for 3 hours a day, and sleeps for 8 hours a day. Half the remaining time is spent eating, and the remainder doing other things. Draw a pie chart to illustrate this information.

7 Susy receives an allowance of £20 a month. She usually spends £9 on clothes and £6 on toiletries. £2 is spent on stationery and she saves the rest. Show this on a pie chart.

8 Usha is a vet. Last week she treated 40 animals. They included 17 dogs, 11 cats, 5 hamsters and 4 lizards. Draw a pie chart to illustrate Usha's week.

9 David draws a pie chart to show the favourite subjects studied by the Year 8 pupils at his school. There are four sectors, labelled Mathematics, English, Art and Other. The largest sector is for mathematics, an angle of 156° representing 52 pupils.
a) Find the total number of pupils in Year 8.
b) English is the favourite subject of 37 pupils. Find the corresponding angle.
c) Art is represented by an angle of 81°. Find the number of pupils who named art as their favourite subject.

What is your favourite subject?

10 The diagram shows the number of hours spent on sports coverage by a cable TV station last week.
a) Explain why the use of a 3-D style pie chart appears to distort the information shown in the diagram.
b) Re-draw the diagram as an ordinary flat pie chart, so that the representation is fair.
c) What sort of people do you think might wish to use a diagram which deliberately distorts the information?

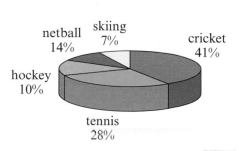

netball 14% skiing 7% cricket 41%

hockey 10%

tennis 28%

23.2 Line graphs

In this Section you will be using two quite different types of line graphs.

Vertical line graph
This is rather like a bar chart. It is used when the *x*-axis consists of categories – e.g. red, green, blue or Monday, Tuesday, Wednesday – with no possibility of any in-between values.

Time series graph (line graph)
This is a continuous line, consisting of several straight segments. It is used when the *x*-axis is continuous (e.g. a plot of time). In-between values may be estimated from the graph.

Example   A toy shop sells 23 dolls on Monday, 15 on Tuesday, 6 on Wednesday, 12 on Thursday and 32 on Friday.

Display this information in a suitable graph.

Solution

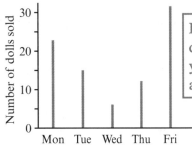

Here a **vertical line graph** is used. Although days of the week are plotted on the *x*-axis you cannot have a value between Monday and Tuesday, for example.

Example   During a busy period on the stock market the share prices of *Easiclean Appliances* change very quickly. The price was 225p at 0900, 275p at 1100 and 295p at 1230. During the afternoon the price peaked at 310p at 1400, then fell to 195p at 1500 before recovering to 240p by 1700.

Display this information in a suitable graph.

Solution

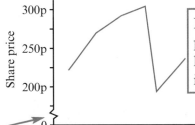

Here a **time series graph** is used. Time is plotted along the *x*-axis, and the straight line segments indicate that there are values in between 0900 and 1100, for example.

This zigzag shows that the *y*-axis has been interrupted.

Exercise 23.2

In questions **1–6** decide whether the data should be displayed using a vertical line graph or a time series graph, and then construct the graph.

1 ✔ In a survey of pets, seven children say they have 1 pet, twelve children have 2 pets, three children have 3 pets and five children have no pets at all.

2 ✔ The depth of water in a river was 10 cm on 1 July, 12 cm on 1 August, 14 cm on 1 September and 15 cm on 1 October.

3 The midday temperature in my garden was 17° on Monday, 19° on Tuesday, 14° on Wednesday, 17° on Thursday and 11° on Friday.

4 Yesterday my pulse rate was 70 at 0900, 75 at 1000, 80 at 1100 and 65 at 1200. It slowed to 55 at 1300 before increasing to 70 at 1600.

5 A shoe shop sold eight pairs of size 44 boots, eleven pairs of size 45, four pairs of size 46 and one pair of size 47.

6 In her summer mathematics examinations Florence scored 84% in Year 7, 72% in Year 8, 66% in Year 9 and 77% in Year 10.

In questions **7** and **8** the graph contains some kind of error. Explain briefly what it is, and draw a corrected version of the graph.

7 The number of words in an eight-page leaflet were counted, to the nearest 25 words. They were:

Page 1   850 words
Page 2   775 words
Page 3   800 words
Page 4   650 words
Page 5   850 words
Page 6   800 words
Page 7   750 words
Page 8   775 words

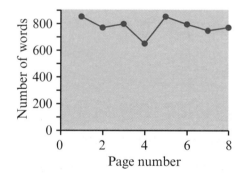

8 The table shows the average rate of spending on health by a new government during the first 400 days after it came to power.

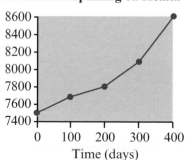

Government Spending on Health

Time (days)	Spending (£ thousands)
0	7500
100	7700
200	7800
300	8100
400	8600

23.3 Other statistical graphs

You should already be familiar with the bar chart and the pictogram.

Example   On Puddleduck Farm there are 15 ducks, 20 pigs, 30 cattle, 4 dogs and 42 sheep. Illustrate this data with a bar chart.

Solution

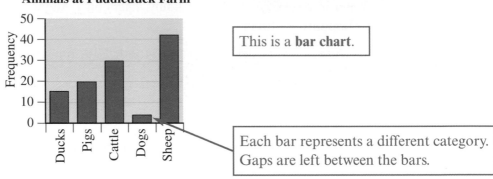

This is a **bar chart**.

Each bar represents a different category. Gaps are left between the bars.

Example   On Puddleduck Farm there are 15 ducks, 20 pigs, 30 cattle, 4 dogs and 42 sheep. Illustrate this data with a pictogram.

Solution

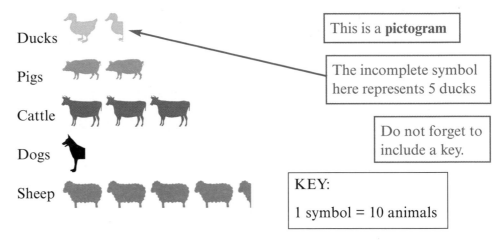

This is a **pictogram**

The incomplete symbol here represents 5 ducks

Do not forget to include a key.

KEY:

1 symbol = 10 animals

Example   The table shows the breakdown of the animals at Puddleduck Farm in a little more detail. Illustrate with a bar chart.

	Male	Female
Ducks	3	12
Pigs	10	10
Cattle	2	28
Dogs	3	1
Sheep	15	27

Solution

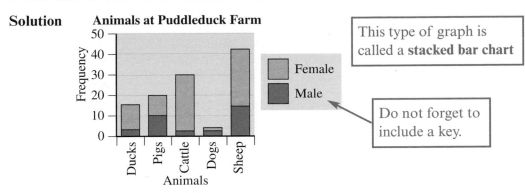

Animals at Puddleduck Farm

Female

Male

This type of graph is called a **stacked bar chart**

Do not forget to include a key.

There are many other types of statistical diagrams. You will meet some more of them in the Review exercise at the end of this Unit.

Exercise 23.3

1 The table shows a comparison between two small zoos:

	Monkeys	Penguins	Zebra	Eagles	Elephants
Zoo A	24	10	6	5	8
Zoo B	15	18	4	3	4

Draw two pictograms to illustrate the number of animals at each zoo. Use symbols of your choice, and a key of 1 symbol = 5 animals.

2 Four friends are comparing the amount they spend on various essentials each week. The figures are given in this table.

	Doris	Maurice	Horace	Boris
Supermarket	£25	£35	£85	£30
Petrol	£20	£35	£30	£5
Electricity	£30	£20	£45	£25

a) Illustrate this data with a stacked bar chart.
b) One of these friends is married and has children; the other three are single. Which one do you think is married?
c) One of these friends uses the train to travel to work; the others drive. Which one do you think uses the train?

Summary

In this Unit you have learnt how to construct pie charts, by scaling all the values until they add up to 360. You have used time series charts for data with a continuous scale along the x-axis (e.g. time), but drawn vertical line graphs when there is no possibility of any in-between values.

You have used pictograms with a key, and constructed stacked bar charts where appropriate. You have made deductions and comments about data presented in a table or a chart.

Review Exercise 23

1 An outdoor pursuits centre spends £1080 on new equipment. £450 is spent on tents, £270 on rucksacks and £240 on waterproof clothing; the rest is spent on maps. Illustrate this expenditure in a pie chart.

2 A daily newspaper allows 40% of its space to be used for news, 25% for photographs and 35% for advertising. On Sundays the proportions change to 35% news, 15% photographs and 50% advertising.
Draw two pie charts to illustrate the use of space in the daily and Sunday editions.

3 On a sports afternoon 42% of the school play hockey, 23% go cross-country running, 20% play squash and the rest swim. Illustrate this information with a pie chart.

4 A packet of coloured beads contains 23 red, 16 blue, 9 green and 14 yellow beads.
a) State the total number of beads in the packet.
b) Calculate the angles required for a pie chart to be drawn, rounding your answer to the nearest degree.
c) Construct the pie chart.

5 Mr Tughard is a dentist. He keeps a note of how many fillings 30 patients need:

1 0 0 1 2   1 2 0 0 1   3 0 1 2 1

1 0 1 1 3   0 1 2 1 1   0 0 1 1 0

a) Draw up a tally chart and find the total frequencies.
b) Display this data in a suitable type of line graph.

6 Four friends are comparing the number of CDs they own. Annabel has 22, Henrietta has 11, Daniel has 7 and David has 18. Using a key of 1 symbol to 5 CDs, draw a pictogram to show how many CDs the four friends have.

7 In the first three months of the new soccer season City won 3 matches, drew 4 and lost 4, Rovers won 7, drew 3 and lost 5, while United won 4, drew 2 and lost 11. Illustrate this data with a stacked bar chart.

8 Felicity is drawing a pie chart to show land use at a local farm. 40 acres are arable; this is represented by an angle of 30°. Dairy farming has an angle of 120°, and there are 120 acres of woodland.
a) How many acres are dairy?
b) What angle represents woodland?
c) How many acres does the farm have in total?

9* The table shows the amount of petrol in my car's fuel tank during a long journey:

Time	1000	1100	1200	1300	1400
Petrol (litres)	55	40	26	14	50

a) Display this information using a vertical line graph.
b) Explain why it would be misleading to join the points up into a time series chart.

10* The 'doughnut diagram' shows the relative sizes of the different rooms in a flat:

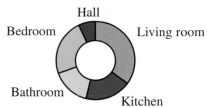

Rooms in a flat

a) Using a protractor, measure the angle of each section as accurately as possible.

b) Redraw the diagram as a pie chart.

11* Mike, John and Abdul have drawn a 'radar chart' to compare the number of minutes per week that they spend doing homework in each of five subjects.

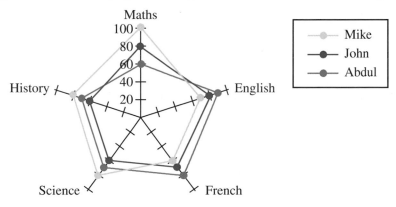

a) Who spends the longest on mathematics?

b) Who spends the least time on science?

c) Estimate the total time that the three boys spend on English.

12* The table shows the temperature at a town on the equator. Time 0 hours indicates midday on January 1, so 24 is midday on January 2, and so on. A × indicates that no reading was taken on that occasion.

Time	0	24	48	72	96	120	144	168
Temperature °C	32°	28°	29°	×	31°	32°	32°	31°

a) State the date on which no reading was taken.

b) Draw a time series chart, and use it to estimate the missing temperature.

c) Explain why it would be unwise to use the time series chart to estimate the temperature at time 60.

Unit 24
Theoretical and experimental probability

In this Unit you will learn how to:
- understand and use a probability scale from 0 to 1;
- calculate probabilities and justify them;
- use experimental probability.

A calculator will be needed for some of these exercises.

24.1 Likely and unlikely outcomes

When an experiment is conducted the outcome might be:
- impossible
- unlikely
- reasonably likely
- very likely
- certain

Example Decide whether each of these is impossible; unlikely; reasonably likely; very likely or certain:
  a) that today will last for more than 24 hours;
  b) that my Walkman batteries will one day run out;
  c) that a coin tossed in the air comes down heads;
  d) that one day a woman will become president of the USA.

Solution a) impossible;
  b) certain;
  c) reasonably likely;
  d) very likely.

The probability scale runs from 0 to 1.
A probability of 0 means an outcome is impossible.
A probability of 1 means an outcome is certain.
A probability of 0.5 indicates that something has a 50% chance of occurring.

Example Indicate on a probability scale the probability that a letter chosen at random from the letters of the word MOUSE is a vowel.

Solution Since three of the five letters are vowels, the probability of choosing a vowel is more likely than not, so the scale will look like this:

Exercise 24.1

Decide whether each of these outcomes is impossible; unlikely; reasonably likely; very likely or certain. Illustrate each answer with a probability scale from 0 to 1.

1 A word chosen at random from a dictionary begins with a letter Q.

2 It will rain somewhere in England during next October.

3 ✔ One day mathematicians will discover a whole number between 8 and 9.

4 A tossed coin will land on end.

5 A throw of a fair dice will result in an even number.

6 The sun will eventually stop shining.

7 ✔ Someone in my class will become Prime Minister when they grow up.

8 My washing machine will break down sometime during the next 30 years.

9 ✔ A drawing pin dropped on the floor will land point up.

10 The score when an ordinary dice is thrown is at least 1.

24.2 Theoretical probability

Suppose an experiment has more than one different possible outcome.

Then the probability of getting a particular result =

$$\frac{\text{number of ways of getting that result}}{\text{total number of all possible outcomes}}$$

A probability of 0 means that something is *impossible* – it *cannot* happen.

A probability of 1 means that something is *certain* – it *must* happen.

Example A bag contains 3 red counters, 4 blue ones and 7 yellow ones. One counter is chosen at random. Find the probability that it is red.

Solution There are 14 possible outcomes in total (3 + 4 + 7). 3 of them give a red counter.

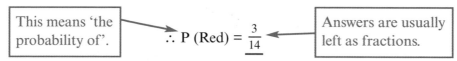

This means 'the probability of'.   ∴ P (Red) = $\frac{3}{14}$ Answers are usually left as fractions.

Many questions in probability are about games involving cards or dice, or numbers involving prime numbers, multiples or factors. You may find the following information useful.

There are 52 cards in an ordinary pack. They are divided into four *suits* – clubs, diamonds, hearts, spades. Clubs and spades are black, diamonds and hearts are red.

Each suit contains 13 cards: 2, 3, 4, 5, 6, 7, 8, 9, 10, Jack, Queen, King, Ace.

Multiples are the result of multiplying by a whole number.
The multiples of 7 are 7, 14, 21, 28 and so on.

Factors are numbers which divide exactly into another number.
The factors of 12 are 1, 2, 3, 4, 6 and 12.

A *prime number* does not have any factors, other than 1 and itself.
2, 3, 5, 7, 11, etc. are prime numbers (but 1 is not).

Example   The whole numbers from 1 to 12 are written on discs and placed in a bag. One disc is then chosen at random. Find the probability that the number on the disc is prime.

Solution   The numbers are   1 2 3 4 5 6 7 8 9 10 11 12
The primes are   ↑ ↑   ↑   ↑   ↑

There are 5 primes altogether.

$$\therefore \text{P (Prime)} = \frac{5}{12}$$

Example   A card is chosen at random from an ordinary pack of 52. Find the probability that it is:
a) an Ace   **b)** a six or a seven   **c)** a diamond.

Solution   **a)** $\text{P(Ace)} = \frac{4}{52} = \frac{1}{13}$

b) $\text{P(6 or 7)} = \frac{8}{52} = \frac{2}{13}$

c) $\text{P(diamond)} = \frac{13}{52} = \frac{1}{4}$

Exercise 24.2

In this exercise you should give your answers as fractions.

1 A card is chosen at random from an ordinary pack. Find the probability that it is:
a) red   **b)** a 7   **c)** the 7 of hearts   **d)** not the 7 of hearts.

2 ✔ A bag contains 5 red balls, 6 blue balls and 7 yellow balls. A ball is chosen at random. Find the probability that it is:
a) red   **b)** blue   **c)** green.

3 A raffle organiser sells 200 tickets for a top prize, and Anton buys 5 of them. Calculate the probability that Anton wins the top prize.

4 I have a collection of 100 stamps. 50 are British, 30 are French and the rest are German. I choose one stamp at random. Calculate the probability that it is:
a) British   **b)** French   **c)** not German   **d)** Italian.

5 In a game of 'Hangman' I have one guess remaining, to find one missing letter. I am sure that it must be either A, E or Y. I guess at random; find the probability that my guess is correct.

6 An ordinary pack of playing cards is shuffled, and a card is chosen at random. Find the probability that it is:
a) red   **b)** an 8, 9 or 10   **c)** a court card (i.e. an Ace, King, Queen or Jack).

7 ✔ The diagram shows a spinner. Scores of 1, 2, 3 and 6 are possible. The spinner is spun once. Find the probability that the score is:
a) 1   **b)** 6   **c)** even   **d)** prime.

8 The whole numbers from 1 to 20 are written on twenty cards and placed in a bag. A card is chosen at random. Find the probability that the number on it is:
a) odd   **b)** a multiple of 6   **c)** prime   **d)** a factor of 36.

9 A cereal company decides to put a toy aircraft in each packet of its new breakfast flakes. There are five toys altogether: Jaguar, Tornado, Phantom, Lightning and Spitfire. A box is chosen at random. Find the probability that the toy it contains is:
a) a Spitfire   **b)** a Jaguar or Tornado   **c)** not a Phantom.
What assumption(s) are you making about the toy aircraft?

10 Ten discs numbered 11, 12, 13, …, 20 are placed in a bag, and one of the discs is chosen at random. Find the probability that it is:
a) even   **b)** prime   **c)** a multiple of 6.

24.3 Experimental probability

In some situations it is not possible to calculate the probability of an outcome just by thinking about it: an experiment must be set up to collect some data first. Then the following result is used:

experimental probability of getting a particular result =
number of times that result occurred
    total number of experiments

Example   An experiment was conducted to find the probability that a
drawing pin lands point up when it is dropped. A drawing pin
was thrown 250 times, and it landed point up 138 times.
Calculate the theoretical probability of this pin landing point up.

Solution   Probability (point up) $= \dfrac{138}{250}$

$$= \dfrac{69}{125}$$

It is important to remember that experimental probabilities are not as
reliable as theoretical ones. If this experiment were to be repeated another
250 times, for example, then you would probably not get the pin landing
point up 138 times, so the experimental probability would be slightly
different. For this reason you should always do as many trials as possible.
For a very large number of trials the experimental probability is close to
theoretical probability.

Exercise 24.3

In this exercise you should give your answers as fractions.

1 An astronomer notices that during a typical July there are 24 clear nights and
7 cloudy ones. Find the experimental probability that a July night is cloudy.

2 A restaurant offers a choice of fries or salad with its main courses. One evening
120 customers are served, and 95 of them choose fries. Find the experimental
probability that a customer chooses:
a) fries   **b)** salad.

3 Rick enjoys shooting clay pigeons. On his last shoot he fired at 60 clay pigeons,
hitting 21 of them. Find the experimental probability that he misses when he fires
at a clay pigeon.

4 I reckon that I know the answers to 44 of the 80 questions in a general knowledge
quiz box. A question is chosen at random from the box. Find the probability that:
a) I know the answer   **b)** I do not know the answer.
What happens if you add together your answers to parts **a)** and **b)**?
Can you explain why?

5 ✔ A ferry company looks at records of 100 sailings, and finds that 60 arrived late,
35 arrived on time and 5 arrived early. Find the experimental probability that:
a) a sailing arrives early   **b)** a sailing does not arrive late.

Summary

In this Unit you have used probabilities between 0 and 1 to describe the likelihood of something happening. Probabilities close to 1 indicate highly likely events, while those close to 0 indicate unlikely events. A probability of 1 indicates certainty, 0 impossibility.

Probabilities are calculated as fractions, dividing the number of favourable outcomes by the total number of all possible outcomes. If this can be done just by thinking then we obtain a *theoretical probability*; if data must be collected first then we obtain an *experimental probability* instead.

The probability that something occurs and the probability that it does not occur must add up to 1.

Review Exercise 24

In questions **1–10** calculate the required probability. Mark it on a probability scale from 0 to 1.

1 A bag contains 8 red and 12 green balls. A ball is chosen at random; find the probability that it is red.

2 A bag contains 6 red, 4 blue and 18 green balls. A ball is chosen at random; find the probability that it is not red.

3 A number is chosen at random from the whole numbers from 1 to 40 inclusive. Find the probability that it is prime.

4 A number is chosen at random from the whole numbers from 51 to 100 inclusive. Find the probability that it is a multiple of 7.

5 A card is chosen at random from an ordinary pack of playing cards. Find the probability that it is the 6 of diamonds.

6 A card is chosen at random from an ordinary pack of playing cards. Find the probability that it is red.

7 The 26 letters of the alphabet are written on 26 discs, and placed in a bag. One disc is chosen at random. Find the probability that the letter on the disc is a consonant.

8 Six of the children in class 5B travel to school by car, and the other 24 walk. Find the probability that a randomly chosen child from class 5B travels to school by car.

9 My school cricket team's recent results were 3 wins, 11 draws and 6 games lost. Find the experimental probability that the team loses a randomly chosen match.

10 'You should only eat mussels when there's an R in the month.' The name of a month is chosen at random. Find the probability that it contains an R.

11* The table shows the result of rolling a dice 600 times:

Score	1	2	3	4	5	6
Frequency	99	101	120	106	91	83

    a) Illustrate this information in a suitable line graph.

    b) Calculate the experimental probability of each score, correct to 2 decimal places.

    c) Comment briefly on whether you think this is a fair dice or not.

12* A spinner is divided into 24 equal segments. Some of them are coloured yellow; of the rest, half are blue and half are purple. When the spinner is spun the probability of getting a yellow is 0.25. Find the number of segments of each colour.

13* A bag contains 8 red balls and n green ones. A ball is chosen at random; the probability that it is red is found to be 0.2. Calculate the value of n.

14* At a school fete I notice that 60 people have played at the 'Roll the Penny' stall, and 8 of them won prizes. It costs 10p to play, and the prize is 50p.

    a) Calculate the experimental probability of winning a prize.

    b) Explain whether you would expect the stall to make money or lose it, overall.

15* Jemma and Emma have collected some data about a spinner, on which the score is always 0 or 1. Jemma spun the spinner 100 times, and Emma spun it 400 times.

	Number of 0s	Number of 1s
Jemma	34	66
Emma	102	298

    a) Calculate the experimental probability of getting a 1, using Jemma's results.

    b) Repeat this calculation, using Emma's results instead.

    c) Explain briefly which of these answers is more reliable.

    d) Suggest a way of obtaining an even more reliable answer.

Level 5 Review

Exercise 1

Do this exercise as mental arithmetic – do not write down any working.

1 Find 8×12.

2 Find $63 \div 7$.

3 Find 11×11.

4 Find $42 \div 6$.

5 Write in figures four million, seventy thousand, two hundred and eight.

6 Write in words $2\,406\,541$.

7 Find 788×1000.

8 Find $12\,500 \div 100$.

9 Find $46\,250 \times 100$.

10 Find $800\,000 \div 10$.

11 Find $15\,000 \div 300$.

12 Find 650×20.

13 Find 8000×500.

14 Find $12\,000\,000 \div 20$.

15 Work out $17.56 + 8.74$.

16 Work out $57.09 - 28.66$.

17 Find the value of $8 + -3 - 7$.

18 Find the value of $12 - 3 \times 2$.

19 Add up £12.99 and £17.25.

20 Find 10% of 2500.

Exercise 2

Do this exercise as mental arithmetic – do not write down any working.

1 Bags of crisps weigh 35 grams each. Find the total weight of 20 bags.

2 Alan has 48 sweets and shares them out amongst 6 people. How many sweets does each person receive?

3 Sheets of stickers cost 99 pence each. Roughly how much would it cost for 20 sheets?

4 Burger meals cost £2.88 plus another 30p to 'go large'. Roughly how much would it cost for 19 people to purchase 'go large' burger meals?

5 Write 5793 correct to 2 significant figures.

6 Pencils cost 19 pence each. How much change should I receive from £1 when I buy five?

7 Find the total number of days in the months from August to December (inclusive).

8 Last year my car insurance cost £140; this year it is 20% more. Find this year's cost.

9 A card is chosen at random from an ordinary pack. Find the probability that it is an Ace.

10 A tape is chosen at random from my collection of 5 classical, 12 rock and 3 jazz tapes. What is the probability that it is a jazz tape?

11 A certain number is an odd number between 80 and 90; it is neither prime nor a multiple of 3. What is the number?

12 A shop sells 805 CDs at £10.99 each. Roughly how much money is taken in total?

13 Shares which were worth 250 pence each have fallen to 90% of their value. Find the new value of the shares.

14 I buy 8 packs of stickers at 99 pence each. Find the exact value of the total cost.

15 An ordinary six-sided dice is thrown. Find the probability that a 5 or a 6 is obtained.

16 In the old Imperial system of measures, one fathom is equal to six feet.
   a) Roughly how many centimetres are there in half a fathom?
   b) Roughly how many fathoms are there in 200 feet?

17 The human body contains about 8 pints (one gallon) of blood. Is this approximately 2 litres, 4.5 litres, or 16 litres?

18 'Angles in a pie chart must always add up to 360°.' True or false?

19 'Five kilometres is roughly the same as eight miles.' True or false?

20 '2.5 kilograms is exactly the same as 250 grams.' True or false?

Exercise 3

You should show all necessary working in this exercise.

1 Work out 6592 + 1277.

2 Work out 8432 – 1966.

3 Work out 9477 + 8061.

4 Work out 11 255 – 958.

5 Add £8.08, £15.44 and £19.99.

6 How much change do I receive from a £20 note when I buy two items, one for £6.50 and the other for £8.75?

7 Work out 126×32.

8 Work out 3622×47.

9 Work out 9854 ÷ 13. (The answer should be an exact whole number.)

10 Work out 9429 ÷ 21. Give the answer as a whole number with a remainder.

11 Find $\frac{3}{4}$ of 360.

12 Find 80% of 500.

13 Usha says 'This fossil is 70 000 000 years old. Next year it will be 70 000 001 years old.' Explain carefully why Usha's statement is not really true.

14 Two of the angles in a triangle are 71° and 22°. Find the third angle, and say whether it is acute or obtuse.

15 Three of the angles in a quadrilateral are 71°, 44° and 103°. Find the fourth angle, and say whether it is acute or obtuse.

16 Leonardo says 'the angle at each corner of a regular pentagon is 118°'. Leonardo is wrong. Explain carefully how you tell that he is wrong, and state the correct value of the angle.

17 My scores in four tests are 17, 19, 19 and 16. Calculate the mean. Find also the range and the mode.

18 The daytime temperature on Mercury reaches 330°C, and at night it falls to –180°C. Find the difference between the daytime and night-time temperatures.

19 I buy eleven filing trays, which cost £2.77 each. Find the total cost.

20 Archie tiles a wall. One row needs 18 complete tiles, plus half a tile on each end, to reach across the full width of the wall. Tiles are 15 cm wide. Find the width of the wall, in metres.

Exercise 4

1 Find seven-ninths of 153.

2 Find 23% of 2600.

3 Simplify $15a - 11b + 4a$.

4 Simplify $7 \times x \times x + 11 \times x \times x$.

5 Increase £10.99 by 23%.

6 Find the value of $16a^2 - 11a$ when $a = 2.5$.

7 Here are some instructions for a number machine:
Input; multiply by 3; add seven; output.
a) Find the output when the input number is 11.
b) Find the input if the output number is 31.

8 Last year Janet was earning £1300 a month, and John was earning £1400 a month. This year Janet's pay has increased by 16% and John's has increased by 8%. Find out who is the higher earner this year, and by how much.

9 A certain number has two digits. The digits add up to 8 and the number is odd but not prime. What is the number?

10 Simplify $5a + 6b - 7a + 8b$ and find the value of this expression when $a = 10.5$ and $b = -0.8$.

11 I have £100 in my savings account but I spend £5 every month. How much do I have left after n months? Is there any limit to the value of n?

12 The number of people attending five theatre shows on different nights are 188, 192, 241, 177 and 288. Find the mean number of people attending per night.

13 The table shows the number of letters delivered to me each day, over a period of n days.

Number of letters	0	1	2	3	4	5	6 or more
Frequency	10	5	7	12	4	2	0

a) Illustrate this information with a suitable line graph.
b) Find the modal number of letters.
c) State the value of n. Hence find the experimental probability that I receive no more than one letter on a given day.

14 The table shows some coursework scores for Year 11 pupils:

Ned	Abdul	Andrew	Kim	Hannah	Rana
23	19	19	19	17	19

a) Find the mean score.
b) State the modal score and the range.

15 Abdul and Rana have to take six examinations, each one being marked out of 70.

a) Abdul has taken five examinations so far, and has a mean score of 53. How many marks must he obtain in the sixth test in order to average 55 marks overall?

b) Rana has also taken five examinations so far, with a mean score of 51. Explain carefully why she cannot end up with an average of 55 marks over all six examinations.

16 The formula $x^2 + x + 41$ is being used to work out numbers which could be prime.

a) Work out the answer when $x = 1$.

b) Work out the answer when $x = 2$.

c) Work out the answer when $x = 41$.

d) One of these three answers is not a prime number. Which one is that?

17 Make a neat copy of this grid in your book:

$\frac{3}{4}$	50%	$\frac{3}{5}$	30%	$\frac{1}{5}$	5%
35%	$\frac{7}{10}$	15%	$\frac{9}{10}$	60%	$\frac{1}{4}$
$\frac{3}{10}$	75%	$\frac{1}{20}$	20%	$\frac{4}{5}$	55%
90%	$\frac{1}{2}$	25%	$\frac{11}{20}$	70%	$\frac{3}{20}$

a) The grid contains pairs of fractions and matching percentages. Colour in each fraction and its matching percentage.

b) When you have finished there will be one fraction and one percentage left over. What fraction is equivalent to the left over percentage? What percentage is equivalent to the left over fraction?

18 Look at this extract from John's mathematics exercise book:

$$\underline{1} \quad 1966 \times 204 = 41064$$
$$\underline{2} \quad 28 \times 88 = 2464$$
$$\underline{3} \quad 10\,146 \div 89 = 114$$

By rounding the numbers off to one significant figure, make estimates of the answers. If you think that John has made any serious mistakes then use your calculator to obtain the correct answer, and explain what you think he did wrong.

19 Ted is recording the depth of water at the end of a pier at hourly intervals. Here are his results:

Time	1400	1500	1600	1700
Depth (metres)	4.75	3.8	2.9	2.4

a) Explain whether it is better to draw a vertical line graph or a time series graph to display this information.

b) Construct your graph, and use it to estimate the depth of water at 4:30 p.m.

20 A newspaper carries out a survey about watching TV in which 4000 people are asked to state their favourite type of programme. The results are:

Soaps/sitcoms	35%
Sports	27%
News	18%
Other	20%

a) Display this information in a pie chart.
b) Which angle corresponds to Sports?
c) How many people stated that their favourite type of programme is News?

Exercise 5 Calculator Crossword

Work out each clue on your calculator, then turn it upside down to make a word. Write the word into a copy of the grid.

Down

1 247×15 (fish)

2 $30 \times 200 - 7$ (breakfast ingredient)

3 $17 \times 20 - 17 \times 19$ (Chinese money)

4 $8^3 + 7^3 - 3^4 - 1$ (old unit)

5 $31^2 - 3 \times 8$ (cricket side)

8 $87 \times 79 + 8 \times 29$ (make dirty)

10 19% of 2000 (medal)

12 Increase 4568 by 25% (lubricates)

13 $0.07 \times 11 - 0.4$ (star sign)

15 $699 \div 5000$, correct to 3 decimal places (place in USA)

16 21.3×18 (mythological servant)

17 Mean of 566, 799, 1047 (found in the kitchen)

18 $29 \times 31 - 2^4$ (to recede)

21 $\sqrt{5329}$ (Spanish word)

Across

1 15.469×5 (found on the beach)

4 $27^2 + 4$ (swimmer)

6 $1511.16 \div 19.6$ (not well)

7 $81 \times 77 - 15 \times 20$ (supports)

9 $9^3 + 178$ (record)

11 0.047×15 (alone)

14 $0.85^2 - 0.001 \times 5.5$ (air bed)

17 $\sqrt{92\,416}$ (garden tool)

19 203×15 (item of clothing)

20 $\sqrt{114\,244}$ (it flies)

22 $(9^2 + 20) \times 8$ (boy's name)

23 $7 + 5 \times 7000$ (free)

Level 6 Unit 25
Rounding and approximation

In this Unit you will learn how to:
- order and approximate decimals;
- use trial and improvement methods;
- solve problems using trial and improvement.

 A calculator will be required for this Unit.

25.1 Decimal places and significant figures

Decimal places are the figures that occur after the decimal point.

Example   Write these numbers correct to 3 decimal places:
   a) 14.5631   **b)** 0.205 817   **c)** 2.009 84

Solution   **a)** 14.563⦙1
   This will round to
   14.653 correct to 3 d.p.

> If this figure is 4 or less then we round down and if it is 5 or more we round up.

   b) 0.205⦙817
   This will round to
   0.206 correct to 3 d.p.

   c) 2.009⦙84
   This will round to
   2.010 correct to 3 d.p.

> **Warning!** It would be a mistake to write 2.01 as this would suggest that you don't know very much about the third decimal place.

Significant figures are the figures that give information about place value. Significant figures are counted from the left. For whole numbers you stop counting when a final block of zeroes is encountered, but for decimals you must keep counting until the last decimal place, even if it is a zero.

Example   Write these numbers correct to 3 significant figures:
   a) 19 245   **b)** 207 740   **c)** 0.007 087   **d)** 0.088 966

Solution   **a)** 19 2⦙45
   This will round to
   19 200 correct to 3 s.f.

> If this figure is 4 or less then we round down
> and if it is 5 or more we round up.

   b) 207⦙740
   This will round to
   208 000 correct to 3 s.f.

> The zeroes in 0.00 do not count as significant figures – they just make the figures that follow occur in the correct columns. The zero in 708 **does** count as a significant figure.

   c) 0.007 08⦙7
   This will round to
   0.007 09 correct to 3 s.f.

d) 0.088 9|66
This will round to
<u>0.0890</u> correct to 3 s.f.

> Do not write 0.089 –
> this would only be 2 s.f.

To arrange decimals in order, compare the **most significant figures** first.
The most significant is the figure furthest towards the left.

Example   Arrange these decimals in order of size, largest first:
   10.45   166   8.25   70.5   8.1444

Solution   First, write the numbers so that the place values line up:

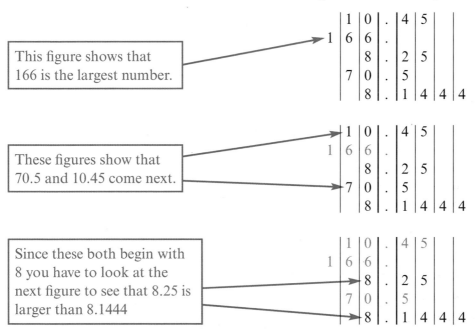

This figure shows that
166 is the largest number.

These figures show that
70.5 and 10.45 come next.

Since these both begin with
8 you have to look at the
next figure to see that 8.25 is
larger than 8.1444

In order of size the decimals are: 166, 70.5, 10.45, 8.25, 8.1444

Exercise 25.1

Round each of these numbers to the given number of decimal places.

1 13.562 (1 d.p.)   **2** ✔ 104.849 (1 d.p.)   **3** 3.0671 (2 d.p.)

4 88.2219 (3 d.p.)   **5** 16.4587 (2 d.p.)   **6** ✔ 12.204 (2 d.p.)

Round each of these numbers to the given number of significant figures.

7 3.14159 (4 s.f.)   **8** 60.2544 (3 s.f.)   **9** 17.281 901 (3 s.f.)

10 ✔ 46.204 (4 s.f.)   **11** 14.2247 (3 s.f.)   **12** 0.002 034 (3 s.f.)

Arrange these in order of size, largest first :

13 6.065, 6.21, 4.3, 4.03, 4.601   **14** 12.109, 12.01, 12.66, 12.2, 12.901

15 ✔ 4.21, 1.24, 1.024, 4.021, 4.201   **16** 0.010, 0.001, 0.03, 0.2, 0.02

Arrange these in order of size, smallest first:

17 14.2, 10.42, 14.02, 1.402, 1.61

18 33.6, 33.13, 36.3, 30.63, 36.03

19 4.7, 4.81, 4.07, 4.87, 4.17

20 ✓ −2.14, −1.44, −3.6, 0.26, 0.77

25.2 Trial and improvement

Some equations are too difficult to solve by exact methods. In the trial and improvement method you start with a solution that is roughly right, and gradually improve it. You will not usually get an exact solution, but one which is correct to a certain number of figures.

Example   The equation $x^2 + x - 5 = 0$ has a solution between $x = 1$ and $x = 2$. Use a trial and improvement method to find this solution correct to 2 decimal places.

Solution   Consider the value of the expression $x^2 + x - 5$.

When $x = 1$ then $1^2 + 1 - 5 = -3$

When $x = 2$ then $2^2 + 2 - 5 = 1$

> One of these is **positive** and the other **negative.** This change of sign indicates a solution between $x = 1$ and $x = 2$.

When $x = 1.6$ then $1.6^2 + 1.6 - 5 = -0.84$

When $x = 1.7$ then $1.7^2 + 1.7 - 5 = -0.41$

When $x = 1.8$ then $1.8^2 + 1.8 - 5 = 0.04$

> This change of sign shows that the solution is between $x = 1.7$ and $x = 1.8$.

When $x = 1.78$ then $1.78^2 + 1.78 - 5 = -0.0516$

When $x = 1.79$ then $1.79^2 + 1.79 - 5 = -0.0059$

When $x = 1.80$ then $1.80^2 + 1.80 - 5 = 0.0400$

> Now we can see the solution is between $x = 1.79$ and $x = 1.80$.

Since the value of −0.0059 is much closer to zero than is 0.0400 then it seems reasonable to deduce that the solution is $x = \underline{1.79 \text{ correct to 2 d.p.}}$

N.B. If you have access to a computer algebra system package such as *Derive* then you can easily verify that the solution is 1.791 28 correct to 6 significant figures.

Exercise 25.2
Solve the equations in the following table by trial and improvement. Remember to show all your working, as in the example above. Stop when you have reached the required level of accuracy.

	Equation	First trial x-value	Find solution correct to
1	$x^2 + 3x - 7 = 0$	$x = 2$	2 decimal places
2	$x^2 - 7x - 9 = 0$	$x = 8$	2 decimal places
3 ✔	$x^2 - x - 5 = 0$	$x = 3$	3 decimal places
4	$x^2 + 5x - 5 = 0$	$x = 1$	2 decimal places
5	$x^2 - x - 10 = 0$	$x = 4$	2 decimal places
6	$x^2 - 6x + 7 = 0$	$x = 2$	2 decimal places
7	$x^2 - 10x + 23 = 0$	$x = 6$	2 decimal places
8	$x^2 + 10x - 120 = 0$	$x = 7$	2 decimal places
9	$2x^2 - 5x + 3 = 0$	$x = 2$	2 decimal places
10 ✔	$x^2 + 5x - 1 = 0$	$x = 0$	2 decimal places

25.3 Harder problems on trial and improvement

The equations in trial and improvement problems do not always have a convenient '= 0' on the right-hand side, so it may be necessary to rearrange them first. You will not always be told the approximate solution, so you might need to hunt around at first.

Both these aspects are illustrated in the next worked example.

Example   Find a solution to the equation $x^3 = 10x - 4$, giving your answer correct to 1 decimal place.

Solution   First rearrange the equation:

$$x^3 = 10x - 4$$
$$\therefore x^3 - 10x = -4$$
$$\therefore \underline{x^3 - 10x + 4 = 0}$$

> This equation can now be solved by trial and improvement.

Since no starting value is given, try $x = 1$, $x = 2$ and so on.

When $x = 1$ then $1^3 - 10 \times 1 + 4 = 1 - 10 + 4 = -5$

When $x = 2$ then $2^3 - 10 \times 2 + 4 = 8 - 20 + 4 = -8$

When $x = 3$ then $3^3 - 10 \times 3 + 4 = 27 - 30 + 4 = 1$

> This change of sign shows that there is a solution between $x = 2$ and $x = 3$.

When $x = 2.9$ then $2.9^3 - 10 \times 2.9 + 4 = -0.611$

When $x = 3.0$ then $3.0^3 - 10 \times 3.0 + 4 = 1$

> This change of sign shows that there is a solution between $x = 2.9$ and $x = 3.0$.

It is a good idea to try 2.95 next.

When $x = 2.95$ then $2.95^3 - 10 \times 2.95 + 4 = 0.172\,375$

Since $x = 2.9$ gives a negative result and $x = 2.95$ gives a positive result then the solution is between $x = 2.9$ and $x = 2.95$.

One solution of the equation $x^3 = 10x - 4$ is $\underline{x = 2.9}$ correct to 1 d.p.

If you have the use of a computer spreadsheet such as *Excel* or *Works* then you can solve trial and improvement problems very easily. You only need to type the equation in once; the computer can then replicate it for you. Just type the trials down one column, and the result can be seen alongside.

Excel screenshot:

	A	B	C	D	E
1	1	−5			
2	2	−8			
3	3	1			
4	2.8	−2.048			
5	2.9	−0.611			
6	2.95	0.172375			
7	2.94	0.012184			
8	2.93	−0.14624			
9	2.936	−0.0514			
10	2.937	−0.03553			
11	2.938	−0.01964			
12	2.939	−0.00374			
13	2.940	0.0912184			
14					

The expression $x^3 - 10x + 4$ is typed as '= A1^3 – 10*A1 + 4' so that it picks up the x-value in cell A1. Then use the mouse to copy down the column.

The change of sign from negative to positive shows that the solution lies between 2.939 and 2.940. By comparing the sizes of −0.003 74 and 0.091 218 4 it looks as if 2.939 is the better answer.

Exercise 25.3

In this exercise you may use a calculator or a computer program such as *Excel*.

In questions **1–8** rearrange the equation so that the right-hand side is zero. Then use trial and improvement to find a positive solution for each equation, giving your answer correct to 1 decimal place.

1 $x^3 = 8x - 3$

2 ✔ $x^3 = 4x - 1$

3 $x^2 = 10 - x$

4 $x^3 = 12x - 7$

5 $2x^3 - x = 4$

6 $x^3 - x^2 = 12$

7 $10 - x^3 = 5x$

8 ✔ $x^2 = 5x + 17$

9 ✓ The equation $x^3 = 13x - 11$ has two positive solutions. Use trial and improvement to find both of them, giving each answer correct to 2 decimal places.

10 The equation $x^2 = 15x - 11$ has a solution between 0 and 1. Use a trial and improvement method to find its value correct to 3 decimal places.

Summary

In this Unit you have learnt how to round decimals to a given number of decimal places or significant figures, and how to use place value in ordering decimals.

You have also learnt how to find approximate solutions to equations, using a trial and improvement method. Remember to rearrange the equation so that the right-hand side is zero before starting a trial and improvement method.

Review Exercise 25

1 Round each of these numbers to the stated number of decimal places:

a) 44.2209 (3 d.p.)   b) 6.666 666 (2 d.p.)   c) 0.000 313 (4 d.p.)

d) 8.425 049 (4 d.p.)   e) 3.818 18 (3 d.p.)   f) 2.000 22 (2 d.p.)

2 Round each of these numbers to the stated number of significant figures:

a) 83.2117 (4 s.f.)   b) 405.22 (2 s.f.)   c) 319.03 (4 s.f.)

d) 452 271 (3 s.f.)   e) 0.000 356 (2 s.f.)   f) 1200.056 (3 s.f.)

g) 0.9999 (3 s.f.)   h) 12.002 66 (4 s.f.)   i) 0.999 99 (1 s.f.)

3 Show that $x^3 = 64 + x$ has a solution between 4 and 5. Use trial and improvement to find its value correct to 2 decimal places.

4* Asher and Isabel are trying to solve the equation $x^4 + 4x = 4x^2 + 1$.

Asher says 'I think the solution lies between 0 and 1'.
Isabel says 'I think that the solution lies between –2 and –3'.

a) Explain how it is possible for both of them to be right.
b) Find two solutions, giving each correct to 2 decimal places.

5* The equation $x^2 = 2x + 17$ has two solutions. One of them lies between 4 and 6, while the other lies between –3 and –4.

a) Use trial and improvement to find the positive solution correct to 2 decimal places.
b) Use trial and improvement to find the negative solution correct to 1 decimal place.

6* Tim, Anwar and Natalie are each trying to find the positive solutions of the equation $x^3 - 11x^2 + 21x + 37 = 0$ by a trial and improvement method.

Tim says 'I think there is a solution between 4 and 5'.
Anwar says 'I think there is a solution between 5 and 7'.
Natalie says 'I think there is a solution between 7 and 8'.

Two of them are right but one is wrong.

a) Which two of them are right?
b) Find the two positive solutions of the equation.

7* Usha is working with the equation $x^3 - 7x^2 + 13x - 3 = 0$. She knows that it has three solutions, which she calls a, b and c. Only solution a is a whole number.

a) Work out the value of the expression $x^3 - 7x^2 + 13x - 3$ when $x = 0$, 1, 2, 3 and 4. Hence state the value of the whole number a.
b) Solution b lies between 3.5 and 4. Use a trial and improvement method to find the value of b correct to 3 significant figures.
c) From your answers to part **a)** state two whole numbers between which the third solution c must lie. Use trial and improvement to find the value of c correct to 2 decimal places.

Unit 26
Number patterns

In this Unit you will learn how to:
- extend number patterns, describing them in words;
- use position-to-term and term-to-term rules;
- find algebraic rules for a given linear number pattern.

A calculator may be used for harder problems.

26.1 Number patterns

Here are some of the more widely used number patterns:

1	3	5	7	9	...	**odd** numbers
2	4	6	8	10	...	**even** numbers
1	4	9	16	25	...	**square** numbers
1	8	27	64	125	...	**cube** numbers
2	3	5	7	11	...	**prime** numbers
1	2	4	8	16	...	**powers of 2**
1	3	6	10	15	...	**triangular** numbers

It is often a good idea to look at the differences between terms in a number pattern. This can help to unlock the pattern so that you can generate more terms.

Example   Describe in words the number pattern 4, 7, 10, 13, 16 ... and find the next two terms.

> Each number is called a **term.** This example gives you five terms to start with.

Solution   Here are the terms and their differences:

The pattern starts at 4 and goes up 3 at a time.
The next two terms are 19 and 22.

Exercise 26.1
Describe each of these number patterns in words, and find the next two terms.

1 5, 7, 9, 11, 13, ...   **2** 11, 16, 21, 26, 31, ...

3 ✔ 16, 19, 22, 25, 28 ...   **4** ✔ 11, 9, 7, 5, 3, ...

5 40, 36, 32, 28, 24 ...   **6** 1, 2, 4, 8, 16, ...

7 ✔ 1, 3, 6, 10, 15, ...   **8** 45, 54, 63, 72, 81, ...

9 11, 22, 33, 44, 55, ...   **10** 100, 99, 97, 94, 90, ...

26.2 Position-to-term and term-to-term rules

The terms in a number pattern are often written algebraically. The symbol u_1 represents the first term, u_2 the second term and so on.

A **position-to-term** rule tells you how to find each term if you know its position.

$u_n = 2n + 5$ is an example of a position to term rule.

Example   Find the first five terms of the number pattern described by the position-to-term rule:
$u_n = 2n + 5$.

Solution   For the first term, set $n = 1$.
$u_1 = 2 \times 1 + 5 = \underline{7}$

For the second term, set $n = 2$.
$u_2 = 2 \times 2 + 5 = \underline{9}$

For the third term, set $n = 3$.
$u_3 = 2 \times 3 + 5 = \underline{11}$

Similarly $u_4 = 2 \times 4 + 5 = \underline{13}$ and $u_5 = 2 \times 5 + 5 = \underline{15}$.

The first five terms are $\underline{7, 9, 11, 13, 15}$

A **term-to-term** rule tells you how to find each term if you know the one before. You also need to know the value of the first term.

$u_{n+1} = 2u_n + 3$ and $u_1 = 4$ is an example of a term-to-term rule.

Example   Find the first five terms of the number pattern described by the term-to-term rule:
$u_{n+1} = 2u_n + 3$ and $u_1 = 4$

Solution   The first term is given: $u_1 = 4$
For the second term, set $n = 1$ so that $n + 1 = 2$.
$u_2 = 2u_1 + 3 = 2 \times 4 + 3$
$\quad = \underline{11}$

For the third term, set $n = 2$ so that $n + 1 = 3$.
$u_3 = 2u_2 + 3 = 2 \times 11 + 3$
$\quad = \underline{25}$

Similarly $u_4 = 2u_3 + 3 = 2 \times 25 + 3 = \underline{53}$ and
$\qquad\qquad u_5 = 2u_4 + 3 = 2 \times 53 + 3 = \underline{109}$

The first five terms are $\underline{4, 11, 25, 53, 109}$

Exercise 26.2

In questions **1–10** find the first five terms of the number patterns given by these position-to-term rules.

1 $u_n = 2n + 3$ **2** $u_n = 5n + 9$ **3** ✔ $u_n = 4n - 2$

4 $u_n = 3n - 2$ **5** $u_n = n + 100$ **6** ✔ $u_n = 10 - 2n$

7 $u_n = 30 + n$ **8** $u_n = 10(n + 2)$ **9** $u_n = n \times (n - 1)$

10 ✔ $u_n = n^2$

In questions **11–20** find the first six terms of the number patterns given by these term-to-term rules.

11 $u_{n+1} = 2u_n$ and $u_1 = 1$ **12** ✔ $u_{n+1} = 2u_n + 1$ and $u_1 = 1$

13 $u_{n+1} = 3u_n - 2$ and $u_1 = 3$ **14** $u_{n+1} = 3(u_n - 2)$ and $u_1 = 4$

15 $u_{n+1} = 3(u_n - 2)$ and $u_1 = 3$ **16** $u_{n+1} = 10 - u_n$ and $u_1 = 4$

17 $u_{n+1} = u_n - 10$ and $u_1 = 4$ **18** ✔ $u_{n+1} = u_n + n$ and $u_1 = 1$

19 $u_{n+1} = 2 \times u_n$ and $u_1 = 32$ **20** $u_{n+1} = \frac{1}{2} \times u_n$ and $u_1 = 32$

26.3 Finding a position-to-term rule for a number pattern

A **linear** pattern is one which goes up in equal steps: 5, 8, 11, 14, 17 ...

Example   Find a position-to-term rule for the number pattern whose first five terms are:

5, 8, 11, 14, 17

Solution   Here are the terms and their differences:

As the difference is always 3, try the position-to-term rule $u_n = ③n$. This rule gives:

3   6   9   12   15

in which all the numbers are 2 less than those in the pattern, so 2 must be added on to the suggested rule.

The position-to-term rule is $\underline{u_n = 3n + 2}$

Example   Find a position-to-term rule for the number pattern whose
first five terms are:

25, 23, 21, 19, 17 ←

> When the numbers go **down** like this you will always have a **negative** number here.

Solution   Here are the terms and their differences:

$$\overset{-2}{25 \frown 23} \overset{-2}{\frown 21} \overset{-2}{\frown 19} \overset{-2}{\frown 17}$$

As the difference is always –2, try the position-to-term rule $u_n = -2n$.
This rule gives:

–2   –4   –6   –8   –10

in which all the numbers are 27 less than those in the pattern, so 27
must be added on to the suggested rule.

The position-to-term rule is $\underline{u_n = 27 - 2n}$

Exercise 26.3

In questions **1–10** find the next two terms in the number pattern. Find also
the position-to-term rule.

1 11, 13, 15, 17, 19, …   **2** ✔ 10, 13, 16, 19, 22, …

3 6, 7, 8, 9, 10, …   **4** 10, 15, 20, 25, 30, …

5 50, 45, 40, 35, 30, …   **6** 10, 12, 14, 16, 18, …

7 20, 23, 26, 29, 32, …   **8** ✔ 10, 7, 4, 1, –2, …

9 4, 11, 18, 25, 32, …   **10** 100, 89, 78, 67, 56, …

In questions **11–20** you are given the first five terms of a number pattern. Say
whether each one is linear or not. For those that are linear, find a position-to-
term rule. For those that are not linear, describe the pattern in words.

11 21, 23, 25, 27, 29, …   **12** ✔ 21, 23, 26, 30, 35, …

13 ✔ 21, 24, 27, 30, 33, …   **14** 21, 24, 29, 36, 45, …

15 2, 4, 8, 16, 32, …   **16** 8, 5, 2, –1, –4, …

17 8, 18, 28, 38, 48, …   **18** 2, 3, 5, 7, 11, …

19 60, 80, 100, 120, 140, …   **20** 1, 8, 27, 64, 125, …

Summary

In this Unit you have learnt how to extend number patterns, using a description in words, a term-to-term rule or a position-to-term rule. You have learnt to recognise linear patterns as those which go up (or down) in equal steps, and practised finding position-to-term rules for linear patterns. The ability to describe a number pattern using algebra is a key skill which can be extremely valuable when you come to do your GCSE coursework.

Review Exercise 26

In questions **1–4** copy down the given number pattern, and continue it for three more terms.

1 122, 116, 111, 107, 104, …   **2** 7, 12, 17, 22, 27, …

3 13, 14, 16, 19, 23, …   **4** 22, 20, 18, 16, 14, …

In questions **5–12** you are given a rule describing a number pattern. Say whether it is a term-to-term rule or a position-to-term rule, and find the first six terms in the number pattern.

5 $u_n = 3n - 3$ **6** $u_{n+1} = u_n + 3$ and $u_1 = 1$

7 $u_n = n^2 + 1$ **8** $u_n = 5n - 11$

9 $u_n = n^2 + n + 1$ **10** $u_{n+1} = 3u_n$ and $u_1 = 1$

11 $u_n = 18 + 2n$ **12** $u_n = 3u_{n-1} + 2$ and $u_1 = 20$

In questions **13–20** you are given the first few terms in a number pattern. If the pattern is linear then find a position-to-term rule for the pattern; if it is not linear then find a term-to-term rule instead.

13 60, 63, 66, 69, 72, …   **14** 10, 30, 90, 270, …

15 80, 40, 20, 10, 5, …   **16** –7, 3, 13, 23, …

17 1, 5, 25, 125, …   **18** 8, 6, 4, 2, …

19 10, 16, 22, 28, …   **20** 243, 81, 27, 9, 3, …

21* At my local library there is a system of fines if books are overdue. In the first week the fine is 40 p, in the second week it is 70 p, in the third week £1 and so on.

     a) Write down the fines, in pence, for each of the first six weeks.
     b) Find a rule for the fine, in pence, in the nth week.
     c) Rewrite your answer to **b)** so that it is now in pounds.

22*a) Find the first five terms of the number pattern generated by the rule
$u_{n+1} = u_n + 2$ and $u_1 = 1$.

b) What name is given to this set of numbers?

c) Without working out any more terms, describe carefully the sets of numbers which are generated by each of these rules:

    (i) $u_{n+1} = u_n + 2$ and $u_1 = 2$

    (ii) $u_{n+1} = u_n + 1$ and $u_1 = 1$

    (iii) $u_{n+1} = u_n + n + 1$ and $u_1 = 1$

23*Richard is investigating linear number patterns, and writes down this example:

$$8 \quad 14 \quad 22 \quad 26 \quad 32 \ldots$$

Unfortunately Richard has made one mistake in this list.

a) Write out the list with the mistake corrected.

b) Find a term-to-term rule connecting the terms u_{n+1} and u_n.

c) Find a position-to-term rule for the nth term u_n.

24*Rosemarie is going on a long car journey. She looks at the number of kilometres recorded on the car's distance meter at the start of the journey, and at regular half-hourly intervals during the first part of the journey. Here are the first four readings:

33 576   33 618   33 660   33 702

a) Find a position-to-term rule for these numbers, and check that $u_{11} = 33\,996$.

b) Explain why this value of u_{11} is likely to be meaningless in reality.

25*The mathematician Leonardo of Pisa used this number pattern:

$$u_{n+2} = u_{n+1} + u_n \text{ and } u_1 = 1, u_2 = 1$$

a) Work out the first ten terms of the pattern.

b) Calculate the values of $\frac{u_8}{u_9}$ and $\frac{u_9}{u_{10}}$, as decimals correct to 3 decimal places. What do you notice?

c) Now continue the pattern until you are able to find $\frac{u_{14}}{u_{15}}$. What do you notice?

d) Look in a reference book about mathematics, and see if you can find the nickname by which Leonardo of Pisa is better known.

Unit 27
Fractions, decimals and percentages

In this Unit you will learn how to:
- add and subtract fractions by using a common denominator;
- write one number as a fraction or percentage of another;
- convert fractions to decimals and vice versa;
- convert decimals to percentages and vice versa;
- solve problems using fractions, decimals, percentages and ratios.

A calculator will be required for this Unit.

27.1 Adding and subtracting fractions

Sometimes you will need to add or subtract two fractions. If they already have the same denominator (bottom number) then there is no problem.

Example   Add $\frac{3}{11} + \frac{5}{11}$.

Solution $\frac{3}{11} + \frac{5}{11}$

$= \frac{3+5}{11}$

$= \frac{8}{11}$

> First, check the denominators: 11 and 11.
>
> Since they are both the same, you can just add 2 and 5 to get 8 for the final numerator (top number).
>
> Note that the bottom stays as 11, you don't add the two 11s together.

If the denominators are not the same, you have to use the idea of equivalent fractions, and rewrite them as necessary. This example shows how you might need to rewrite one fraction.

Example   Add $\frac{2}{5} + \frac{3}{10}$.

Solution   First, we have to change $\frac{2}{5}$ into an equivalent fraction with 10 in the bottom.

$\frac{2}{5}$ is equivalent to $\frac{4}{10}$.

Therefore $\frac{2}{5} + \frac{3}{10}$

$= \frac{4}{10} + \frac{3}{10}$

$= \frac{4+3}{10}$

$= \frac{7}{10}$

> You need to change $\frac{2}{5}$ into $\frac{*}{10}$.
>
> 5 needs to be multiplied by 2 to make 10. Therefore 2 is multiplied by 2 as well, to make 4.
>
> So $\frac{2}{5}$ is equivalent to $\frac{4}{10}$.

In more difficult cases you might have to rewrite **both** fractions, by looking for the **lowest common denominator**. This next example shows you how.

Example   Find $\frac{3}{4} - \frac{2}{7}$.

Solution   First, look at the two denominators. They are 4 and 7.

The smallest number that both 4 and 7 go into exactly is $4 \times 7 = 28$.

So rewrite $\frac{3}{4}$ as $\frac{21}{28}$ and rewrite $\frac{2}{7}$ as $\frac{8}{28}$.

Therefore $\frac{3}{4} - \frac{2}{7}$

$= \frac{21}{28} - \frac{8}{28}$

$= \frac{21-8}{28}$

$= \frac{13}{28}$

Finally, you might find that the answer can be cancelled down. This last example shows how it works, but remember that this won't happen in every question you do.

Example   Find $\frac{5}{6} - \frac{11}{15}$.

Solution   First, look at the two denominators. They are 6 and 15.
The smallest number that both 6 and 15 go into exactly is 30.

So rewrite $\frac{5}{6}$ as $\frac{25}{30}$ and rewrite $\frac{11}{15}$ as $\frac{22}{30}$.

Therefore $\frac{5}{6} - \frac{11}{15}$.

$= \frac{25}{30} - \frac{22}{30}$

$= \frac{25-22}{30}$

$= \frac{3}{30}$ This answer can be cancelled down, because 3 goes into both 3 and 30.

$= \frac{1}{10}$

Exercise 27.1

Work out the value of each of these. Remember to show all of the steps in your working.

1 $\frac{3}{7} + \frac{2}{7}$ **2** $\frac{5}{13} + \frac{7}{13}$ **3** $\frac{10}{11} - \frac{4}{11}$

4 $\frac{5}{12} + \frac{1}{4}$ **5** $\frac{3}{8} + \frac{1}{2}$ **6** $\frac{9}{10} - \frac{3}{5}$

7 $\frac{1}{3} + \frac{1}{2}$ **8** $\frac{2}{5} + \frac{1}{4}$ **9** $\frac{17}{20} - \frac{3}{4}$

10 $\frac{17}{18} - \frac{2}{3}$ **11** $\frac{2}{5} + \frac{1}{6}$ **12** $\frac{1}{6} + \frac{4}{9}$

13 $\frac{5}{8} - \frac{1}{6}$ **14** $\frac{19}{20} - \frac{2}{3}$ **15** $\frac{5}{14} + \frac{4}{21}$

16 Add together four-sevenths and two-ninths.

17 One morning Susie eats one-third of a bag of sweets, and in the afternoon she eats another two-fifths. What fraction of the bag has she eaten altogether?

18 In a youth club one-eighth of the members are boys aged 9 or under, and three-fifths are boys aged over 9. What fraction of the youth club members are boys?

19 During a Duke of Edinburgh expedition Simon has to walk for three days. On the first day he covers two-ninths of the total journey, and on the second day he covers one-third.

  a What fraction of the total journey does Simon cover during the first two days?
  b What fraction needs to be covered on the third day?
  c On which day does he cover the largest part of the journey?

20 In Greenview School there is a Reception Class, an Infants School and a Junior School. Three-tenths of the children are in the Infants school, and one-half are in the Junior School. What fraction are in the Reception Class?

27.2 Fractions and percentages

To write one number as a fraction of another, simply set up the fraction and cancel if possible.

You can also check this using the fraction key on your calculator. Key in

and the cancelled result should be displayed.

Example Express 42 as a fraction of 78.

Solution $\dfrac{\cancel{42}}{\cancel{78}} = \dfrac{\cancel{21}}{\cancel{39}} = \dfrac{7}{13}$

Example Express 55 cm as a fraction of 3.6 m.

Solution 3.6 m = 360 cm

$\dfrac{\cancel{55}}{\cancel{360}} = \dfrac{11}{72}$

You must convert both lengths into the same units first.

To write one number as a percentage of another, set up a fraction and multiply by 100%.

Example Express 63 as a percentage of 180.

Solution $\dfrac{63}{180} = \dfrac{7}{20}$

Then $\dfrac{7}{20} \times \dfrac{100\%}{1} = \underline{35\%}$

Exercise 27.2

1 Express the first quantity as a fraction of the second.
  Cancel down where possible.

a) 70, 95   **b)** 44, 77   **c)** ✔ 38, 48

d) 39, 91   **e)** 35, 95   **f)** 84 cm, 1.64 m

g) 350 g, 2.25 kg   **h)** 25 min, 2 h   **i)** 65 mm, 19 cm

j) ✔ 65 ml, 13 cl

2 Express the first quantity as a percentage of the second.

a) ✔ 48, 60   b) 19, 25   c) 3, 20

d) 18, 45   e) 56, 80   f) 7, 40

g) ✔ 74 cm, 2 m   h) 18 min, 1 h   i) 850 m, 5 km

j) 750 g, $2\frac{1}{2}$ kg

27.3 Fractions and decimals

> To change a fraction into a decimal simply carry out the division, using a calculator if necessary.

Example   Express $\frac{5}{8}$ as a decimal.

Solution   Using a calculator to work out $5 \div 8$,

$$\frac{5}{8} = \underline{0.625}$$

Example   Express $3\frac{5}{7}$ as a decimal, correct to 4 decimal places.

Solution $5 \div 7 = 0.714285...$

So $3\frac{5}{7} = \underline{3.7143}$ correct to 4 d.p.

> To change a decimal into a fraction set up a fraction out of 10, 100, 1000 etc., then cancel.

Example   Change 4.72 into a fraction, using mixed fraction notation.

Solution $0.72 = \frac{72}{100} = \frac{36}{50} = \frac{18}{25}$

$$\therefore 4.72 = 4\frac{18}{25}$$

Example   Write 3.725 in the form $\frac{a}{b}$ where a and b are whole numbers.

Solution $0.725 = \frac{725}{1000} = \frac{145}{200} = \frac{29}{40}$

$$3.725 = 3\frac{29}{40} \quad \longleftarrow \boxed{\text{This is a } \textbf{mixed fraction.}}$$

$$= \frac{3 \times 40 + 29}{40}$$

$$= \frac{120 + 29}{40}$$

$$= \frac{149}{40} \quad \longleftarrow \boxed{\text{This is the same answer, converted into a } \textbf{top-heavy fraction.}}$$

Exercise 27.3

1 Change these fractions into decimals, correct to 4 decimal places where necessary:

a) ✔ $\frac{3}{8}$ **b)** $2\frac{7}{10}$ **c)** $5\frac{1}{4}$ **d)** $\frac{3}{11}$ **e)** $2\frac{1}{3}$

f) $\frac{4}{9}$ **g)** $\frac{5}{12}$ **h)** $3\frac{1}{7}$ **i)** $\frac{7}{16}$ **j)** ✔ $4\frac{9}{14}$

2 Write these decimals as fractions, giving your answers as mixed fractions where necessary.

a) ✔ 0.88   **b)** 0.124   **c)** 0.225   **d)** 4.15   **e)** ✔ 3.64

f) 0.036   **g)** 2.95   **h)** 0.66   **i)** 1.85   **j)** 0.316

27.4 Decimals and percentages

> To change a decimal into a percentage, multiply by 100%. This moves the decimal point 2 places right.

Example   Express 0.225 as a percentage.

Solution $0.225 \times 100\% = \underline{22.5\%}$

> To change a percentage into a decimal, divide by 100%. This moves the decimal point 2 places left.

Example   Express 37.8% as a decimal.

Solution $37.8\% \div 100\% = \underline{0.378}$

Example   Express $12\frac{1}{2}\%$ as a decimal.

Solution $12\frac{1}{2}\% = 12.5\%$

               $12.5\% \div 100\% = \underline{0.125}$

Exercise 27.4

1 Change these decimals into percentages:

a) 0.38   **b)** ✔ 0.7   **c)** 0.315   **d)** 0.205   **e)** 1.43

f) ✔ 6.2   **g)** 1.707   **h)** 0.080   **i)** 0.1   **j)** 4.4

2 Change these percentages into decimals:

a) 65%   **b)** ✔ $33\frac{1}{3}\%$ **c)** 2.5%   **d)** 18%   **e)** 150%

f) 77%   **g)** 6%   **h)** ✔ $7\frac{1}{2}\%$ **i)** 105%   **j)** 88%

27.5 Using multiplying factors

To increase an amount by a certain percentage, a **multiplying factor** can be used.

For a 3% increase the factor is 1.03, for a 12% increase it is 1.12 and so on.

For a 3% decrease the factor is 0.97, for a 12% decrease it is 0.88 and so on.

Example Increase £425 by 3%.

Solution The multiplying factor is 1.03.
£425 × 1.03 = £437.75

Example Decrease 1600 litres by 9%.

Solution The multiplying factor is 0.91.
1600 litres × 0.91 = 1456 litres

Example A shop increases all its prices by 12%. The price of a jacket after the increase is £61.60. Find its price before the increase.

Solution Let the price before the increase be £x.
The multiplying factor for a 12% increase is 1.12.

$$1.12 \times x = 61.60$$
$$x = 61.60 \div 1.12$$
$$= 55$$

The original price was £55.

> **Warning!**
> If you decrease £61.60 by 12% you get an incorrect answer (£54.21)
> This is because 12% of the new price is £7.39, but 12% of the original price is £6.60

Exercise 27.5

1 Use a multiplying factor to make the required increase or decrease.

a) Increase 25 000 by 13%. **b)** ✓ Increase 350 by 6%. **c)** Decrease 7500 by 18%.

d) Increase $140 by 65%. **e)** ✓ Decrease £975 by 4%.

2 Last season the average number of people who watched Swindon Town play soccer each week was 26 300. Town have now been promoted, and the manager expects to see a 15% increase in attendance.

a) Write down the multiplying factor for a 15% increase.

b) Find the average weekly attendance this season, assuming the manager's prediction to be right. (Give your answer to the nearest hundred.)

3 Last summer I went on holiday to France. The ferry fare was £39. This year the ferry company has reduced all its fares by 11%.

  a) Write down the multiplying factor for an 11% decrease.
  b) Find the ferry fare this year.

4 A computer is advertised for a price of £699 plus VAT. The present rate of VAT is $17\frac{1}{2}$%.

  a) Write down the multiplying factor for a $17\frac{1}{2}$% increase.
  b) Find the total cost of the computer including VAT.

5 ✔ My bill in a restaurant was £20.72 including a service charge of 12%.

  a) Write down the multiplying factor for a 12% increase.
  b) Use this factor to find the cost before the service charge was added.

6 A packet of cereal says: 16% extra – FREE. The packet contains 435 g. Find the amount of cereal that the packet would contain without the extra 16%.

27.6 Using ratios

Questions involving **ratios** can often be treated in a similar way to fractions.

It is important to add up the parts of a ratio first, so the total can be used to identify the fractions represented by the component parts. For example, in a ratio of 3:4 the total is 7, so the two parts are equivalent to fractions of $\frac{3}{7}$ and $\frac{4}{7}$.

Example Two chemicals are mixed in the ratio 3:4. Find the amount of each chemical, if 350 g of the mixture is to be made.

Solution $3 + 4 = 7$
$350 \div 7 = 50$
$3 \times 50 = 150$
$4 \times 50 = 200$

> Here we are finding that each share is 50 g so 3 shares is 150 g and 4 shares is 200 g.

The amounts are 150 g and 200 g.

Example In Year 5 at Greenview school 14 children catch the bus to school, 21 walk and 49 come by car.

  a) Write this information as a ratio in its simplest form.

  b) Assuming that this ratio applies throughout the school, find the total number who come by car. There are 324 children at the school altogether.

Solution   **a)** The ratio is $14:21:49$
which can be written as
$\underline{2:3:7}$

> All three numbers can be divided by 7 to cancel the ratio down.

b) $2+3+7=12$. The children who come by car
comprise $\frac{7}{12}$ of the school.

$324 \div 12 = 27$ ← Find $\frac{1}{12}$

$27 \times 7 = 189$ ← Find $\frac{7}{12}$

$\underline{189 \text{ children}}$ come by car.

Exercise 27.6

1 Cancel down each ratio into its simplest form.

a) $20:35$ **b)** ✔ $18:24$ **c)** $15:12$ **d)** $60:84$

e) $350:550$ **f)** $125:225$ **g)** $40:60:75$ **h)** ✔ $100:65:55$

i) $18:36:42$ **j)** $35:90:65$ **k)** $35\,\text{cm}:2.4\,\text{m}$ **l)** $450\,\text{g}:3.5\,\text{kg}$

2 A sheet of Christmas gift-wrap paper is 1.2 m long. It is cut into two pieces, the shorter one being 75 cm in length. Find the ratio of the lengths of the two pieces, giving your answer in its simplest form.

3 ✔ During a school week I have 6 periods of mathematics, 10 periods of science and 24 periods of other subjects.
a) Write this information as a ratio, in its simplest form.
b) I plan to do five hours of revision next Sunday. The amount of time spent on each subject is to be in the same ratio as the number of periods I get each week. How much time should I spend on mathematics revision?

4 Henrietta has a collection of music cassettes in which 18 of them are rock music, 30 are jazz, and the remaining 24 are classical.

a) Write this information as a ratio.

Henrietta's friend Susan has a similar but smaller collection. Susan has 16 cassettes of classical music.

b) How many cassettes does Susan have in total?
c) How many of Susan's cassettes are jazz?

Summary

In this Unit you have compared one number with another, using fractions, percentages, decimals and ratios. When units are mixed (e.g. centimetres and metres) remember to change both measurements into the same unit before comparing them.

You have practised adding and subtracting fractions using a common denominator and changing fractions into decimals, or decimals into percentages, and vice versa.

Multiplying factors are a convenient shortcut in many problems about percentage increase or decrease, and offer the best way of dealing with 'find the original price' problems.

In the Review Exercise which follows you will practise all these skills again, and solve problems using fractions, percentages, decimals and ratio.

Review Exercise 27

1 Write the first quantity as a fraction of the second, and also as a percentage of the second. Simplify your answers where possible.

a) 24, 60   **b)** 132, 240   **c)** 5000, 8000   **d)** 63, 105

e) 30 s, $2\frac{1}{2}$ min   **f)** 230 ml, 4 l   **g)** 78 cm, 1.2 m   **h)** 81 min, $1\frac{1}{2}$ h

2 Change these fractions into decimals, correct to 3 decimal places where necessary:

a) $\frac{17}{20}$ **b)** $\frac{5}{8}$ **c)** $\frac{5}{7}$ **d)** $4\frac{7}{10}$

e) $\frac{8}{9}$ **f)** $3\frac{1}{3}$ **g)** $\frac{37}{50}$ **h)** $2\frac{7}{100}$

3 Change these decimals into fractions, and also into percentages:

a) 0.06   **b)** 0.65   **c)** 0.28   **d)** 0.44

e) 0.025   **f)** 0.125   **g)** 2.6   **h)** 1.08

4 Change these percentages into decimals:

a) 25%   **b)** 9%   **c)** $22\frac{1}{2}$%   **d)** 204%

5 Lois and Richard buy some tickets in a school raffle. Lois buys 13 tickets and Richard buys 7 tickets. They agree to share any prize between them, in the ratio of the number of tickets they bought.
When the raffle is drawn Lois wins a prize of £15. Calculate the amount that each receives when they share this prize.

6 In Bluebell Wood there are 20 silver birch trees, 8 maple trees and 12 oak trees.

a) Write down the ratio of silver birch : maple : oak trees in Bluebell Wood, giving your answer in its simplest form.

b) In Shelley Wood there are 200 trees in total. Assuming that they are all silver birch, maple, or oak, and in the same ratio as in Bluebell Wood, find the number of trees of each kind in Shelley Wood.

7 The number of bacteria in a certain colony grows by 30% every day. On Day 1 there are 6000 bacteria. Find out how many there will be on:

a) Day 2;   **b)** Day 3;   **c)** Day 7.

8 As part of a computer upgrade I decide to buy a new hard disk drive. The same unit is available from two suppliers, who advertise as follows:

BARGAIN PC SUPPLIES	None Better Peripherals
Superturbo 1.4 Gb hard disk	Superturbo 1.4 Gb hard disk
only £149 + VAT	only £177 including VAT

Work out whether Bargain PC Supplies or None Better Peripherals is giving the cheaper overall cost, assuming a VAT rate of $17\frac{1}{2}\%$.

9 A sweet shop sells coloured sweets in mixed bags. The sweets are red, green and yellow in the ratio $4:5:11$.

a) What percentage of the sweets are red?
b) How many of each colour would you expect to find in a bag containing 80 sweets?

10 Express the ratio $26:65:91$ in its simplest form.

11* Express the ratio $10^3:10^4:10^5$ in its simplest form.

12* A square measures 15 cm by 15 cm, and a second square measures 20 cm by 20 cm.

a) Find the ratio of their perimeters.
b) Find the ratio of their areas.

13* A camera costs \$126.50 including sales tax of 15%. Calculate its cost before the sales tax is added.

14* My photocopier is set to produce copies which are 41% larger than the originals. A copy comes out of the machine; it contains a diagram which is 98 mm wide. How wide (to the nearest millimetre) was the original diagram?

15* A company decides to give all its workers a 12% pay rise and, after this has been applied, to give the managing director a further rise of 20%.

a) Write down a multiplying factor for a 12% increase.
b) Write down a multiplying factor for a 20% increase.
c) Using your answers to a) and b), explain why the managing director's increase is not 32%.

16* Last time I went to France £6 was worth 50 francs.

a) Write the ratio of pounds:francs in its simplest form.
b) How many francs did I get for £90?

The exchange rate has altered, and now £5 is worth 50 francs.

c) Write this new ratio in its simplest form.
d) How many francs do I now get for £90?
e) Find the percentage increase in the exchange rate.

Unit 28
Linear equations

In this Unit you will learn how to:
- solve simple linear equations using one operation;
- solve more difficult linear equations using several operations;
- formulate and solve problems using linear equations.

A calculator will be required for some exercises in this Unit.

28.1 Linear equations with one operation

This section looks at techniques for solving equations using the operations of adding, subtracting, multiplying and dividing. Study each example carefully before going on to the Exercise.

Set your working out in detail, just as in the examples.

Example   Solve the equation $x + 5 = 30$.

Solution
$$x + 5 = 30$$
$$x = 30 - 5$$
$$x = 25$$

To get the x on its own you need to remove the $+5$. This is done by **subtracting** 5 from both sides of the equation.

Example   Solve the equation $x - 7 = 10$.

Solution
$$x - 7 = 10$$
$$x = 10 + 7$$
$$x = 17$$

This time you need to remove the -7. This is done by **adding** 7 to both side of the equation.

Example   Solve the equation $5x = 30$.

Solution
$$5x = 30$$
$$x = 30 \div 5$$
$$x = 6$$

$5x$ means 5 times x. To get the x on its own you must **divide** both sides by 5.

Example   Solve the equation $\frac{x}{3} = 4$.

Solution
$$\frac{x}{3} = 4$$
$$x = 4 \times 3$$
$$x = 12$$

$\frac{x}{3}$ means $x \div 3$.

To get the x on its own you must **multiply** both sides by 3.

Note

Always copy the question as the first line of your working. Set out the lines that follow so that the = signs are aligned.

Exercise 28.1

Solve these linear equations, showing all your working.

1 $x+4 = 19$ **2** $x+6 = 23$ **3** ✓ $x+11 = 4$ **4** $x-3 = 29$

5 $x-11 = 5$ **6** $x-4 = -5$ **7** $3x = 24$ **8** ✓ $8x = 56$

9 $4x = 22$ **10** $\frac{x}{3} = 9$ **11** ✓ $\frac{x}{11} = 3$ **12** $\frac{x}{6} = 13$

13 ✓ $x-14 = 9$ **14** $x+9 = 14$ **15** $\frac{x}{7} = 13$ **16** $6x = 18$

17 $x+2 = 1$ **18** $x-9 = 9$ **19** $\frac{x}{3} = 4$ **20** $9x = 45$

28.2 Linear equations with two operations

In this section two operations will be used. Study each example carefully before going on to the Exercise.

Set your working out in detail, just as in the examples. Do not try to solve the equation in one line – the key is to break the problem down into small steps.

Example   Solve the equation $2x + 5 = 31$.

Solution
$$2x + 5 = 31$$
$$2x = 31 - 5$$
$$2x = 26$$
$$x = 26 \div 2$$
$$x = 13$$

First of all, treat this as a problem to find $2x$.

Then finish off by finding x.

Example   Solve the equation $4x - 7 = 17$.

Solution
$$4x - 7 = 17$$
$$4x = 17 + 7$$
$$4x = 24$$
$$x = 24 \div 4$$
$$x = 6$$

First of all, treat this as a problem to find $4x$.

Then finish off by finding x.

Example   Solve the equation $5x = 30 + 2x$.

Solution
$$5x = 30 + 2x$$
$$5x - 2x = 30$$
$$3x = 30$$
$$x = 30 \div 3$$
$$x = 10$$

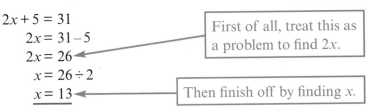

$5x$ appears on one side of the equation, and $2x$ on the other side. The first step is to subtract $2x$ from both sides of the equation. This leaves a simple one-operation problem to finish off.

Example Solve the equation $3x = 15 - 2x$.

Solution
$$3x = 15 - 2x$$
$$3x + 2x = 15$$
$$5x = 15$$
$$x = 15 \div 5$$
$$\underline{x = 3}$$

$3x$ appears on one side of the equation, and $-2x$ on the other side. The first step is to add $2x$ from both sides of the equation. This leaves a simple one-operation problem to finish off.

Exercise 28.2

Solve these linear equations, showing all your working.

1 $5x + 1 = 31$
2 $4x + 9 = 45$
3 ✓ $7x + 2 = 51$

4 $3x - 1 = 8$
5 $7x - 9 = 12$
6 $11x - 7 = 59$

7 $7x = 60 + 2x$
8 $4x = 18 + x$
9 ✓ $11x = 21 + 4x$

10 $3x = 72 - 3x$
11 $5x = 28 - 2x$
12 $4x = 63 - 5x$

13 ✓ $6x - 7 = 29$
14 $2x + 17 = 9$
15 $8x = 15 - 2x$

16 $14x = 55 + 3x$
17 $9x + 5 = 41$
18 $2x - 3 = 2$

19 ✓ $4x = 15 - 2x$
20 $35x = 48 + 29x$

28.3 Harder linear equations

These equations are a little harder. Once again, the key is to break the problem down into small steps.

Example Solve the equation $7x + 6 = 41 + 2x$.

Solution
$$7x + 6 = 41 + 2x$$
$$7x - 2x + 6 = 41$$
$$5x + 6 = 41$$
$$5x = 41 - 6$$
$$5x = 35$$
$$\therefore x = 35 \div 5$$
$$\underline{x = 7}$$

The first stage is to subtract $2x$ from both sides. This makes the equation much simpler.

The next stage is to subtract 6 from both sides. This makes the equation even simpler.

The final step is simply to divide by 5.

Example Solve the equation $5x + 7 = 42 - 2x$.

Solution
$$5x + 7 = 42 - 2x$$
$$5x + 2x + 7 = 42$$
$$7x + 7 = 42$$
$$7x = 42 - 7$$
$$7x = 35$$
$$\therefore x = 35 \div 7$$
$$\underline{x = 5}$$

This time, begin by adding $2x$ to both sides.

Next, subtract 7 from both sides.

Finally, divide both sides by 7.

Example   Solve the equation $5x + 7 = 31 + 9x$.

Solution
$$5x + 7 = 31 + 9x$$

> You might begin by subtracting $9x$ from both sides …

$$5x - 9x + 7 = 31$$
$$-4x + 7 = 42$$

> … but this will lead to a **negative** number of x's.

To avoid this situation, begin again and collect the x-terms on the **right-hand side** of the equation.

$$5x + 7 = 31 + 9x$$
$$7 = 31 + 9x - 5x$$
$$7 = 31 + 4x$$
$$7 - 31 = 4x$$
$$-24 = 4x$$
$$-24 \div 4 = x$$
$$\therefore \ x = -6$$

> The first stage is to take $5x$ from both sides

> Next, subtract 31 from both sides

> The final step is simply to divide by 4.

Exercise 28.3

Solve these linear equations, showing all your working. You will need a calculator for some of the later ones, where the answers are not whole numbers.

1 $6x + 4 = 20 - 2x$ **2** ✔ $3x + 5 = 37 - x$ **3** $2x + 3 = 11 + x$

4 $2x - 1 = 8 - x$ **5** $7x - 4 = 2x + 31$ **6** $4x + 21 = 3 - 2x$

7 ✔ $9x + 7 = 63 + x$ **8** $3x + 7 = 2x + 7$ **9** $x - 4 = 17 - 6x$

10 $6x + 3 = 23 + x$ **11** $15x - 4 = 9x + 23$ **12** $6 - x = 20 - 4x$

13 $7x + 4 = 4x - 3$ **14** $8x + 5 = 3x + 23$ **15** ✔ $15x - 37 = 15 - x$

16 $17 - 2x = 51 - 7x$ **17** $28 - x = 17 + 3x$ **18** $5x + 11 = 20x - 64$

19 $45x + 11 = 20x - 54$ **20** ✔ $21 + 2x = 35 + 12x$

28.4 Setting up and solving equations

Sometimes you will meet a problem given in words, or in a diagram.

Turn the problem into an equation, then solve it using the methods you have practised.

Example   I think of a number and multiply it by 6, then I add 5 to the answer. I end up with 59. What number did I first think of?

Solution   Let the number I think of be x.
When I multiply by 6 it becomes $6x$.
When I add 5 it becomes $6x + 5$.

$$6x + 5 = 59$$
$$6x = 59 - 5$$
$$6x = 54$$
$$x = 54 \div 6$$
$$\underline{x = 9}$$

Example   The length of a rectangle is 6 cm more than its breadth. The perimeter is 40 cm. Find the dimensions of the rectangle.

Solution   Let the breadth be x cm.
Then the length is $x + 6$ cm.

$x + 6$

x

The perimeter is
$$x + (x + 6) + x + (x + 6) = 4x + 12$$
$$4x + 12 = 40$$
$$4x = 40 - 12$$
$$4x = 28$$
$$x = 28 \div 4$$
$$\underline{x = 7}$$

> Remember to answer the original question – which was to find the dimensions of the rectangle

The dimensions of the rectangle are 7 cm by 13 cm.

Exercise 28.4

Write equations to describe each of these problems, then use the equation to solve the problem.

1 I think of a number and multiply it by 3, then add 11. The answer is 59. What number did I think of?

2 The length of a rectangle is 9 cm more than its breadth. The perimeter is 70 cm. Find the dimensions of the rectangle.

3 ✔ Rana likes to collect toy dogs. If she had 84 more dogs then she would have four times as many as she actually has. How many does she have?

4 I think of a number and multiply it by 6, then add 7. The answer is 61. What number did I think of?

5 Tim and Gavin are the same age. If you multiply Tim's age by 5 and then add 7 you get the same answer as if you had multiplied Gavin's age by 10 and taken away 43. How old are Tim and Gavin?

6 ✔ Flora, Natalie and Usha are playing a numbers game. Flora whispers the same number to Natalie and to Usha.

Natalie multiplies the number by 7, then adds 4.
Usha takes the number away from 100.
They both end up with the same number.

What number did Flora whisper to the other two girls?

Summary

In this Unit you have solved linear equations involving one or more steps. Remember to write down the given equation, and then solve it in a number of small steps rather than trying to do everything all in one go.

In harder problems you have usually collected the x-terms together on the left-hand side of the equation, or on the right-hand side if this helps to avoid problems with negative numbers. You have also practised setting up and solving equations from information given in words. This will become an increasingly important skill as your knowledge of mathematics develops.

Review Exercise 28

1 Solve these equations, showing all your working clearly.

a) $x+3 = 31$ **b)** $x-2 = 11$ **c)** $x-8 = 0$

d) $x+17 = 12$ **e)** $3x = 96$ **f)** $\frac{x}{4} = 17$

g) $11x = 121$ **h)** $\frac{x}{11} = 3$

2 Solve these equations, showing all your working clearly.

a) $3x-7 = 17$ **b)** $5x+6 = 51$ **c)** $11x = 16+3x$

d) $4x = 77-3x$ **e)** $2x+17 = 9$ **f)** $4x = 25+9x$

g) $8x+5 = 79$ **h)** $7x = 55-3x$

3 Solve these equations, showing all your working clearly.

a) $13+3x = 21+x$ **b)** $33+7x = 23+2x$ **c)** $3x+23 = 7x-1$

d) $2+8x = 57-3x$ **e)** $8-x = 18-3x$ **f)** $2x+12 = 5x-12$

4 One side of a square is labelled $(3x+4)$ cm and another side is labelled $(28-x)$ cm.

     a) Write this information in an equation.
     b) Solve the equation, and hence find the perimeter of the square.

5 I think of a number and multiply it by 7, then I add 13 to the result. The final answer is 69.

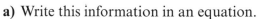

     a) Write this information in an equation.
     b) Solve the equation, to find the number I thought of.

6 John has been counting his marbles, which are either red, blue or yellow.

     He has n red marbles.
     He has two more blue marbles than he has red.
     He has twice as many yellows as he has red.
     In total he has 62 marbles.

a) Write down, in terms of n, the number of blue marbles he has.
b) Write down, in terms of n, the number of yellow marbles he has.
c) Write down an equation for the total number of marbles, and solve it.
d) Write down how many marbles of each colour John has.

7* Séan is told 'Think of a number, multiply it by 3, then add 8'.
By mistake he multiplies it by 8, then adds 3. He ends up with the number 75. If he had followed the instructions correctly what number would he have ended up with?

8* Two of the sides of an equilateral triangle are labelled $(4x-7)$ mm and $(33-x)$ mm.

a) Find the value of x.
b) Find the perimeter of the triangle.

9* I asked my grandma to tell me how old she was. She replied 'If you multiply my age by 3 and then subtract 100 you get the same answer as if you took my age and added 34'.

a) Write this information in an equation, using x to represent grandma's age.
b) Solve the equation, to find grandma's age.

10* Richard and Ben went shopping. They each began with the same amount of spending money.

Richard says:

Ben says:

a) Express this information in an equation.
b) Solve your equation, to find the cost of a pencil.

11* The diagram shows an isosceles triangle ABC.
The sides AB and AC are equal in length.

a) Set up an equation in x and solve it.
b) Hence state the lengths of the three sides.
c) Find the perimeter of the triangle.

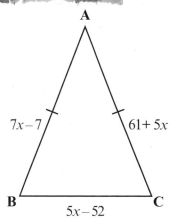

Unit 29
Functions and graphs

In this Unit you will learn how to:
- represent functions using mapping diagrams;
- draw graphs of linear functions, giving straight line graphs;
- draw graphs of other functions, giving curves;
- draw graphs using all four quadrants.

A calculator may be used with some of the harder exercises.

29.1 Mapping diagrams

When two quantities x and y are connected by an equation such as $y = 2x + 3$ or $y = 3x^2 - 2x - 5$ then we say that y is a **function** of x.

$y = 2x + 3$ is an example of a **linear** function – its graph is a straight line (see 25.2).

$y = 3x^2 - 2x - 5$ is an example of a **quadratic** function – its graph is a curve (see 25.3).

All functions can be illustrated by means of a **mapping diagram.**

Example Draw a mapping diagram to illustrate this function:

x	1	2	3	4
y	7	9	11	13

Solution

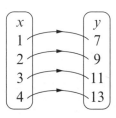

The two boxes show the sets of values for x and y.
The arrows show how the function relates the values

Example Draw a mapping diagram to illustrate the function $y = 3x - 1$ for $x = 1, 2, 3$ and 4.

First, draw up a table of values.

x	1	2	3	4
y	2	5	8	11

When $x = 4$

$y = 3 \times 4 - 1$
$= 12 - 1$
$= 11$

Solution

Use the table to construct the mapping diagram.

Exercise 29.1

In questions **1–6** construct a mapping diagram for the given table.

1

x	1	2	3	4
y	10	11	12	13

2 ✓

x	1	2	3	4
y	20	18	16	14

3

x	1	2	3	4	5
y	1	3	6	10	15

4

x	1	3	5	7
y	4	2	0	–2

5

x	1	2	3	5	10
y	3	6	9	15	30

6

x	10	15	20	30
y	30	25	20	10

In questions **7–14** you are given some sets of (x, y) coordinates. Write them in tables, and then construct a mapping diagram for each function.

7 ✓ (1,6) (2,8) (3,10) (4,12)

8 (1,2) (2,4) (3,8) (4,16)

9 (1,2) (3,4) (5,6) (7,8)

10 (1,3) (2,5) (5,11) (10,21)

11 (1,5) (2,9) (3,13) (10,41)

12 ✓ (5,5) (6,4) (7,3) (8,2)

13 (1,1) (2,2) (3,3) (4,4)

14 (1,0) (2,1) (3,2) (4,3)

In questions **15–20** you are given the rule for a function. Using the values $x = 1, 2, 3$ and 4 construct a table of values, and use it to make a mapping diagram.

15 ✓ $y = 3x + 4$

16 $y = 4x + 3$

17 $y = 5x - 2$

18 $y = 6x + 1$

19 $y = 10 - x$

20 ✓ $y = x^2 + 4$

29.2 Graphs of linear functions

A **linear function** has the form $y = ax + b$, for example $y = 2x + 3$.

Linear functions are so called because their graphs are straight lines.

The number a in front of the x tells you how steep the graph will be. It is called the **gradient.**

To draw a graph of a linear function, work out the coordinates of **three points,** then join them up with a straight line.

Example   Draw the graph of $y = 2x + 3$ for values of x from –2 to 4.

Solution

x	–2	1	4
y			

> First, choose three x-values at different parts of the range, e.g. –2, 1 and 4.

When $x = -2$, $y = 2 \times -2 + 3 = -4 + 3 = -1$
When $x = 1$, $y = 2 \times 1 + 3 = 2 + 3 = 5$
When $x = 4$, $y = 2 \times 4 + 3 = 8 + 3 = 11$

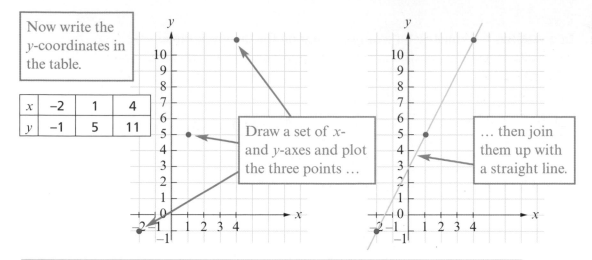

Now write the *y*-coordinates in the table.

x	−2	1	4
y	−1	5	11

Draw a set of *x*- and *y*-axes and plot the three points …

… then join them up with a straight line.

Note

- The straight line should pass through all three points, and continue slightly beyond them.
- Remember to label the *x*- and *y*- axes

Example   Draw the graph of $y = -\frac{1}{2}x + 6$ for values of *x* from −4 to 10.

Solution   Consider the points where *x* = −4, 0 and 10.

x	−4	0	10
y			

When $x = -4$, $y = -\frac{1}{2} \times -4 + 6 = 2 + 6 = 8$

When $x = 0$, $y = -\frac{1}{2} \times 0 + 6 = 0 + 6 = 6$

x	−4	0	10
y	8	6	1

When $x = 10$, $y = -\frac{1}{2} \times 10 + 6 = -5 + 6 = 1$

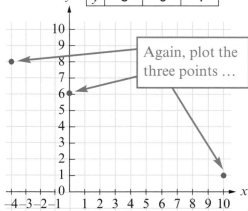

Again, plot the three points …

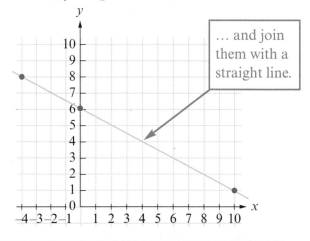

… and join them with a straight line.

Comparing these examples you should notice that:

$y = 2x + 3$ has a **positive gradient** of 2. It goes up as you move to the right.
$y = -\frac{1}{2}x + 6$ has a **negative gradient** of $-\frac{1}{2}$. It goes down as you move to the right.

Exercise 29.2

In questions **1–10** calculate the coordinates of three points on the line.
Then draw a pair of coordinate axes, and plot the line over the given range
of values of x.

1 $y = x + 1$ for values of x from –5 to 5

2 ✔ $y = 3x + 2$ for values of x from –5 to 5

3 $y = 4x - 1$ for values of x from 0 to 5

4 $y = \frac{1}{2}x + 3$ for values of x from 0 to 20

5 $y = \frac{1}{4}x + 12$ for values of x from –12 to 12

6 $y = 6 - x$ for values of x from 0 to 6

7 $y = 10 - 2x$ for values of x from –2 to 6

8 ✔ $y = -3x + 1$ for values of x from –1 to 3

9 $y = -\frac{1}{2}x + 12$ for values of x from –10 to 10

10 $y = 4x$ for values of x from 0 to 5

29.3 Graphs of curves

Functions of the form $y = ax^2 + bx + c$, for example $y = x^2 + 2x + 3$, do not
have straight line graphs. They are non-linear functions.

To draw a graph of a non-linear function, work out the coordinates of
many points, then join them up with a smooth curve. You may need to
compute extra points where the curve bends most.

Example   Draw the graph of $y = x^2 + 2x + 3$ for values of x from –2 to 4.

Solution   First, choose whole number x-values throughout the range from –2 to 4.

x	–2	–1	0	1	2	3	4
y							

When $x = -2$, $y = (-2)^2 + 2 \times -2 + 3 = 4 - 4 + 3 = 3$
When $x = -1$, $y = (-1)^2 + 2 \times -1 + 3 = 1 - 2 + 3 = 2$
When $x = 0$, $y = (0)^2 + 2 \times 0 + 3 = 0 + 0 + 3 = 3$
When $x = 1$, $y = (1)^2 + 2 \times 1 + 3 = 1 + 2 + 3 = 6$
When $x = 2$, $y = (2)^2 + 2 \times 2 + 3 = 4 + 4 + 3 = 11$
When $x = 3$, $y = (3)^2 + 2 \times 3 + 3 = 9 + 6 + 3 = 18$
When $x = 4$, $y = (4)^2 + 2 \times 4 + 3 = 16 + 8 + 3 = 27$

Now write the y-coordinates in the table.

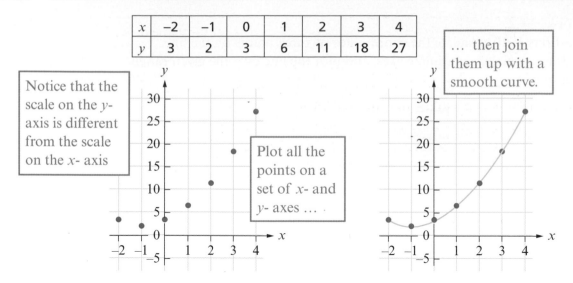

x	−2	−1	0	1	2	3	4
y	3	2	3	6	11	18	27

Notice that the scale on the y-axis is different from the scale on the x-axis

Plot all the points on a set of x- and y-axes …

… then join them up with a smooth curve.

Sometimes it can be helpful to break the formula up into several steps in order to calculate the values of y in the table. The next example illustrates this.

Example Draw the graph of $y = 10 + 2x - x^2$ for values of x from −3 to 3.

Solution

x	−3	−2	−1	0	1	2	3
10							
+2x							
−x^2							
y							

First, draw up this table

x	−3	−2	−1	0	1	2	3
10	10	10	10	10	10	10	10
+2x							
−x^2							
y							

Fill in the 10s …

x	−3	−2	−1	0	1	2	3
10	10	10	10	10	10	10	10
+2x	−6	−4	−2	0	2	4	6
−x^2							
y							

… then the +2x …

x	−3	−2	−1	0	1	2	3
10	10	10	10	10	10	10	10
+2x	−6	−4	−2	0	2	4	6
−x^2	−9	−4	−1	0	−1	−4	−9
y							

… then the −x^2 …

Finally, add the three parts in each column to get the value for y.

x	-3	-2	-1	0	1	2	3
10	10	10	10	10	10	10	10
$+2x$	-6	-4	-2	0	2	4	6
$-x^2$	-9	-4	-1	0	-1	-4	-9
y	-5	2	7	10	11	10	7

Plot all the points on a set of x- and y- axes …

… then join them up with a smooth curve.

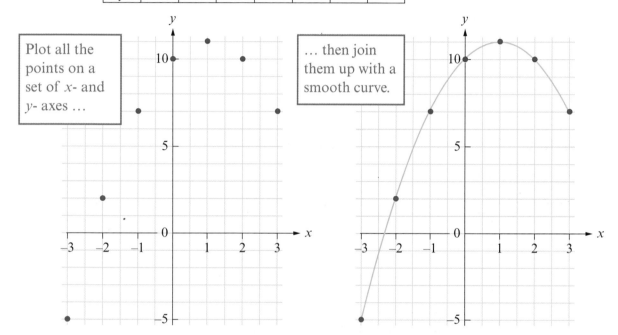

 Exercise 29.3

In questions **1–3** you are given a function and a table of values. Copy and complete the table, then plot the graph of the function.

1 ✔ $y = x^2 + 4x - 3$

x	-4	-3	-2	-1	0	1	2	3
x^2	16	9		1	0		4	
$+4x$	-16	-12	-8		0	4		
-3	-3	-3	-3	-3	-3	-3	-3	-3
y	-3	-6						

2 $y = 10 + 2x - x^2$

x	-3	-2	-1	0	1	2	3
10	10	10	10	10	10	10	10
$+2x$		-4	-2			4	
$-x^2$	-9	-4				-4	
y		2					

3 $y = 2x^2 - 4x - 1$

x	-2	-1	0	1	2	3	4
$2x^2$	8					18	
$-4x$	8				-8		
-1	-1						
y	15						

4 Draw the graph of $y = x^2 - 4x + 6$ for values of x from -1 to 5.

5 Draw the graph of $y = x^2 - 6x + 1$ for values of x from -1 to 5.

6 ✔ Draw the graph of $y = 5 - x - x^2$ for values of x from -3 to 2.

7 Draw the graph of $y = x^2 + 3x + 2$ for values of x from -4 to 1.

8 Draw the graph of $y = 3 + 3x - x^2$ for values of x from -1 to 4.

9 Draw the graph of $y = 2x^2 - 2x - 3$ for values of x from -2 to 3.

10 Draw the graph of $y = 4 - 0.5x^2$ for values of x from -3 to 3.

Summary

In this Unit you have represented functions by the use of tables, coordinate pairs and mapping diagrams. You have drawn the graphs of linear functions by plotting three points. Remember that a linear function such as $y = 3x - 5$ has gradient 3; a positive gradient indicates that the graph goes up as you move to the right, while a negative gradient means that it goes down.

The graphs of quadratic functions like $y = x^2 + 3x - 5$ give rise to curves; in order to draw their graphs you need to calculate the positions of as many points as possible.

Review Exercise 29

1 Draw a mapping diagram to illustrate the given function for $x = -1, 0, 1, 2, 3$.

    a) $y = x + 2$ **b)** $y = 2x + 3$ **c)** $y = 2 - x$ **d)** $y = x^2 - 1$

2 Copy the mapping diagram and fill in the missing values. Find the rule that has been used for the mapping, giving your answer **a)** as a rule in words; **b)** as an algebraic equation.

a)

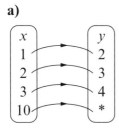

b)

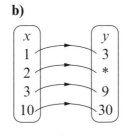

c)

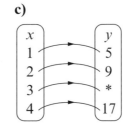

d)

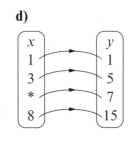

3 The table shows some values for the function $y = 2x - 3$.

x	−3	0	2	5
y		−3		7

a) Copy the table, and fill in the missing values.
b) Plot the graph of $y = 2x - 3$ on a coordinate grid in which x can run from −3 to 5.

4 The table shows some values for the function $y = -3x + 5$.

x	−1	0	2	4
y	8		−1	

a) Copy the table, and fill in the missing values.
b) Plot the graph of $y = 2x - 3$ on a coordinate grid in which x can run from −1 to 4.

5 Draw the graph of $y = \frac{1}{2}x - 1$ for values of x from −6 to 6.

6 Draw the graph of $y = 2 - x$ for values of x from −10 to 10.

7 Draw up a table of values for $x = -5, -4$ and so on, up to $x = 5$ and work out the corresponding y-values. Hence plot the graph of each curve, using a pair of coordinate axes in which x and y can each run from −5 to 5. You will need four separate diagrams.

a) $y = x^2 - 3x - 4$ b) $y = 5 - x^2$

c) $y = x^2 - x - 1$ d) $y = 0.1x^2 - 2$

8* Draw a pair of coordinate axes in which x and y can each run from −10 to 10.

a) Plot three points on the line $y = 3x - 2$ and join them up to obtain the graph of the line.
b) On the same diagram, draw the graph of $y = 2x + 5$.
c) Write down the coordinates of the point where these two lines cross.

9* The diagram on the right shows four straight lines, labelled A, B, C and D. Match up the lines to the four equations below:

a) $y = x + 2$
b) $y = 2x - 1$
c) $y = -x - 1$
d) $y = 6 - x$

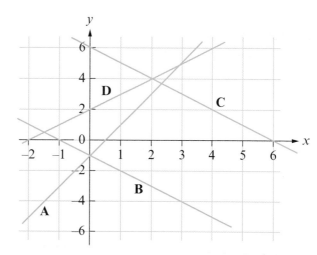

10* The diagram on the right shows four curves, labelled A, B, C and D. Match up the lines to the four equations below:

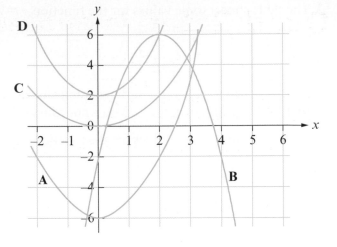

a) $y = x^2 + 2$

b) $y = x^2 - 6$

c) $y = -2 + 8x - 2x^2$

d) $y = \frac{1}{2}x^2$

11* The height y of a ball above the ground at a time x is given by $y = 10 + 3x - x^2$.

Copy and complete this table of values:

x	0	1	2	3	4	5	6
y	10				6		

a) Plot these points on a graph, and join them up to form a smooth curve.

b) Find the maximum height reached by the ball.

c) Find the time at which the ball lands.

Unit 30
Quadrilaterals and angles

In this Unit you will learn how to:
- classify quadrilaterals by properties;
- use vertically opposite, alternate and corresponding angles;
- solve problems using angle properties.

A calculator may be used with some of the harder exercises.

30.1 Types of quadrilateral

A **quadrilateral** is a 2-D geometric shape with four straight sides.

The properties of some special quadrilaterals are summarised in the table below.

Quadrilateral		Properties
Square		▪ Four equal sides ▪ Opposite sides are parallel ▪ Four equal angles of 90° ▪ Rotational symmetry of order 4 ▪ Four lines of symmetry
Rhombus		▪ Four equal sides ▪ Opposite sides are parallel ▪ Two pairs of equal angles ▪ Rotational symmetry of order 2 ▪ Two lines of symmetry
Rectangle		▪ Two pairs of equal sides ▪ Opposite sides are parallel ▪ Four equal angles of 90° ▪ Rotational symmetry of order 2 ▪ Two lines of symmetry
Parallelogram		▪ Two pairs of equal sides ▪ Opposite sides are parallel ▪ Two pairs of equal angles ▪ Rotational symmetry of order 2 ▪ No line of symmetry
Kite		▪ Two pairs of equal sides ▪ One pair of equal angles ▪ One line of symmetry

Quadrilateral		Properties
Arrowhead		■ Two pairs of equal sides ■ One pair of equal angles ■ One line of symmetry
Trapezium		■ One pair of parallel sides ■ Some trapeziums have a line of symmetry, others do not

Example   Draw a pair of coordinate axes in which x and y can each run from 0 to 10.

Plot the points A (2, 5), B (7, 3), C (9, 5) and D (7, 7) and join them up, in order, to form a closed quadrilateral. Name the type of quadrilateral that is obtained. Mark any line(s) of symmetry on your diagram.

Solution

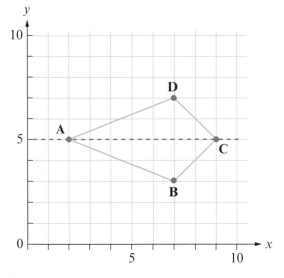

There is *one* line of symmetry.

The shape is a *kite*.

Exercise 30.1

In each of these questions you will need to draw a coordinate grid in which x and y can range from 0 to 10.

1 ✔ Plot the points A (2, 2), B (8, 3), C (8, 7) and D (2, 6) and join them up, in order, to form a closed quadrilateral. Name the type of quadrilateral that is obtained. Mark the angle DAB on your diagram, and mark another angle which is equal to it.

2 Plot the points P (1, 6), Q (5, 4), R (9, 6) and S (5, 8) and join them to form the quadrilateral PQRS. Name the type of quadrilateral that is obtained. Mark any line(s) of symmetry on your diagram.

3 Plot the points A (5, 2), B (8, 7), C (3, 10) and D (0, 5) and join them up, in order, to form a closed quadrilateral. Name the type of quadrilateral that is obtained.

4 ✔ Plot the points P (2, 2), Q (8, 2), R (7, 7) and S (5, 7) and join them up, in order, to form a closed quadrilateral. Name the type of quadrilateral that is obtained.

5 Plot the points A (6, 9), B (2, 7), C (5, 1) and D (9, 3) and join them up, in order, to form a closed quadrilateral. Name the type of quadrilateral that is obtained. Find also the coordinates of the point X at the centre of the quadrilateral.

6 Plot the points P (7, 5), Q (6, 1), R (1, 5) and S (2, 9) and join them up, in order, to form a closed quadrilateral. Name the type of quadrilateral that is obtained. State whether the quadrilateral has any lines of symmetry.

7 Plot the points A (3, 2), B (2, 7), C (7, 8) and D (8, 3) and join them up, in order, to form a closed quadrilateral. Name the type of quadrilateral that is obtained. State also the order of rotational symmetry of this quadrilateral.

8 Plot the points P (2, 2), Q (2, 9), R (8, 8) and S (8, 3) and join them up, in order, to form a closed quadrilateral. Name the type of quadrilateral that is obtained. State whether this quadrilateral has any lines of symmetry.

9 Plot the points A (2, 2), B (2, 9), C (4, 7) and D (3, 3) and join them up, in order, to form a closed quadrilateral. Name the type of quadrilateral that is obtained. Mark on your diagram any line of symmetry.

10 A certain quadrilateral has rotational symmetry of order 2 but no line of symmetry. What is it?

30.2 Angles and parallels

> The angles inside a quadrilateral add up to 360°.

Example   Find the missing angle a.

Solution
$$80 + 123 + 105 + a = 360$$
$$308 + a = 360$$
$$a = 360 - 308$$
$$\underline{a = 52°}$$

(not to scale)

In the next Exercise you will need to use the fact that angles in a quadrilateral add up to 360°. You will also need to know the following properties of angles and parallel lines:

Angles at a point add up to 360°.   Z-angles (alternate angles) are equal.

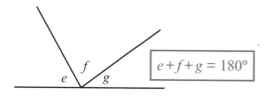

$$a+b+c+d = 360°$$

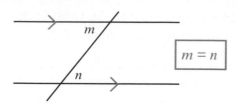

$$m = n$$

Angles on a straight line add up to 180°. F-angles (corresponding angles) are equal.

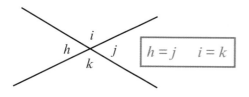

$$e+f+g = 180°$$

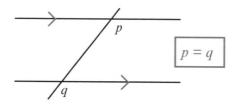

$$p = q$$

Vertically opposite angles are equal.   Interior angles add up to 180°.

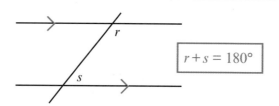

$$h = j \qquad i = k$$

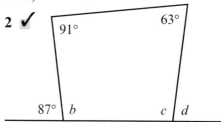

$$r + s = 180°$$

Exercise 30.2

Find the angles represented by letters in these diagrams. Give a brief reason
in each case. (*The diagrams are not drawn to scale.*)

1

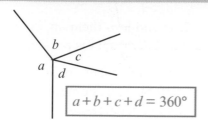

2 ✔

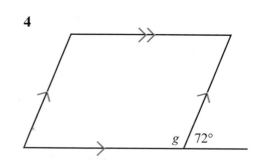

3 ✔

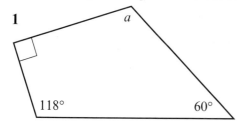

4

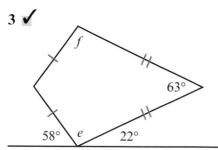

5

6

110°
130°
i

h 120°

7

8

60°
k 100°

31° *j*

9

10

n
35° *l*
m

42°
p

11

12 ✔

r
55°
q

60° *s* 30°
t *u*

13

14

105°
w
v

z 48°
y *x*

30.3 Using equations to solve angle problems

Example Find the angles in this quadrilateral.

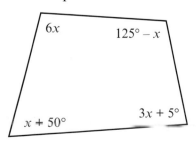

6*x*   125° − *x*

x + 50°   3*x* + 5°

Solution　　　The four angles add up to 360°.

$$(x + 50) + 6x + (125 - x) + (3x + 5) = 360$$

First, set up this equation …

$$9x + 180 = 360$$
$$9x = 360 - 180$$

… simplify …

$$9x = 180$$
$$x = 180 \div 9$$
$$x = 20$$

… and solve, to find x.

Then $x + 50 = 70$; $6x = 120$; $125 - x = 105$; $3x + 5 = 65$.

The angles are $\underline{70°, 120°, 105°, 65°}$

Then use $x = 20$ to find the values of the angles.

Exercise 30.3

Find the values represented by letters. You should set up and solve an equation where possible.

1 ✔
$110° - a$
$60° + 2a$

2
$85°$　b　$b + 15°$

3 ✔
$2c + 14°$
$3c - 24°$

4
$66° + d$
$26° + 4d$　$88°$

5
$2f + 90°$　$e + 60°$
$5f + 63°$
$3e + 36°$

6 ✔
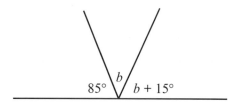
$44° + g$
$86° - 2g$

7
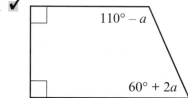
$h + 40°$
$h + 10°$

8
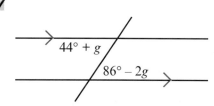
$95° + j$
$65° + 3j$

9
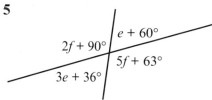
$52° + k$
$5k + 20°$

10
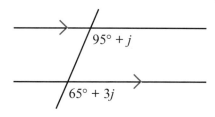
m
$36°$
n

Summary

In this Unit you have used symmetries to classify types of quadrilateral, including square, rhombus, rectangle, parallelogram, kite, arrowhead and trapezium.

Angles in any quadrilateral add up to 360°. Angles at a point also add up to 360°, while angles on a straight line add up to 180°.

You have learnt that vertically opposite angles are equal, Z-angles are equal and F-angles are equal, while interior angles add up to 180°.

You have solved problems using these results, sometimes by setting up an equation first.

Review Exercise 30

1 A quadrilateral has four right angles and two lines of symmetry. What type of quadrilateral is it?

2 A quadrilateral has two lines of symmetry and rotational symmetry of order 2, but none of the internal angles are right angles. What type of quadrilateral is it?

3 Sanjay says: 'Any quadrilateral with four equal sides must be a square'. Is he right or is he wrong?

4 Gita says: 'Any quadrilateral with rotational symmetry of order 4 must be a square'. Is she right or is she wrong?

5 Make a copy of this table in your exercise book:

Four lines of symmetry	Two lines of symmetry	One line of symmetry	No line of symmetry

Put the words 'arrowhead, kite, parallelogram, rectangle, rhombus, square and trapezium' in the correct columns.

In questions **6–13** find the angles represented by letters.

6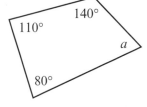

7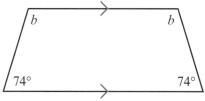

8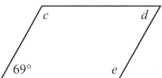

9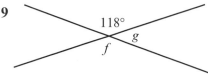

10

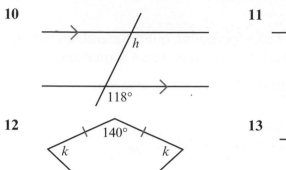

11

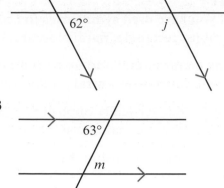

12

13

In questions **14–17** set up and solve an equation to find the value of each letter.

14

$50° - w$
$130° + w$
$110° - 2w$ $5w + 25°$

15

$142° - m$
$114° + 3m$

16

$150°$
$7y - 4°$ $50° + y$
$92°$

17

$z - 5°$ $2z$ $3z - 25°$

18* Find the value of the angle represented by the letter a:

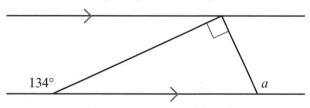

$134°$ a

19* The four angles in a quadrilateral are $5x$, $10x - 30°$, $124° - x$ and $3x + 28°$ (in order, as you go around the quadrilateral). Find x, and hence decide what type of quadrilateral it is.

20* Find the values represented by letters in this diagram:

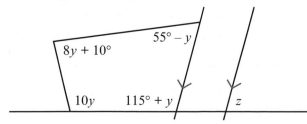

$55° - y$
$8y + 10°$
$10y$ $115° + y$ z

Unit 31
Making shapes using *Logo*

In this Unit you will learn how to:

- follow *Logo* instructions to make shapes;
- write simple *Logo* programs;
- construct polygons and stars using *Logo*;
- use procedures to build up more complicated shapes;
- use 2-D representations for 3-D objects.

A calculator is not required for this Unit, but you will need access to a computer, such as a PC running 'Logo for Windows'. The instructions in this Unit are for MSW's 'Logo for Windows'; you might need to change them slightly if you are operating a different version.

31.1 Getting started

Look at the pattern on the right.

It was made using the computer package *Logo*.

It may look complicated, but the instructions to make the pattern can be written using one line of computer code.

> You have probably met **Logo** before, as a software package for drawing geometric shapes. A marker called a Turtle moves around the screen, and this type of application is therefore sometimes called Turtle Graphics.

Here are examples of some of the commands which you will use most often:

Command	Shortened Form	What it does:
forward 20	fd 20	moves the turtle forwards 20 units
back 30	bk 30	moves the turtle backwards 30 units
left 90	lt 90	turns the turtle 90° to the left
right 75	rt 75	turns the turtle 75° to the right
clean	–	cleans the screen
home	–	returns the turtle to the centre
clearscreen	cs	cleans the screen and returns the turtle to the centre

Several commands may be joined together, either by writing them in a line (with spaces in between) or by using several lines.

Example   Describe the shape formed by this set of instructions:

fd 50 rt 90
fd 70 rt 90
fd 50 rt 90
fd 70 rt 90

Solution   You could run these instructions on a computer, or draw the pattern on squared paper using a scale of (say) 1 square to 10 units. The result will look like this:

and so you obtain a <u>rectangle measuring 50 by 70 units.</u>

> If a set of instructions contains a lot of repetition then the **Repeat** command may be helpful.

The instructions in the previous example could have been written like this:

repeat 2 [fd 50 rt 90 fd 70 rt 90]

| Some versions of *Logo* do not like a space in here | These four instructions get carried out in order, then repeated |

Example   Using the repeat command, write a set of instructions to draw:

a) a square of side 80 units;
b) a rectangle measuring 40 by 70 units.

Solution   **a)** For the square,   <u>repeat 4 [fd 80 rt 90]</u>

b) For the rectangle,   <u>repeat 2 [fd 40 rt 90 fd 70 rt 90]</u>

Exercise 31.1

In questions **1–10** you are given some lines of *Logo* code. Describe as accurately as you can the shape that you think is being drawn, then run the code on a computer to see if you were right.

1 repeat 4 [fd 75 rt 90]
2 repeat 2 [fd 20 rt 90 fd 30 rt 90]
3 fd 60 rt 90 fd 60 rt 90 fd 60 rt 90 fd 60 rt 90
4 fd 50 rt 90 fd 50 rt 135 fd 71 rt 45
5 repeat 3 [fd 60 rt 120]

  6 repeat 5 [fd 50 rt 72]
  7 repeat 6 [fd 50 rt 60]
  8 repeat 5 [fd 50 rt 144]
  9 repeat 2 [fd 20 rt 110 fd 30 rt 70]
10 repeat 10 [fd 10 rt 90 fd 10 lt 90]

31.2 Setting up procedures

By now you should have learnt to recognise that the code 'repeat 4 [fd 50 rt 90]'
will draw a square of side 50 units. It is possible to teach the computer to draw
a square, like this:

Call up the editor screen (your teacher will need to show you how to do this
for your version of *Logo*).

Then type in:

```
to square
repeat 4 [fd 50 rt 90]
end
```

and return to the main *Logo* program. If you now type the command
square then *Logo* will look up these instructions and carry them out.
You have taught *Logo* how to do something new!

Exercise 31.2

Here are some more procedures. Type them into your computer's editor
screen, and then try them out. Describe the effect of each procedure.

You might find it helpful to hide the turtle first – using the command **hide.**

Remember to clear the screen – **cs** – after you have run each one.

1
```
to fred
fd 50 rt 90 fd 70 rt 90
fd 50 rt 90 fd 70 rt 90
end
```

2
```
to flag
fd 100
repeat 4 [fd 30 rt 90]
end
```

3
```
to shape
repeat 3 [fd 70 lt 120]
end
```

4
```
to star
repeat 5 [fd 70 rt 144]
end
```

5
```
to wriggle
repeat 10 [fd 20 rt 70 fd 20 lt 70]
end
```

6
```
to letter
fd 100 lt 90 fd 20 bk 40
end
```

7
```
to octopus
repeat 8 [fd 30 rt 45]
end
```

8
```
to roof
rt 45 fd 14 rt 45 fd 8 rt 45 fd 14
rt 135 fd 28 rt 90
end
```

9
```
to platypus
repeat 20 [fd 10 rt 36]
end
```

10
```
to frame
repeat 2 [fd 50 rt 80 fd 50 rt 100]
end
```

Warning!

When you come to shut down *Logo* the computer will forget all the new procedures you have taught it, unless you save them first. The usual way to do this is to use the **Save** command from the menu, and tell the software a filename – such as **Alan**. All the procedures you have been using will all be saved together under that one heading.

When you start your next *Logo* session you should begin by using the **Load** command, followed by the filename **Alan** (or whatever you used when you did your Save). All your procedures will then become active again.

31.3 Writing your own procedures

It is now time to try writing procedures by yourself. The ability to write computer instructions comes with practice, so don't worry if you find this a little difficult at first – and remember that there is often more than one good way to achieve the same result.

In the example and exercises which follow you should imagine that the shape has been drawn on a grid whose squares are 50 units apart, and the the turtle begins at the point marked **Start**. Assume that the turtle is facing straight up the page to begin with.

Example   Write a procedure to draw this shape:

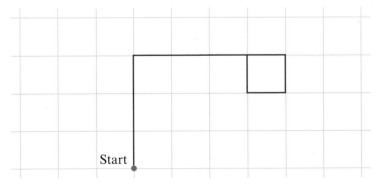

Solution

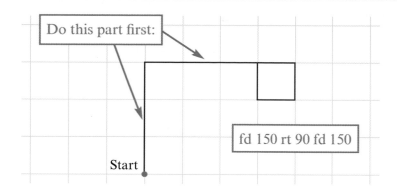

Do this part first:

fd 150 rt 90 fd 150

Start

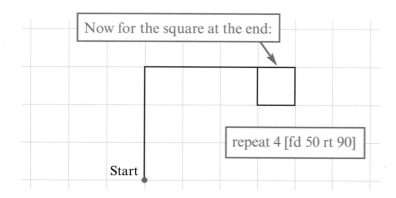

Now for the square at the end:

repeat 4 [fd 50 rt 90]

Start

Putting it all together we have:

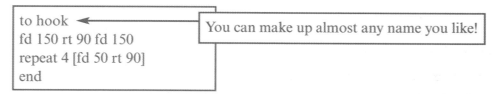

```
to hook
fd 150 rt 90 fd 150
repeat 4 [fd 50 rt 90]
end
```

You can make up almost any name you like!

Exercise 31.3

Write procedures to draw each of these shapes. In each case the turtle begins at the point marked **Start** and is facing up the page. Take each square to be 10 units across.

1   **2**

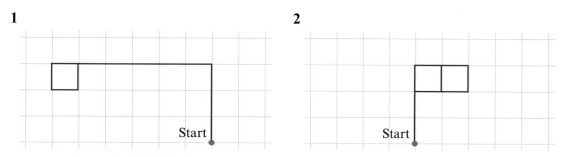

Start   Start

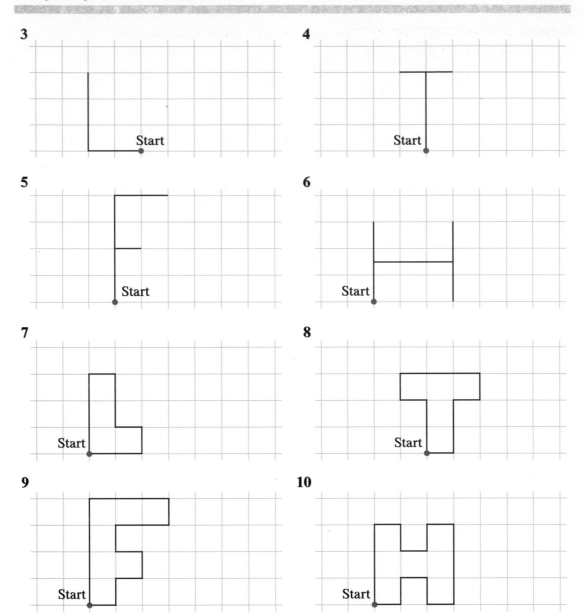

3

4

5

6

7

8

9

10

31.4 Polygons and stars

Try this procedure on your computer:

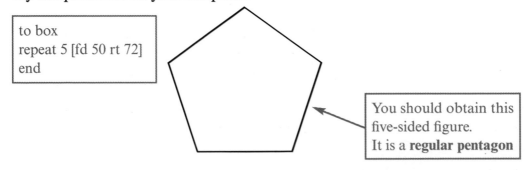

```
to box
repeat 5 [fd 50 rt 72]
end
```

You should obtain this five-sided figure.
It is a **regular pentagon**

To learn how to make a regular polygon with any number of sides, look again at the code for a pentagon:

repeat 5 [fd 50 rt 72]

This is the number of sides.

This is 360° ÷ the number of sides. For a pentagon, 360° ÷ 5 = 72°.

Warning! Regular polygons are often described by their **interior angles** but *Logo* constructs them by turning through **exterior angles**:

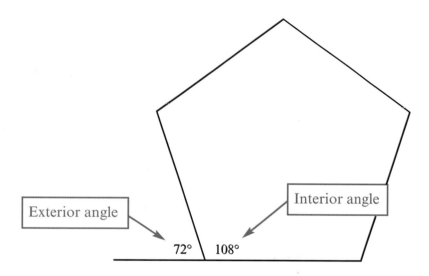

Exterior angle

Interior angle

72°   108°

Here is another procedure for you to try. Type this into your computer and see what happens.

```
to star
repeat 5 [fd 50 rt 144]
end
```

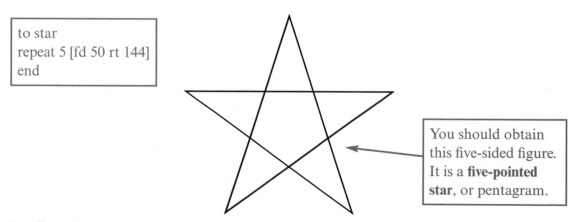

You should obtain this five-sided figure. It is a **five-pointed star**, or pentagram.

In effect this is the same code as was used for the pentagon, but doubling the angle to 144° makes the turtle turn around itself twice. The result produces a star instead of a polygon.

Here is a table of interior and exterior angles for some of the more common regular polygons. You will find it helpful when you work through the next exercise.

Name of polygon	Number of sides	Interior angle	Exterior angle
Square	4	90°	90°
Regular pentagon	5	108°	72°
Regular hexagon	6	120°	60°
Regular octagon	8	135°	45°
Regular nonagon	9	140°	40°
Regular decagon	10	144°	36°
Regular dodecagon	12	150°	30°
Regular 15-gon	15	156°	24°
Regular 18-gon	18	160°	20°

Exercise 31.4

For each of these, write a *Logo* procedure to draw the required shape, then check it by running it on your computer.

1 A square of side 70 units.

2 A regular pentagon with sides 40 units long.

3 A regular hexagon of side 50 units.

4 A regular 15-gon with sides 10 units long.

5 A regular dodecagon of side 12 units.

6 A regular 18-gon with sides 25 units long.

7 A regular decagon of side 30.

8 A regular octagon with sides 45 units long.

9 A regular nonagon of side 40.

10 A regular nine-pointed star with sides 40 units long.

31.5 3-D Shapes

It is important not to confuse the language of 2-dimensional and 3-dimensional objects. For example an **octagon** is a flat 2-D shape with 8 **edges**, while an **octahedron** is a 3-D solid object with 8 **faces**.

Here is a reminder of some of the more common 3-D solids. They are drawn here using 2-D sketches; look for examples of them in your classroom or elsewhere.

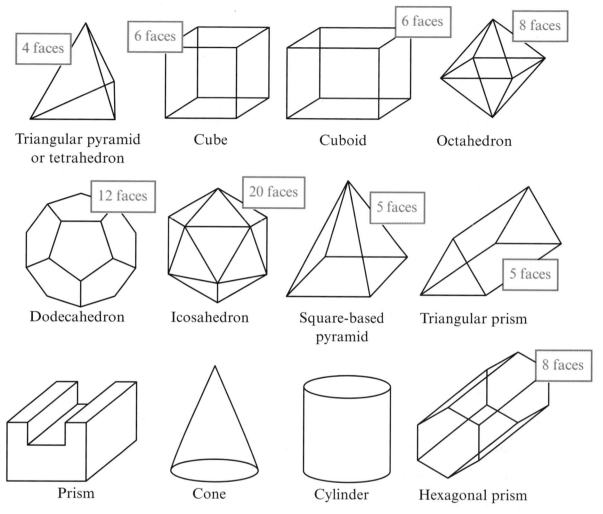

| 4 faces | 6 faces | 6 faces | 8 faces |

Triangular pyramid or tetrahedron   Cube   Cuboid   Octahedron

| 12 faces | 20 faces | 5 faces | |
| 5 faces |

Dodecahedron   Icosahedron   Square-based pyramid   Triangular prism

| 8 faces |

Prism   Cone   Cylinder   Hexagonal prism

Exercise 31.5

1 Write down the name for a regular 2-D shape with 12 straight edges. Write down also the name for a regular 3-D shape with 12 flat faces. What shape are the faces?

2 Andrew is making a 3-D model out of equilateral triangles. He wants to make a regular polyhedron. There are two different models that he can make. Name the two different polyhedra, and state the number of triangles needed for each one.

3 Rana wants to make a model of a regular polyhedron with 8 faces.

a) What name is given to this solid?
b) What shape will Rana need for each face?

4 Samir has made five shapes using *Logo*. He has printed them on card and cut them out. Two of the shapes are equilateral triangles of side 5 cm, and the other three are rectangles measuring 5 cm by 12 cm.

a) Name the 3-D solid that Samir can make using these five shapes.
b) How long is this solid?

5 Katie has made two square-based pyramids. She decides to stick them together by gluing the two bases to each other. What name describes the single 3-D object she makes?

Summary

In this Unit you have learned how to draw shapes using *Logo* commands. It is a good idea to store your commands as procedures, so that they can be saved on your computer disk. You have begun to write *Logo* programs of your own.

To make regular polygons you have used the result that the external angle is 360° divided by the number of sides; this is a powerful result and should be remembered. If you take the standard program for a polygon with an odd number of sides, and then double the angle, the result will be a star rather than a polygon.

You have revised the names for common 3-D solids. Be careful to distinguish between –gon (a flat 2-D shape) and –hedron (a 3-D solid).

Review Exercise 31

1 Look at this line of *Logo* code:

```
repeat 2 [fd 100 rt 90 fd 60 rt 90]
```

Explain what you think it might draw. Then run it on your computer to see if you were right.

2 Look at this line of *Logo* code:

```
repeat 2 [fd 100 rt 100 fd 80 rt 80]
```

Explain what you think it might draw. Then run it on your computer to see if you were right.

3 Look at this line of *Logo* code:

```
repeat 10 [fd 40 rt 36]
```

Explain what you think it might draw. Then run it on your computer to see if you were right.

4 Write a *Logo* procedure to draw a rhombus of side 70 units. The obtuse angles in the rhombus should both be 140°.

5 Write a *Logo* procedure to draw a regular octagon of side 35 units.

6 Write a *Logo* procedure to draw a regular hexagon of side 55 units.

7 Terri writes this piece of code to draw a shape using *Logo*:

```
to pattern
cs
repeat 2 [fd 100 rt 120 fd 100 rt 60]
fd 100 rt 60
repeat 3 [fd 100 rt 60 fd 100 rt 120]
lt 60
fd 100 rt 60 fd 100 rt 120
end
```

   a) Enter this procedure into your computer and run it.

   b) Explain why Terri wrote 'cs' in the second line.

   c) What 3-D solid do you think this 2-D pattern is supposed to represent?

8 Usha is using *Logo* to make a pattern which is supposed to represent a 3-D solid.

The computer prints out the pattern
shown on the right:

a) What solid do you think Usha is
trying to represent?

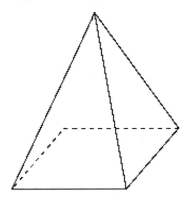

There is a small error in Usha's diagram,
which makes it slightly misleading.

b) Explain how Usha's diagram could
be improved.

9 Damian wants to draw a five-pointed star. He writes this procedure:

```
to star
repeat 5 [fd 50 rt 120 fd 50 lt 120 rt 62]
end
```

   a) Run this procedure on your computer.

   b) Explain what has gone wrong with Damian's procedure.

   c) Change Damian's procedure so that it now draws a five-pointed star correctly.

10* Key this *Logo* procedure into your computer:

```
to fan
repeat 36 [ repeat 4[fd 50 rt 90] rt 10]
end
```

You should obtain a pattern similar to the one at the beginning of section 27.1. See if
you can extend your program and add colour to make an exact copy of that pattern.

Unit 32
Area and volume

In this Unit you will learn how to:

■ find areas of triangles;

■ find areas of quadrilaterals;

■ find areas of compound shapes;

■ find the volume of a cuboid;

■ solve problems involving areas and volumes.

A calculator will be required for this Unit.

32.1 Areas of triangles

> For a triangle with base b and perpendicular height h the area A can be found by using this result: $\qquad A = \dfrac{b \times h}{2}$

Example Find the area of this triangle.

(The diagram is not to scale. All lengths are in centimetres.)

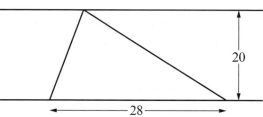

Solution $b = 28$ and $h = 20$

$$A = \frac{b \times h}{2}$$

$$= \frac{28 \times 20}{2}$$

$$= \frac{560}{2}$$

$$= \underline{280 \, \text{cm}^2}$$

Notice that $\dfrac{28 \times 20}{2} = \dfrac{560}{2} = 280$ and ...

$\dfrac{28 \times 20}{2} = 14 \times 20 = 280$ and ...

$\dfrac{28 \times 20}{2} = 28 \times 10 = 280$ and ...

all give the same result.

The same formula can be used even when the triangle is obtuse-angled.

Example Find the area of this triangle.

(The diagram is not to scale. All lengths are in millimetres.)

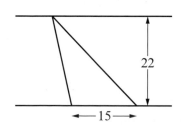

228

Solution $b = 15$ and $h = 22$

$A = \dfrac{b \times h}{2}$

> Explain your working clearly.

$\quad = \dfrac{15 \times 22}{2}$

$\quad = \dfrac{330}{2}$

$\quad = \underline{165\,\text{mm}^2}$

Exercise 32.1

1 Find the areas of these triangles, correct to 3 significant figures where appropriate:

a) ✔ Base 12 cm, perpendicular height 26 cm

b) Base 16 cm, perpendicular height 19 cm

c) Base 40 mm, perpendicular height 49 mm

d) Base 32 cm, perpendicular height 21 cm

e) Base 6 m, perpendicular height 11 m

f) ✔ Base 11 cm, perpendicular height 13 cm

g) Base 12.5 cm, perpendicular height 8.5 cm

h) Base 4.8 m, perpendicular height 8.7 m

i) Base 165 mm, perpendicular height 223 mm

j) Base 340 mm, perpendicular height 420 mm.

Find the areas of the triangles in these diagrams. In some cases you have been given more information than you actually need. (*The diagrams are not drawn to scale. Take all measurements as centimetres.*)

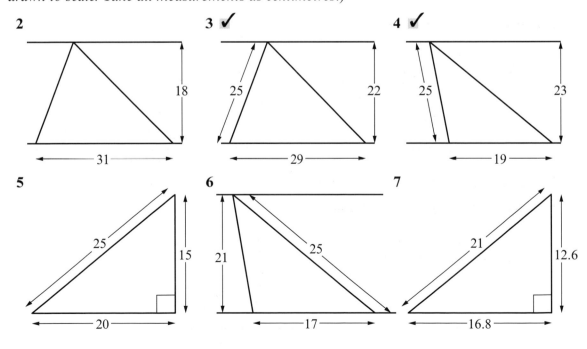

32.2 Areas of quadrilaterals

The area of a square, rectangle, parallelogram, rhombus or trapezium can be found by using one of the following standard results:

Quadrilateral	Area formula	Example
Square	$\text{Area} = a \times a$ $= a^2$	$\text{Area} = 8 \times 8$ $= 64\,\text{cm}^2$
Rectangle	$\text{Area} = a \times b$ $= ab$	$\text{Area} = 8 \times 5$ $= 40\,\text{cm}^2$
Parallelogram	$\text{Area} = b \times h$ $= bh$	$\text{Area} = 8 \times 5$ $= 40\,\text{cm}^2$
Rhombus	$\text{Area} = \frac{1}{2} \times a \times b$ $= \frac{ab}{2}$	$\text{Area} = \frac{1}{2} \times 10 \times 14$ $= \frac{140}{2}$ $= 70\,\text{m}^2$
Trapezium	$\text{Area} = \frac{1}{2} \times (a+b) \times h$ $= \frac{h(a+b)}{2}$	$\text{Area} = \frac{1}{2} \times (10+14) \times 8$ $= \frac{1}{2} \times 24 \times 8$ $= 12 \times 8 = 96\,\text{m}^2$

Example Name this type of quadrilateral, and find its area.

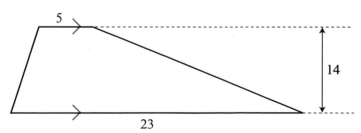

Solution   This is a <u>trapezium</u>, with $a = 5$, $b = 23$ and $h = 14$.

$$\text{Area} = \frac{h(a+b)}{2}$$

$$= \frac{14 \times (5+23)}{2}$$

$$= \frac{14 \times 28}{2}$$

$$= 7 \times 28$$

$$= \underline{196} \text{ square units}$$

Exercise 32.2

Name each of these quadrilaterals, and find its area. (*All lengths are in centimetres.*)

1
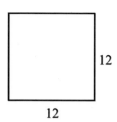
12
12

2 ✔
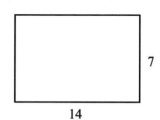
7
14

3
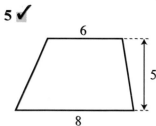
4
9

4 ✔
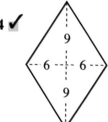
9
6   6
9

5 ✔
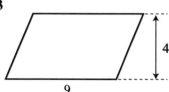
6
5
8

6
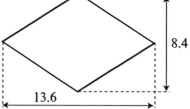
8.4
13.6

7
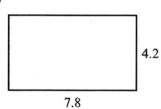
4.2
7.8

8 ✔
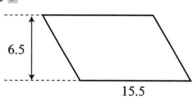
6.5
15.5

32.3 Areas of compound shapes

The areas of more complicated shapes can be found by breaking them up into smaller parts. Each separate area is found, then they are all added together.

Example   Find the area of the letter F. *(All lengths are in centimetres. The diagram is not to scale.)*

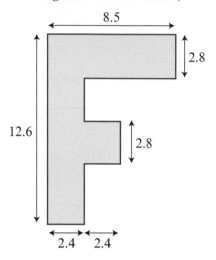

Solution

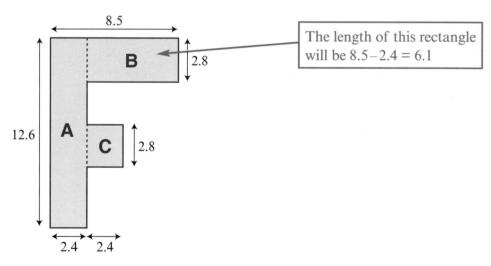

The length of this rectangle will be 8.5 − 2.4 = 6.1

Area of rectangle A = 12.6 × 2.4 = 30.24

Area of rectangle B = 2.8 × 6.1 =   17.08

Area of rectangle C = 2.8 × 2.4 =   6.72

Total   54.04

Remember to include units in your final answer.

The area of the letter F is 54.0 cm² (correct to 3 s.f.)

Exercise 32.3

For each of these compound shapes make a neat sketch and add dotted lines to break it up into simpler pieces. Find the area of each piece, and the total area for each compound shape. *(All the lengths are in centimetres.)*

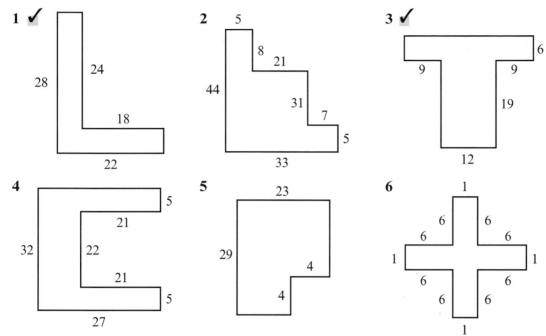

1 ✔

28, 24, 18, 22

2 5, 8, 21, 44, 31, 7, 5, 33

3 ✔ 6, 9, 9, 19, 12

4 5, 21, 32, 22, 21, 5, 27

5 23, 29, 4, 4

6 1, 6, 6, 6, 6, 1, 1, 6, 6, 6, 6, 1

32.4 Volumes of cuboids

> The volume of a **cuboid** is found by multiplying its height, breadth and depth together.

Example   Find the volume of this cuboid:

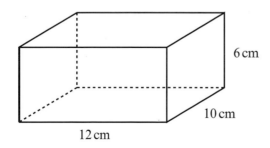

6 cm
10 cm
12 cm

Solution   Volume $= 12 \times 6 \times 10$

$= 72 \times 10$

$= \underline{720\,\text{cm}^3}$

Remember to include units of volume – cubic centimetres, cubic inches etc.

Exercise 32.4

Find the volumes of these cuboids:

1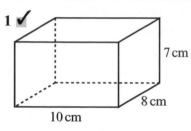

7 cm
8 cm
10 cm

2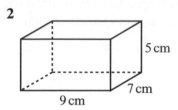

5 cm
7 cm
9 cm

3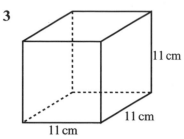

11 cm
11 cm
11 cm

4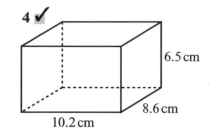

6.5 cm
8.6 cm
10.2 cm

5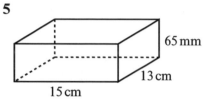

65 mm
13 cm
15 cm

6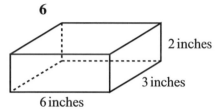

2 inches
3 inches
6 inches

Summary

In this Unit you have calculated areas of triangles and quadrilaterals using standard formulae. You have found areas of compound shapes by breaking them up into smaller pieces.

You have also found the volume of a cuboid, by multiplying its three dimensions together.

The Review Exercise includes some questions about applying these results in order to solve problems.

Review Exercise 32

1 Find the areas of these triangles. (*All the lengths are in centimetres.*)

a)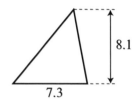

8.1
7.3

b)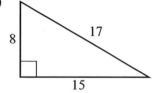

8
17
15

c)

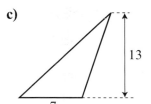

d)

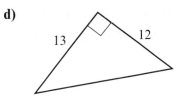

2   Find the areas of these quadrilaterals.

a)

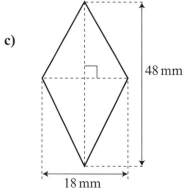

b)

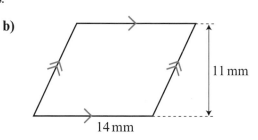

c)

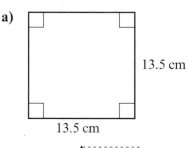

d)

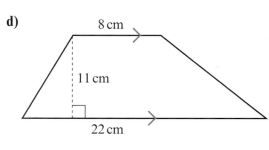

e)

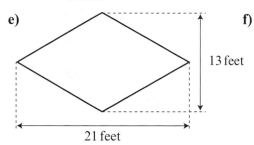

f)

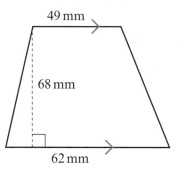

3   A cuboid measures 21 cm by 19 cm by 14 cm. Find its volume, correct to 2 significant figures.

4   A cuboid measures 20 cm by 50 mm by 70 mm. Find its volume in cubic centimetres.

5* Two of the dimensions of a cuboid are 21 cm and 25 cm. Its volume is 15 225 cm³. Find the third dimension.

6* A cube has a volume of 6859 cm³. Find its dimensions.

7* A cuboid measures 26 cm by 130 cm by 2.3 m.

Find
a) the total area of all 6 faces
b) the volume of the cuboid

[Hint: decide whether to work in centimetres or metres, then use the same units throughout]

8* A farmer surveys a field by dividing it into pieces. Each piece is in the shape of a right-angled triangle or a trapezium, as shown in the sketch below:

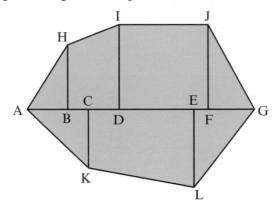

The following lengths are measured: AB = 10 m, BC = 2 m, CD = 6 m, DE = 9 m, EF = 6 m, FG = 11 m, BH = 12 m, DI = 15 m, JF = 15 m, CK = 8 m, EL = 9 m.

Find the area of each of the separate parts of the field. Hence find the total area.

Unit 33
The circle: area and circumference

In this Unit you will learn how to:

- find the circumference of a circle, using $C = 2\pi r$ or $C = \pi d$;
- find the area of a circle, using $A = \pi r^2$;
- solve inverse problems to find a radius.

A calculator will be required for this Unit.

33.1 Circumference of a circle

The **circumference** of a circle is the distance all the way around its outside.

The circumference is just over three times the diameter; more precisely, about 3.142 times.

The exact value of this decimal ratio is called 'pi' written π.

A **diameter** is a straight line passing from one side of the circle to the other, through the centre. AB is a diameter; it passes through the centre O.

A **radius** is half a diameter. OC is a radius.

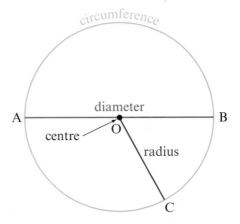

For a circle of radius r or diameter d the circumference C can be found by using either of these results:

$$C = 2\pi r$$
$$C = \pi d$$

Example A circle has radius 12 cm. Find its circumference.

Solution $r = 12$. Using the result $C = 2\pi r$ we have

$C = 2\pi r$
$\quad = 2 \times 3.141\,592\,6 \times 12$
$\quad = 75.398\,222\,4$ (by calculator)
$\quad = \underline{75.4\,cm}$ correct to 3 s.f.

Your calculator should have the value of π stored in it, probably to 10 significant figures. Just use this key sequence:

Example   A circle has diameter 11 cm. Find its circumference.

Solution $d = 11$. Using the result $C = \pi d$ we have

$$C = \pi d$$
$$= 3.141\,592\,6 \times 11$$
$$= 34.557\,518\,6 \text{ (by calculator)}$$
$$= \underline{34.6\,\text{cm}} \text{ correct to 3 s.f.}$$

> It is a good idea to write down several figures…

> …and then round them off to 3 significant figures

Exercise 33.1

Find the circumference of each of these circles, correct to 3 significant figures.

1 $r = 8\,\text{cm}$ **2** $r = 18\,\text{cm}$

3 ✓ $r = 5\,\text{km}$ **4** $d = 20\,\text{cm}$

5 $d = 28\,\text{mm}$ **6** $r = 12\,\text{mm}$

7 $d = 14\,\text{km}$ **8** ✓ $d = 19\,\text{m}$

9 $r = 6\,\text{cm}$ **10** $d = 2\,\text{cm}$

Find the circumference of each of these circles, correct to 4 significant figures.

11 $d = 2.9\,\text{m}$ **12** $r = 1.5\,\text{cm}$

13 ✓ $d = 42.8\,\text{mm}$ **14** $r = 4.1\,\text{cm}$

15 $r = 15\,\text{cm}$ **16** $d = 62.5\,\text{mm}$

17 $d = 0.9252\,\text{km}$ **18** ✓ $r = 12.25\,\text{km}$

19 $r = 1255\,\text{mm}$ **20** $d = 1.008\,\text{km}$

33.2 Area of a circle

> For a circle of radius r or diameter d the area A can be found by using the result $A = \pi r^2$

Example   A circle has radius 12 cm. Find its area.

Solution $r = 12$. Using the result $A = \pi r^2$ we have

$$A = \pi r^2$$
$$= 3.141\,592\,6 \times 12 \times 12$$
$$= 452.389\,334\,4 \text{ (by calculator)}$$
$$= \underline{452\,\text{cm}^2} \text{ correct to 3 s.f.}$$

> You can use the square key x^2 on your calculator. This sequence will work well:

Example   A circle has diameter 11 cm. Find its area.

Solution $d = 11$ so $r = 11 \div 2 = 5.5$.

> For area problems you cannot work with diameter – you **must** find the radius straight away.

Using the result $A = \pi r^2$ we have
$$A = \pi r^2$$
$$= 3.141\,592\,6 \times 5.5 \times 5.5$$
$$= 95.033\,176\,15 \text{ (by calculator)}$$
$$= \underline{95.0\,\text{cm}^2} \text{ correct to 3 s.f.}$$

> Remember to write **cm²**, not just cm

Exercise 33.2

Find the area of each of these circles, correct to 3 significant figures.

1 $r = 8$ cm   **2** $r = 18$ cm

3 ✔ $r = 5$ km   **4** $d = 20$ cm

5 $d = 28$ mm   **6** $r = 12$ mm

7 ✔ $d = 14$ km   **8** $d = 19$ m

9 $r = 6$ cm   **10** $d = 2$ cm

Find the area of each of these circles, correct to 4 significant figures.

11 $d = 2.9$ m   **12** $r = 1.5$ cm

13 ✔ $d = 42.8$ mm   **14** $r = 4.1$ cm

15 ✔ $r = 15$ cm   **16** $d = 62.5$ mm

17 $d = 0.9252$ km   **18** $r = 12.25$ km

19 $r = 1255$ mm   **20** $d = 1.008$ km

33.3 Inverse problems

> Sometimes you are given the circumference or area of a circle, and you find the radius by working backwards.

Example   A circle has circumference 16.5 cm. Find its diameter.

Solution   Using the result $C = 2\pi r$ we have
$$2\pi r = 16.5$$
$$r = \frac{16.5}{2\pi}$$
$$= 2.626\,056\,561\ldots$$

> The question says 'find its diameter' but it is usually best to find the radius first. This can simply be doubled at the end, to obtain the diameter

$$d = 2 \times r$$
$$= 2 \times 2.626\,056\,561\ldots$$
$$= 5.252\,113\,122\ldots$$
$$= \underline{5.25\,\text{cm}} \text{ correct to 3 s.f.}$$

> Beware of rounding too early! The full calculator values are used until the very last line, when the answer is rounded to 3 s.f.

Example   A circle has area 125 cm². Find its radius.

Solution   Using the result $A = \pi r^2$ we have

$$\pi r^2 = 125$$
$$r^2 = \frac{125}{\pi}$$
$$= 39.788\,735\,77\ldots$$
$$r = \sqrt{39.788\,735\,77\ldots}$$
$$= 6.307\,831\,305\ldots$$
$$= \underline{6.31\,\text{cm}} \text{ correct to 3 s.f.}$$

> Concentrate on finding r^2 first, then square root it to find r.

> Once again, rounding is done only at the very last stage.

Exercise 33.3

Find the radius of each of these circles:

1 Circumference 35 mm

2 ✔ Circumference 20 inches

3 ✔ Area 35 mm²

4 Area 4.56 m²

5 Circumference 235 mm

6 Area 865 cm²

7 Circumference 11 m

8 Area 24 cm²

9 Area 1.035 mm²

10 Circumference 8500 km

Summary

In this Unit you have learnt how to find the circumference and the area of a circle, given its radius or diameter. You have also learnt how to work backwards to find the radius given the circumference or the area of the circle.

When using a calculator you should beware of errors which can occur if you round off numbers too soon. It is best to work with full calculator values, only rounding off at the very last line of the solution.

Review Exercise 33

1 A circle has radius 19 cm. Find its circumference.

2 A circle has diameter 29 cm. Find its area.

3 A circle has diameter 48 cm. Find its circumference.

4 A circle has radius 1100 mm. Find its area.

5 A circle has radius 27 cm. Find its circumference and area, each correct to 4 significant figures.

6 A circle has diameter 93 mm. Find its circumference and area, each correct to 2 significant figures.

7 A circle has area 975 cm². Find its radius.

8 A circle has circumference 1185 mm. Find its diameter.

9 Find the diameter of a circle whose area is $75\,cm^2$.

10 Find the radius of a circle whose circumference is $99\,m$.

11* Richard measures the circumference of two tree trunks. The smaller one is $2.35\,m$ and the larger one is $3.77\,m$.

    a) Calculate the radius of the smaller tree trunk.

    b) Calculate the radius of the larger tree trunk.

    c) Richard says '2.35 goes into 3.77 about 1.6 times, so the radius of the larger trunk is about 60% bigger than the radius of the small trunk'. Is Richard right or is he wrong?

12* In 1893 the American engineer G W G Ferris built a 'Big Wheel' for the Chicago Exposition. It could carry 36 cabins, each holding 60 people. This Ferris wheel was $76\,m$ in diameter.

    a) Calculate the total number of people who could travel on the Ferris wheel when it was full.

    b) Calculate the circumference of the Ferris wheel.

13* A circular paddling pool has a circumference of $24.5\,m$.

    a) Find the radius, correct to 3 significant figures.

    b) Hence find the area of the surface of the pool, also correct to 3 significant figures.

14* A machine marks sheets of plastic into small squares measuring $6\,cm$ by $6\,cm$. A circular disc of radius $3\,cm$ is pressed from each square, and the plastic left over is discarded.

    a) Calculate the area of one circular disc.

    b) Write down the area of one small square.

    c) Find the percentage of plastic which is discarded.

15* The Earth travels around its orbit once each year. The Earth's orbit is approximately circular, with a radius of about 93 million miles.

    a) Taking this information as exact, calculate the distance that the Earth travels during one year. Give your answer in miles, correct to 2 significant figures.

    b) Rewrite your answer to part **a)** so that it is in kilometres. (1 mile = 1.609 kilometres)

16* A scientist is studying a colony of penguins. She notices that during a blizzard they huddle together in a circle of circumference $11.2\,m$.

    a) Calculate the radius of the circle.

    b) Calculate the area of the circle.

    c) Calculate the number of penguins in the colony, assuming that each penguin takes up $0.04\,m^2$ of ground space.

17* Damian has two circular discs. One is red; it has an area of 121 cm^2. The other is blue and has a circumference of 52 cm. Which of Damian's discs is larger?

18* The front wheel of my bicycle has diameter 64 cm.
   a) Find the circumference of the wheel, in centimetres.
   b) Write down the number of centimetres in 6 km.
   c) Find out how many times the front wheel turns when I cycle a distance of 6 km.

19* Tammy has cut out a circle of radius 12 cm, and Simon has cut out a circle of radius 6 cm.

Simon says to Tammy:

Your circle is twice the size of mine, so it should have twice the circumference and twice the area ... but something doesn't quite seem right

   a) Find the circumference and area of Simon's circle.
   b) Find the circumference and area of Tammy's circle.
   c) Write down a correct statement that Simon should have made about the circumference and area of Tammy's circle.

20* A sports centre is marking out a new running track. The diagram shows the outline design for the track:

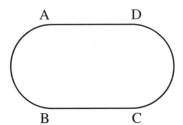

AB is a semicircular arc.
BC is a straight section of length 65 m.
CD is a semicircular arc.
DA is a straight section of length 65 m.
The length of the whole track is 200 m.

Calculate the radius of each semicircular arc.

Unit 34
Enlargement and reflection

In this Unit you will learn how to:
- ■ enlarge a shape using a whole number scale factor;
- ■ find the scale factor and centre of enlargement, given the object and image;
- ■ solve problems using enlargements and reflections.

A calculator is not required for this Unit.

34.1 Enlargement

To **enlarge** a shape you need a **scale factor** and a **centre of enlargement**. The enlargement is constructed by drawing rays outward from the centre of enlargement.

Example Enlarge this flag, using a scale factor of 2 and centre of enlargement (0, 0).

Solution

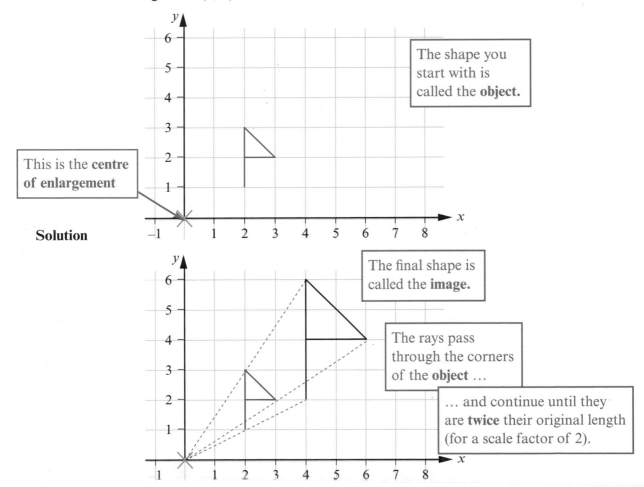

The shape you start with is called the **object.**

This is the **centre of enlargement**

The final shape is called the **image.**

The rays pass through the corners of the **object** …

… and continue until they are **twice** their original length (for a scale factor of 2).

The centre of enlargement does not always have to be at the origin.

Example   Enlarge this flag, using a scale factor of 2 and centre of enlargement (0, 1).

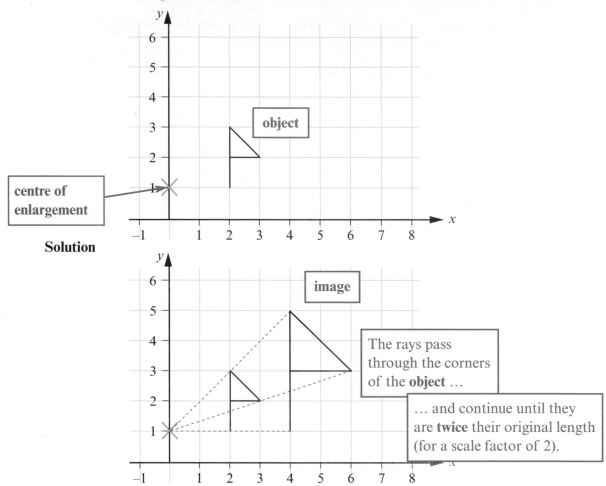

Solution

The rays pass through the corners of the **object** …

… and continue until they are **twice** their original length (for a scale factor of 2).

This example shows a different scale factor.

Example   Enlarge this flag, using a scale factor of 3 and centre of enlargement (–1, 2).

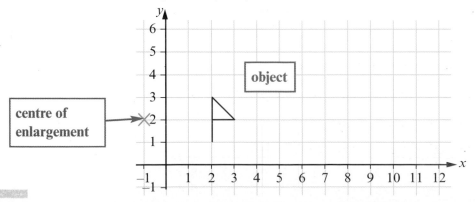

Solution

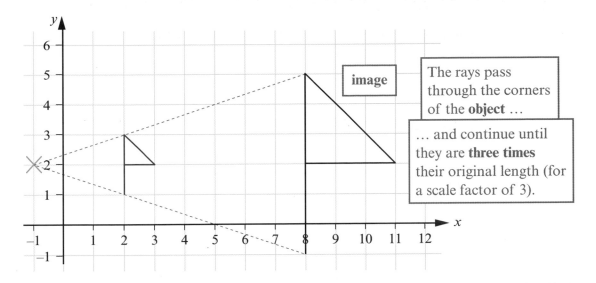

The rays pass through the corners of the **object** …

… and continue until they are **three times** their original length (for a scale factor of 3).

Exercise 34.1

For each of questions **1–4** you will need to make a copy of this grid:

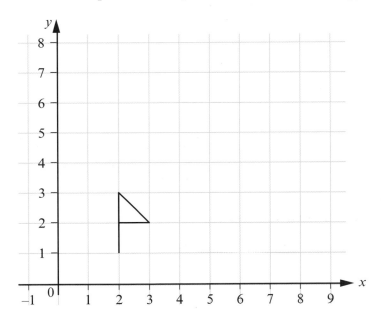

1 Enlarge the flag by scale factor 3, centre of enlargement (0, 0).

2 Enlarge the flag by scale factor 2, centre of enlargement (0, 2).

3 Enlarge the flag by scale factor 3, centre (1, 0).

4 Enlarge the flag by scale factor 2, centre (3, 1).

For each of questions **5–7** you will need to make a copy of this grid:

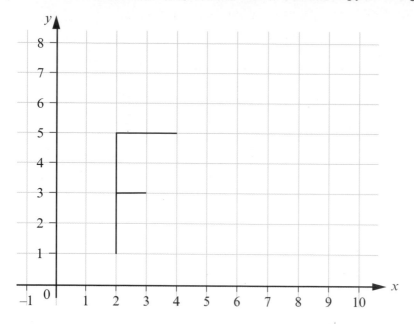

5 Enlarge the letter F by scale factor 2, centre of enlargement (1, 2).

6 Enlarge the letter F by scale factor 2, centre of enlargement (–1, 2).

7 Enlarge the letter F by scale factor 2, centre (5, 2).

8 Draw coordinate axes so that *x* and *y* can each range from –2 to 10.
   a) Construct rectangle ABCD where A is (9, 7), B (9, 9), C (6, 9) and D (6, 7).
   b) Enlarge the rectangle by scale factor 3, centre (10, 10).

9 Draw coordinate axes so that *x* and *y* can each range from –2 to 10.
   a) Construct a kite by joining the points (–1, 8), (2, 10), (4, 8), (2, 6) then back to (–1, 8).
   b) Enlarge the kite by scale factor 2, centre (–1, 10).

10 Draw coordinate axes so that *x* and *y* can each range from –2 to 10.
   a) Construct a triangle by joining the points (2, 2), (4, 5) and (1, 5).
   b) Enlarge the triangle by scale factor 3, centre (1, 3).

34.2 Finding the centre and scale factor

To find the centre and scale factor trace the rays backwards from the image through the object. The rays all come together, or **converge**, at the centre of enlargement.

Example   The large letter T is an enlargement of the smaller one. Find the coordinates of the centre of enlargement and the scale factor.

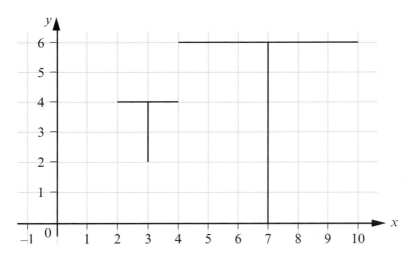

Solution

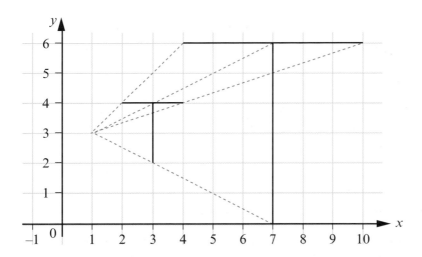

The centre of enlargement is (1, 3)

By comparing the height of the object (2 squares) and image (6 squares) the scale factor can be found:

Scale factor = 6 ÷ 2 = 3

Exercise 34.2

Copy each of these diagrams on to squared paper. The larger shape is an enlargement of the smaller one. Add suitable rays to your diagrams, and hence find the coordinates of the centre of enlargement and the scale factor in each case.

1

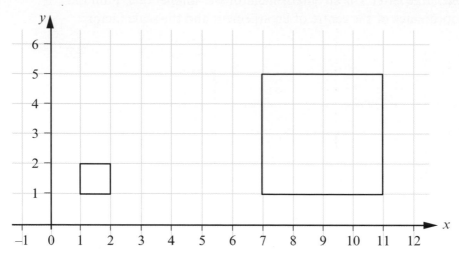

2

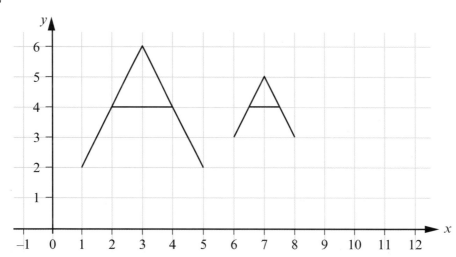

3

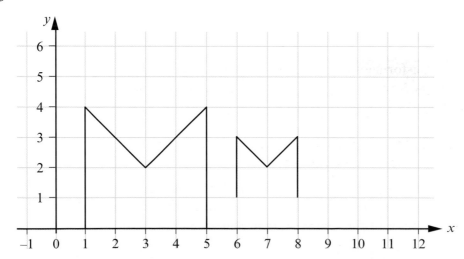

4

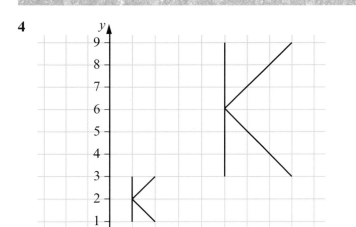

5

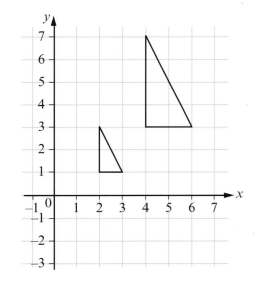

34.3 Enlargement and reflection

Sometimes two transformations are combined – for example, an enlargement followed by a reflection. The transformations must be done in the right order.

Example   Enlarge the given shape by scale factor 3, centre $(0, 2)$.
Then reflect the result in the mirror line $x = 8$.

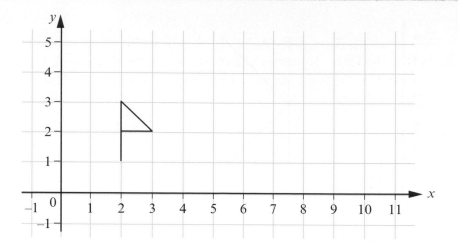

Solution   First, enlarge by scale factor 3, centre (0, 2):

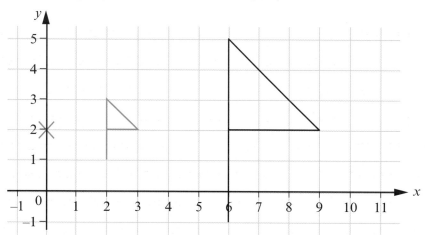

Now reflect in the line $x = 8$:

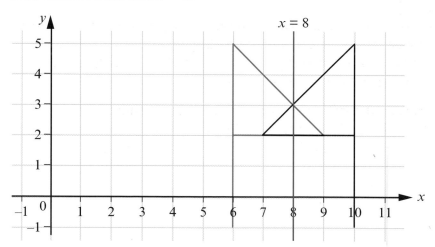

Exercise 34.3

For each of questions **1**–**8** you will need a coordinate grid in which x and y can each run from −5 to 10. On each diagram make a copy of this flag as your starting object. Then carry out the two given transformations. Make sure you do them in the right order!

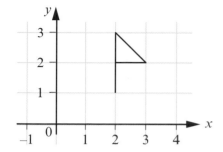

1 Enlargement with scale factor 3, centre (0, 0), followed by reflection in the line $x = 5$.

2 Enlargement with scale factor 3, centre (0, 0), followed by reflection in the line $y = 5$.

3 Enlargement with scale factor 4, centre (1, 2), followed by reflection in the line $x = 7$.

4 Enlargement with scale factor 2, centre (3, 0), followed by reflection in the line $x = 4$.

5 Enlargement with scale factor 2, centre (5, −2), followed by reflection in the line $x = 4$.

6 Reflection in the line $y = 5$, followed by enlargement with scale factor 4, centre (1, 10).

7 Enlargement with scale factor 3, centre (4, 1), followed by reflection in the line $x = 2$.

8 Reflection in the line $x = 2$, followed by enlargement with scale factor 3, centre (4, 1).

Summary

In this Unit you have learnt how to enlarge a shape from a given centre of enlargement, using a whole number enlargement factor. You have also worked backwards from a given object and image, to find the centre and the scale factor of the enlargement.

You have practised combining two transformations, such as an enlargement followed by a reflection. Remember to be careful here – it is important to carry out the transformations in the right order.

Review Exercise 34

For each of questions **1**–**5** you will need a copy of this diagram.

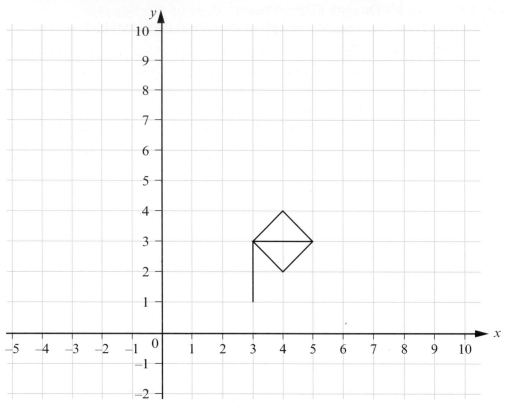

Enlarge the figure in the diagram above by:

1 Scale factor 2, with centre (0, 0).

2 Scale factor 2, with centre (2, 1).

3 Scale factor 3, with centre (4, 1).

4 Scale factor 2, with centre (5, −1).

5 Scale factor 4, with centre (5, 2).

6 Draw coordinate axes so that x and y can each range from −5 to 5.
  a) Construct a rectangle by joining the points (3, 1), (4, 2), (2, 4) and (1, 3).
  b) Enlarge the rectangle by scale factor 3, centre (4, 4).

7 Draw coordinate axes so that x can range from −2 to 12 and y from 0 to 10.
  a) Construct a parallelogram by joining the points (−1, 1), (2, 1), (3, 3) and (0, 3).
  b) Enlarge the parallelogram by scale factor 3, centre (−1, 0).

8 Draw coordinate axes so that x can range from 0 to 10 and y from −2 to 12.
  a) Construct a quadrilateral by joining the points (1, 0), (1, 2), (3, 4) and (5, 4).
  b) Name the type of quadrilateral you have obtained in part **a)**.
  c) Enlarge the quadrilateral by scale factor 3, centre (−1, 0).

9 The triangle formed by joining the points (2, 1), (4, 1) and (4, 2) is enlarged. The image under the enlargement is obtained by joining the points (−2, 5), (8, 5) and (8, 10).

   a) Draw coordinate axes and plot the object and image.

   b) Find the coordinates of the centre of enlargement and state the scale factor.

10 The rectangle formed by joining the points (2, 2), (2, 4), (1, 4) and (1, 2) is enlarged. The image under the enlargement is obtained by joining the points (−2, 4), (−2, 10), (−5, 10) and (−5, 4).

   a) Draw coordinate axes and plot the object and image.

   b) Find the coordinates of the centre of enlargement, and state the scale factor.

11 Make a copy of the T shape given below, making sure that the *x*-axis can run from 0 to 14 and the *y*-axis from 0 to 7.

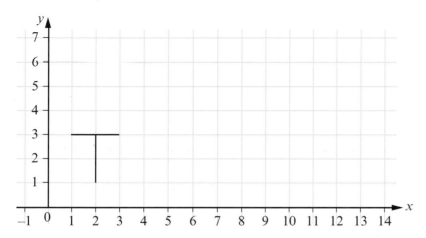

   a) Enlarge the letter T using scale factor 2, centre (1, 1).

   b) Reflect the image in the line $x = 7$.

12* The map below shows two points A and B. A horse is at point A, and wishes to walk to point B. He is thirsty, however, and must stop for a drink in the river on the way. The river flows along the *x*-axis.

   a) Make a copy of this diagram on squared paper.

   b) Find the shortest path the horse might take.

     [Clue: it is helpful to draw the reflection of point B, using the river as a mirror line.]

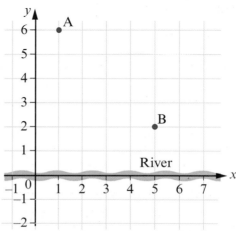

13*Draw coordinate axes in which x can run from 0 to 18 and y from 0 to 11.

   a) Draw a rectangle by joining the points (2, 1), (2, 3), (5, 3) and (5, 1). Enlarge this rectangle by scale factor 3, centre (−1, 1).

   b) Draw a rectangle by joining the four points (1, 1,), (2, 1), (2, 4) and (1, 4). Reflect this rectangle in the line $x = 7$.

   c) Draw a square by joining (9, 5), (10, 5), (10, 6), (9, 6) and another by joining (15, 5), (16, 5), (16, 6), (15, 6). Reflect both squares in the line $y = 4$.

   d) Construct a triangle by joining the points (8, 7), ($12\frac{1}{2}$, 10) and (17, 7).

   When you have finished, you might like to colour in the result.

14*Anna says 'If you do a scale factor 2 enlargement centred at the origin and a reflection in the x-axis, it doesn't matter in which order you do them'. Is Anna right or is she wrong?

15*Jim drew an object using invisible ink. He then enlarged it using scale factor 4 (and ordinary ink) before the object faded from view. The diagram shows the image, drawn on squared paper. The centre of enlargement is at (0, 1).

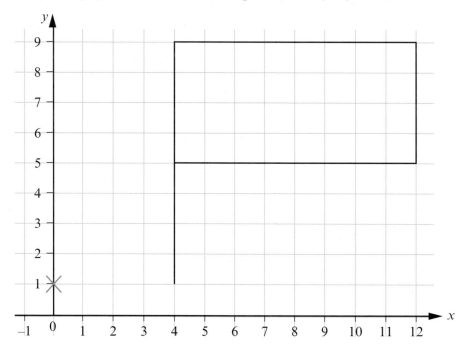

Make a copy of this diagram, and add the position of the object (using ordinary ink).

Unit 35
Frequency diagrams and pie charts

In this Unit you will learn how to:
- collect and record continuous data;
- construct and interpret frequency diagrams;
- construct pie charts.

You will need a calculator and a protractor for some of the later exercises.
You may also find a pie chart scale useful.

35.1 Discrete and continuous data

Quantities like length, time or weight are **continuous**. They are usually obtained by measurement, and can only be recorded to a limited level of accuracy (e.g. 3 significant figures).

Quantities like the number of people on a bus, or the number of marbles in a bag are **discrete**. They are usually obtained by counting, and can be recorded exactly.

Example   Decide whether each of these is discrete or continuous:
   a) the number of pages in a book;
   b) the temperature of a cup of tea;
   c) the area of a sheet of paper.

Solution   **a)** The number of pages can be counted exactly: it is discrete.
   b) The temperature can only be measured approximately: it is continuous.
   c) The area can only be measured approximately: it is continuous.

Exercise 35.1
Say whether each of these is discrete or continuous:

1 ✓ The number of words on a page of a newspaper

2 The length of a CD track, in minutes.

3 The time taken for a girl to run 100 m.

4 The number of files stored on a computer floppy disk.

5 The length of a roll of adhesive tape.

6 The marks scored in a 25-question multiple-choice test.

7 ✓ The area of a wall, in square metres.

8 ✓ The number of 1-litre pots of paint required to paint a wall.

9 The amount of money in my bank account on a given day.

10 The weight of a tomato.

35.2 Frequency tables

When continuous data is recorded it can be rounded off (e.g. to the nearest centimetre) before being written down. Watch out – the data then looks discrete but it is not.

Another method is to record the data using a tally chart (similar to those used for discrete data in Unit 9). The values are divided into **classes**, and each class has a corresponding **frequency**.

Example   The heights of 20 indoor plants have been recorded in centimetres, correct to the nearest millimetre, as follows:

32.1   23.6   30.8   34.1   28.0   21.5   27.5   38.3   19.8   22.9
22.7   17.2   25.2   21.6   29.3   27.0   26.1   32.8   28.9   27.0

a) Use a tally method to construct a grouped frequency table.
b) A plant is chosen at random. Find the probability that its height is less than 25 cm.

Solution   a)

This **tally chart** contains five **classes.**

Height x (cm)	Tally
$15.0 \leq x < 20.0$	
$20.0 \leq x < 25.0$	
$25.0 \leq x < 30.0$	
$30.0 \leq x < 35.0$	
$35.0 \leq x < 40.0$	

This class includes 15.0 but not 20.0.

This mark corresponds to 32.1.

This is the finished **tally chart.**

Height x (cm)	Tally	Frequency
$15.0 \leq x < 20.0$	||	2
$20.0 \leq x < 25.0$	卌	5
$25.0 \leq x < 30.0$	卌 |||	8
$30.0 \leq x < 35.0$	||||	4
$35.0 \leq x < 40.0$			1

b) $P(x < 25.0) = \dfrac{2+5}{20}$

$= \dfrac{7}{20}$

$= \underline{0.35}$

Exercise 35.2

1 The masses of 25 kittens are measured correct to the nearest gram:

144	122	129	150	155		133	147	138	139	121
103	126	131	135	132		141	130	136	142	151
133	138	121	135	146						

    a) Draw up a frequency table using classes of $100 \le x < 110$ and so on.

    b) What percentage of the kittens have a mass above 140 g?

2 The heights of 30 children are measured correct to the nearest centimetre:

101	125	115	122	136		134	103	120	128	114
126	112	124	105	122		112	127	119	108	139
117	149	118	127	111		141	115	129	121	122

    a) Draw up a frequency table using classes of $100 \le x < 110$ and so on.

    b) How many children have a height of less than 130 cm?

3 ✔ The ages of 24 trees are recorded, to the nearest year:

2	15	19	15	15		16	17	19	10	11
17	17	11	13	2		14	16	19	2	15
18	12	13	19							

    a) Draw up a frequency table using classes of $0 \le x < 5$ and so on.

    b) Three of these trees were planted following a storm. How long ago do you think the storm took place?

35.3 Histograms and frequency polygons

When continuous data is grouped in classes the frequencies can be displayed in a number of ways.

A **histogram** looks like a bar chart, but the scale on the *x*-axis is continuous, and there are no gaps between the bars. A **frequency polygon** is obtained by joining the mid-points of the tops of the histogram columns.

Example

Height x (cm)	Tally	Frequency
$15.0 \le x < 20.0$	|	2
$20.0 \le x < 25.0$	⧼⧽⧼⧽	5
$25.0 \le x < 30.0$	⧼⧽⧼⧽ |||	8
$30.0 \le x < 35.0$	||||	4
$35.0 \le x < 40.0$	|	1

Illustrate this data:

a) with a histogram;

b) with a frequency polygon.

Solution **a)**

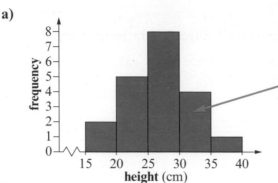

You are graphing a **continuous** quantity – so no gaps between the columns!

This is a **histogram**, not a bar chart.

b)

Remember to include this zigzag if the *x*-axis does not extend all the way back to zero.

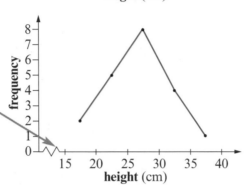

The five points are plotted and then joined with straight line segments.

Do not try to close this polygon on to the *x*-axis.

Exercise 35.3

In questions **1–6** draw a histogram and a frequency polygon to illustrate the data given in the table.

1

Diameter d (mm)	Frequency
$0 \leq d < 10$	8
$10 \leq d < 20$	9
$20 \leq d < 30$	12
$30 \leq d < 40$	7
$40 \leq d < 50$	1
$50 \leq d < 60$	4

2 ✔

Time t (mins)	Frequency
$15 \leq t < 20$	3
$20 \leq t < 25$	1
$25 \leq t < 30$	3
$30 \leq t < 35$	9
$35 \leq t < 40$	7

3

Mass x (grams)	Frequency
$60 \leq x < 70$	3
$70 \leq x < 80$	6
$80 \leq x < 90$	11
$90 \leq x < 100$	8
$100 \leq x < 110$	7
$110 \leq x < 120$	5

4

Temperature T (°C)	Frequency
$-10 \leq T < -5$	12
$-5 \leq T < 0$	7
$0 \leq T < 5$	5
$5 \leq T < 10$	2
$10 \leq T < 15$	1

5

Speed v (m/s)	Frequency
$20 \le v < 30$	6
$30 \le v < 40$	8
$40 \le v < 50$	7
$50 \le v < 60$	2

6

Volume V (ml)	Frequency
$160 < V \le 175$	3
$175 < V \le 190$	2
$190 < V \le 205$	3
$205 < V \le 220$	4
$220 < V \le 235$	10
$235 < V \le 250$	3

35.4 Pie charts

One of the most commonly used statistical diagrams is the **pie chart**; you have met simple cases in Unit 19 earlier in this book. Remember that pie charts should only be used for **categorical** data, i.e. data broken into several categories such as colour, type of animal etc. Continuous statistical data should not be displayed using pie charts: histograms or frequency polygons are more appropriate.

In this section you will practise making pie charts for data which does not always conveniently multiply up to 360°.

Example   The 29 pupils in Class 3 are asked to name their favourite type of drink: 11 say it is cola, 9, milk shake, 6, mineral water and 3 name other drinks. Display this information in a pie chart.

Solution   There are 29 pupils in total, so multiply by $\frac{360}{29}$ to find the angle in degrees:

Drink	Frequency	Angle
Cola	11	137°
Milk shake	9	112°
Mineral water	6	74°
Other	3	37°

$\frac{11 \times 360}{29} = 136.55\ldots$
which is rounded to 137°.

The angle – in degrees – should be marked clearly.

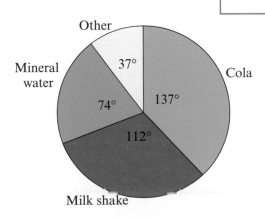

Exercise 35.4

1 ✓ Forty-four motorists are surveyed and asked to name the country in which their car was built: 21 reply Great Britain, 10, France, 5, Germany and the rest Other countries. Draw up a table of angles, and display this information in a pie chart.

2 Littlewood Farm has an area of 1050 acres. Of this 450 acres are used for dairy farming, 220 acres for growing cash crops and 120 acres are woodland. The rest of the farmland provides animal feed. Draw up a table of angles, and display this information in a pie chart.

3 Ginnie has a collection of toy animals, made up of 21 puppies, 11 ponies, 18 kittens and 7 rabbits. Display this information in a pie chart.

4 Last August there were 17 sunny days and 9 overcast days; the rest were wet. Display this information in a pie chart.

Summary

In this Unit you have learnt to recognise the difference between discrete and continuous quantities. Discrete quantities are usually counted to obtain exact answers, whereas continuous quantities are measured to a limited level of precision.

You have drawn up frequency tables for grouped continuous data, and used your tables to display histograms or frequency polygons. Remember that there should be no gaps between the columns of a histogram.

You have also extended construction of pie charts to include those with more difficult totals, rounding the angles to a sensible level of accuracy. Remember that pie charts should only be used for categorical data.

Review Exercise 35

In questions **1–6** say whether the given quantity is discrete or continuous.

1 The number of baby mice on sale in a pet shop.

2 The time it takes to make a cup of tea.

3 The number of photographs in a magazine.

4 The price of a bottle of nail polish.

5 The speed at which an athlete can run.

6 The amount of soft drink in a bottle.

7 The table shows the running time of twenty CD tracks, in minutes and seconds. For example, 2:33 indicates 2 minutes and 33 seconds.

2:08	3:00	3:25	2:24	5:22	3:25	2:08	3:13	4:46	3:06
4:50	3:07	2:24	3:15	2:55	3:21	6:57	0:39	2:04	3:47

a) Draw up a tally chart, using $0 \le t < 1$ and so on, where t is the running time in minutes.

b) The random play function on my CD player chooses one of these tracks. What is the probability that the track is over three minutes long?

8 The table shows the body-length of 24 fish caught at a local lake. The lengths are in millimetres, rounded off to the nearest millimetre.

208	144	177	199	155	166	169	172	177	170
157	183	175	172	161	168	159	195	174	171
141	179	198	160						

a) Draw up a tally chart for the body lengths. Use classes of $140 \le l < 150$ and so on.
b) Display the data in a histogram.
c) What percentage of the fish are under 180 mm in length?

9 During the last month I have seen 16 sparrows, 13 starlings, 5 blackbirds and 1 robin in my back garden. Illustrate this data with a pie chart.

10* Alice carried out a survey among her friends. She asked each person to name the (terrestrial) TV channel which broadcasts their favourite programme. The replies were:

Channel	BBC 1	BBC 2	ITV	Channel 4	Channel 5
Frequency	17	3	14	6	0

a) Display this information in a pie chart.
b) The survey was carried out in 1997, when Channel 5 was only available in certain parts of the country. What does this suggest about the area where Alice lives?

11* Fifty-four people are asked how many hours of vigorous exercise they do per week, on average. Their replies are summarised in this table:

Time t spent exercising (hours)	Number of people
$0 \le t < 1$	18
$1 \le t < 2$	23
$2 \le t < 3$	9
$3 \le t < 4$	3
$4 \le t < 5$	1

a) Explain briefly whether it would be better to display this data in a pie chart or in a frequency polygon.
b) Draw the appropriate diagram.

12* A class of children were asked to name their favourite day of the week. Eleven children say that it is Saturday, and this information is represented on a pie chart using an angle of 172°.

a) Calculate the total number of children in the class.
b) Calculate the angle of the sector representing Sunday, the favourite day of 8 children.

Unit 36
Scatter diagrams and other graphs

In this Unit you will learn how to:
- draw conclusions from scatter diagrams;
- use conversion graphs;
- obtain information from other graphs.

A calculator may be used when necessary in this Unit.

36.1 Scatter diagrams

A **scatter diagram** shows how two statistical quantities might be related. Points are plotted on a set of (x, y) axes, and any **trend** is observed. Often you will see **positive correlation** or **negative correlation**.

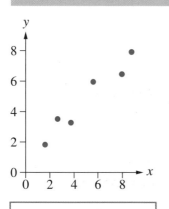

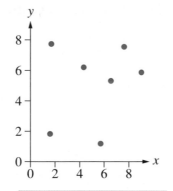

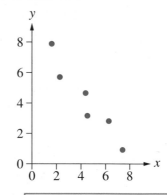

positive correlation:
the points follow a line with a positive gradient (uphill).

no correlation:
the points are scattered with no obvious trend.

negative correlation:
the points follow a line with a negative gradient (downhill).

Example   Look at the graph on the right. It shows the number of cups of tea and glasses of cola sold by a café on ten different occasions.

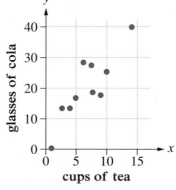

Describe the relationship between the sales of tea and cola. Explain how the graph helps you describe the relationship.

Solution   Sales of tea and cola appear to be show <u>positive correlation</u>.

You can see this because the scatter diagram shows points clustering around a <u>straight line with positive gradient</u>.

Example In an experiment the following values of x and y were recorded:

x	2	3	5	6	7	7	10
y	8	9	4	4	6	5	1

Plot these values on a scatter diagram. Describe the relationship between x and y.

Solution

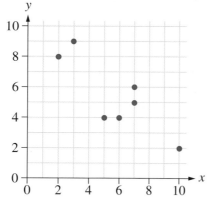

x and y appear to show <u>negative correlation</u>, as the trend line slopes downwards.

Exercise 36.1

In questions **1–5** draw coordinate axes and plot the given points. Say whether there is any evidence of correlation between x and y; if so, indicate whether it is positive or negative and whether you think the correlation is strong or weak.

1 ✔

x	1	8	4	12	8	9	2	5	7
y	3	6	5	8	9	7	3	4	6

2 ✔

x	2	7	5	3	3	9	6
y	5	2	4	6	1	7	8

3 ✔

x	2	3	3	6	6	10	10	12
y	3	1	4	2	7	9	7	5

4 ✔

x	2	4	4	6	8	9
y	9	6	7	5	3	4

5 ✔

x	2	7	10	5	7	4	9	2
y	2	2	4	5	5	7	8	9

6 In a 'Dog of the Year Show' two judges award marks out of 20 to each of eight dogs. The marks are given in the table below:

Dog	Fido	Crystal	Spike	Gnasher	d'Arcy	Spot	Lucky
Judge A	11	18	15	11	14	7	5
Judge B	13	19	13	12	16	4	8

a) Illustrate these marks on a scatter diagram.

b) Comment on the apparent relationship between the two marks.

7 ✔ In an experiment ten seeds are planted in containers of moist soil and left for a period of time. At the end of the experiment small plants have developed, and their heights are measured. Each container had been stored at a different temperature:

Plant	A	B	C	D	E	F	G	H	I	J
Temperature (°C)	5	10	12	14	16	18	20	22	24	25
Height (mm)	0	8	9	16	16	19	23	29	28	32

a) What do you think happened to Plant A?

b) Plot the results for the other nine plants on a scatter diagram. (Temperature on the *x*-axis and height on the *y*-axis.)

c) Comment on the relationship between height and temperature.

36.2 Conversion graphs

If you want to convert miles into kilometres, or French francs into pounds sterling, for example, you can use a **conversion graph**. The graph will often be a **straight line** passing **through the origin**, indicating **direct proportion**.

Example Delphine is planning to go shopping in London this Saturday, and in Paris next Saturday. She expects £1 to be equivalent to 9.40 French francs. Use the conversion graph to convert:

a) £55 into French francs;

b) £14 .99 into French francs;

c) 275 francs into £.

Solution **a)** From the graph on page 243, £55 is worth about 510 francs.

Magenta graph

b) £14.99 cannot be read accurately on this graph – so use £15 instead.

Green graph

From the graph £15 is worth about 140 francs.

Red graph

c) From the graph 275 francs is about £29.

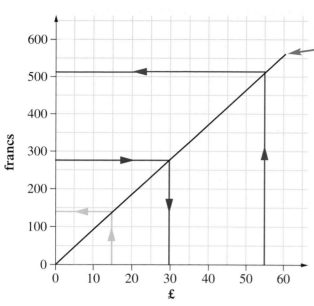

£60 is equivalent to 60 × 9.40 = 564 francs so the line goes through (60, 564)

Exercise 36.2

1 On graph paper draw coordinate axes like this:

a) Plot a point to show that 100 miles is about the same as 160 km. Draw a straight line connecting this point to the origin.

b) ✔ Use your graph to convert 45 miles to kilometres.

c) ✔ Use your graph to convert 140 km to miles.

2 On graph paper draw coordinate axes like this:

a) Plot a point to show that 88 pounds is about the same as 40 kg. Draw a straight line connecting this point to the origin.

b) Use your graph to convert 25 pounds to kilograms.

c) Use your graph to convert 30 kg to pounds.

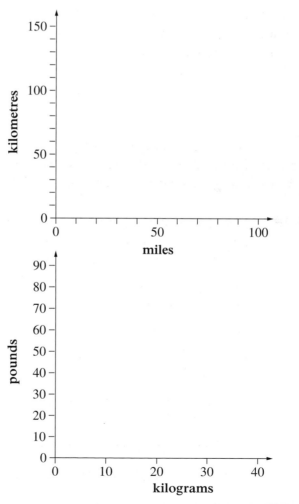

3 Draw coordinates axes in which x can run from 0 to 100 and y from 0 to 200.

   a) Taking £1 to be equal to $1.65 (US dollars), calculate the number of dollars in £100.
   b) Plot a point on your graph to represent your answer to part **a)** and draw a straight line joining it to the origin.
   c) Use your graph to convert £85 into dollars.
   d) Use your graph to convert $65 into pounds.

4 Draw coordinates axes in which x can run from 0 to 40 and y from 0 to 200.

   a) Taking 1 gallon to be equivalent to 4.55 litres, calculate the number of litres in 40 gallons.
   b) Plot a point on your graph to represent your answer to part **a)** and draw a straight line joining it to the origin.
   c) Use your graph to find the number of litres in 25 gallons.
   d) Use your graph to find the number of gallons in 40 litres.

5 ✔ Land areas may be measured in acres or hectares. 1 hectare is about 2.47 acres.

   a) Calculate the number of hectares equivalent to 50 acres.
   b) Using your answer to part **a)**, construct a conversion graph.
   c) Use your graph to convert 15 hectares to acres.
   d) Use your graph to convert 15 acres to hectares.

36.3 Obtaining information from other graphs

Scatter graphs and conversion graphs are only two of the many ways in which graphs can be used to obtain information. In this section you will meet other types of graphs in which information can be obtained by reading from one axis to the graph and then across to the other axis.

Example   The growth chart shows how an average baby girl's weight will increase throughout her first year. Using the graph, find approximate values for:

   a) the weight of an average baby girl, at age 32 weeks;
   b) the age of an average baby girl, whose weight is 6 kilograms.

   From the graph estimate the weight at birth of an average baby girl.

Solution   Reading on to the graph on page 245 as shown:

   a) The average weight at 32 weeks is <u>8.3 kilograms</u>.
   b) The age of a baby girl weighing 6 kilograms is about <u>13 weeks</u>.

   The graph shows an average birth weight of <u>3.5 kilograms</u>.

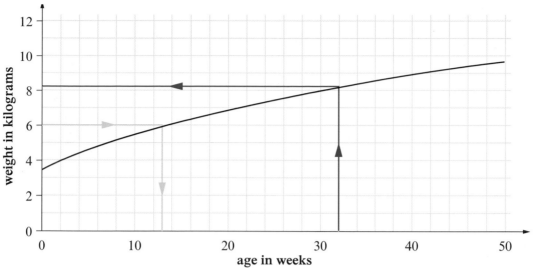

Exercise 36.3

1 A bank publishes this table to show how much an investment of £100 would be worth after up to 20 years:

Years	2	4	6	8	10	15	20
Value (£)	110	121	134	147	162	207	265

a) Draw a graph to illustrate this information.
b) Use your graph to obtain the value of the investment after 12 years.

2 ✔ A stone is dropped over the edge of a high cliff. The table shows its velocity during the next six seconds:

Time (seconds)	0	1	2	3	4	5	6
Velocity (metres per second)	0	5	20	45	80	125	0

a) Illustrate this data on a graph, with time along the x-axis and velocity on the y-axis.
b) Use your graph to estimate the velocity after 4.5 seconds.
c) Use your graph to estimate the time at which the velocity reaches 40 m/s.
d) How many seconds after being dropped does the stone land?

3 The table shows the number of pupils on the roll of Greenview school at 10-year intervals:

Year	1950	1960	1970	1980	1990
Number of pupils	44	292	311	329	351

Greenview School opened in 1950. An oak tree was planted when there were 300 pupils on the roll, and a swimming pool was opened when there were 340 pupils on the roll.
a) Display the information in the table on a graph.
b) Use your graph to estimate the year in which the oak tree was planted.
c) Use your graph to estimate the year in which the swimming pool was opened.

Summary

In this Unit you have learned how to draw scatter diagrams, and used them to identify positive or negative correlation. Remember that for positive correlation the trend line goes up as you move to the right, while for negative correlation it goes down.

You have used conversion graphs to solve problems with change of units, including money. Remember that these graphs are quick and easy to use, but are not as accurate as solving the problem by arithmetic. You have also used other types of graphs to solve problems.

Review Exercise 36

1 In an experiment the following results were obtained:

x	10	3	8	2	9	4	5	7	1	6
y	1	9	3	9	2	6	5	4	12	5

a) Plot the data on a scatter diagram.

b) Describe briefly how the quantities x and y appear to be related.

2 The table shows the scores achieved by eight Year 9 students in an algebra test. The test was divided into two parts, Paper 1 and Paper 2.

Paper 1	18	20	11	8	13	9	12	17
Paper 2	14	18	10	9	11	8	10	17

a) Plot these scores on a scatter diagram, with Paper 1 scores along the x-axis and Paper 2 scores along the y-axis.

b) Describe the relationship between the scores on the two papers.

c) Joe scored 11 on Paper 1 but was absent for Paper 2 so he took it at home. Joe's Paper 2 was then marked to give a score of 19. Explain whether this score fits the rest of the data.

3 In an experiment the following results were obtained:

x	10	15	20	25	30	35	40
y	10	12	15	16	21	20	25

a) Plot the data on a scatter diagram.

b) Describe briefly how the quantities x and y appear to be related.

4 Tomi has been conducting an experiment into verbal and numerical skills. She gives two tests to a set of nine friends, with these results:

Verbal skills (x)	60	65	70	75	80	85	90	95	100
Numerical skills (y)	75	65	75	85	75	60	95	70	75

a) Plot the data on a scatter diagram.

b) Write down the conclusion which Tomi might make about how the verbal and numerical skills appear to be related.

5 Frank is going on holiday to Germany. He decides to make up a conversion chart between German marks (DM) and pounds sterling (£). He works on a rate of £1 = 2.88 DM.

a) Draw up a conversion graph, with £ along the x-axis and DM on the y-axis. Make sure that x can run from 0 to 100 and y from 0 to 300.

b) Frank has to pay a bill for 200 DM. Use your graph to convert this into £.

c) At the end of the holiday Frank changes 120 DM back into £, but is charged £5 commission by the bank. Using your graph, find out how much Frank obtains after he has paid the commission.

6 Astronomers sometimes measure distances in light years, and sometimes in parsecs. One parsec is equivalent to 3.26 light years.

a) Write down the number of light years equivalent to 10 parsecs.

b) Construct a conversion graph which can be used to convert up to 10 parsecs into light years.

c) Use your graph to find the number of light years in 8.5 parsecs.

d) The star Sirius is about 8.6 light years from Earth. Use your graph to convert this distance into parsecs.

7 The energy value of foods used to be measured in kilocalories (kcal); nowadays kilojoules (kJ) are used instead. 1 kcal is equivalent to 4.187 kJ.

a) Using graph paper, construct a conversion graph with kilocalories along the x-axis and kilojoules along the y-axis. Make sure that x can run from 0 to 500 and y from 0 to 2100.

b) Kelly notices that a chocolate mousse has an energy rating of 875 kJ per 100 g. Use your graph to express this in kcal.

c) As part of a healthy-eating programme Kelly decides to eat no more than 400 kcal in total at lunch time. Express this figure in kilojoules.

8* Temperatures can be measured either in degrees Fahrenheit (F) or degrees Celsius (C). A temperature of 0°C is equivalent to 32°F, while 100°C is the same as 212°F.

a) Draw coordinate axes in which x represents °C and y represents °F. Make sure that x can run from 0 to 100 and y from 30 to 220.

b) Plot the points (0, 32) and (100, 212) on your graph, and join them up with a straight line to make a conversion graph.

c) Use your graph to convert 30°C into °F, and 180°F into °C.

d) Does your conversion graph indicate that y is proportional to x?

9* The table shows approximate figures for the world's population at intervals of 100 years:

Year	1500	1600	1700	1800	1900
Population (millions)	425	545	610	900	1625

a) Draw a graph with the year plotted along the *x*-axis and population along the *y*-axis.

b) From your graph estimate the world's population in **i)** 1550; **ii)** 1750.

c) Explain briefly why it would be unwise to estimate the world's population in 1950 from this graph.

10* Andrei asks ten adults to tell him their age and shoe size (British units). Their replies are:

Age (years)	21	22	22	25	26	27	29	30	30	35
Shoe size	8	10	6	11	7	7	8	10	6	9

a) Display Andrei's data in a scatter diagram (age along the *x*-axis).

b) Comment briefly on whether there is any evidence of correlation between age and shoe size for Andrei's data.

c) Naomi asks ten members of her youth club to tell her their age and shoe size. After graphing the results Naomi says:

If you look at my graph there is very clear evidence of strong positive correlation between age and shoe size.

d) Suggest a reason why Naomi's data shows strong correlation but Andrei's does not.

Unit 37
Probability

In this Unit you will learn how to:
- use a sample space diagram for the outcome of two experiments;
- use tables and tree diagrams;
- use the principle that the probabilities of mutually exclusive outcomes add up to 1.

 A calculator will be required for this Unit.

37.1 Sample space diagrams

A **sample space** diagram is a way of showing the combined probability of the outcomes of two experiments. It usually takes the form of a table.

Example   Two fair dice are thrown, and the scores are recorded. Find the probability that the total of the two scores is 9.

Solution   We begin by drawing up a table:

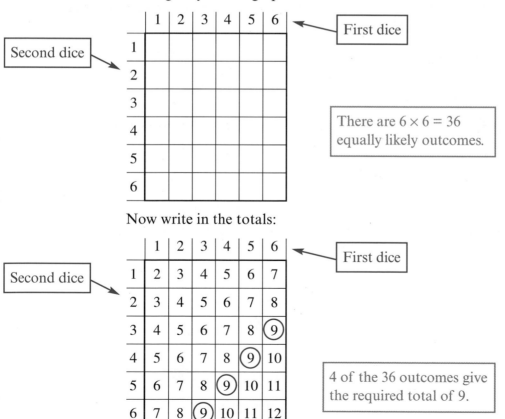

First dice

Second dice

There are $6 \times 6 = 36$ equally likely outcomes.

Now write in the totals:

First dice

Second dice

	1	2	3	4	5	6
1	2	3	4	5	6	7
2	3	4	5	6	7	8
3	4	5	6	7	8	⑨
4	5	6	7	8	⑨	10
5	6	7	8	⑨	10	11
6	7	8	⑨	10	11	12

4 of the 36 outcomes give the required total of 9.

$$P(\text{total of } 9) = \frac{\text{number of ways of getting a total of } 9}{\text{total number of equally likely outcomes}}$$

$$= \frac{4}{36}$$

$$= \underline{\frac{1}{9}}$$

> You could give the answer as a decimal: 0.111 111 …
> but it is usually easier to write it as a fraction.

Exercise 37.1

Draw up a sample space diagram for each of these situations, and use it to answer the question. Answers should be left as fractions, cancelled down where possible.

1 Two fair dice are thrown and the total is recorded. Find the probability that the total is:
a) odd;   **b)** prime;   **c)** five.
What is the most likely total?

2 A spinner has four equal sectors, labelled 1, 2, 3, 4. It is spun twice. Find the probability that the total score is 6.

3 ✔ A spinner has six equal sectors, labelled 1, 2, 2, 3, 3, 6. It is spun twice. Find the probability that the total score is 6.

4 Two coins are tossed. Find the probability that the result is:
a) two heads;   **b)** two tails;   **c)** one head and one tail.

5 One spinner has three equal sectors labelled 1, 2, 3; another spinner has five equal sectors labelled 1, 2, 3, 4, 5. Each spinner is spun, and the total score is obtained. Find the probability that this total is 6. Find also the most likely total.

6 ✔ I have four coins in my left pocket: they are 2p, 5p, 5p and 10p. I have three coins in my right pocket: they are 2p, 5p and 20p. Two coins are chosen at random, one from each pocket. Find the probability that:
a) both coins are 5p;
b) the total value of the coins is 7p.

7 My top drawer contains 3 red socks and 2 black socks, while my second drawer contains 2 red socks and 4 black socks. In the dark I take one sock from each drawer. Find the probability that I end up with: **a)** two red socks;   **b)** two socks of the same colour.

8 A pack of cards is shuffled, and one card is chosen at random; its suit is recorded. From a second shuffled pack another card is chosen, and again its suit is noted. Find the probability that the cards are:

a) both diamonds;   **b)** both black.

[There are two red suits (hearts, diamonds) and two black suits (clubs, spades).]

9 Lenny is in a hurry to order some fast food, so he chooses randomly from beef burger, chicken burger or veggie burger. This is accompanied by either jacket potato, French fries or salad, again chosen randomly. Find the probability that Lenny's chosen meal includes French fries but not a veggie burger.

10 ✔ Two fair dice are thrown and the two scores are multiplied to form a product, which is then recorded. For example, when one dice shows 4 and the other shows 3 then a product of 12 is recorded.

Find the probability that the product is:

a) 12; **b)** 15; **c)** odd; **d)** prime.

37.2 Tree diagrams

A **tree diagram** is used when there are two or more stages to a problem, each with only two or three outcomes. Probabilities are written on the branches, and multiplied to obtain the final total.

Example   The probability that I buy a lottery ticket on a Saturday is 0.3, and the probability that my wife does is 0.4. Draw a tree diagram, and use it to find the probability that

a) we both buy tickets;   **b)** only one of us does.

Solution

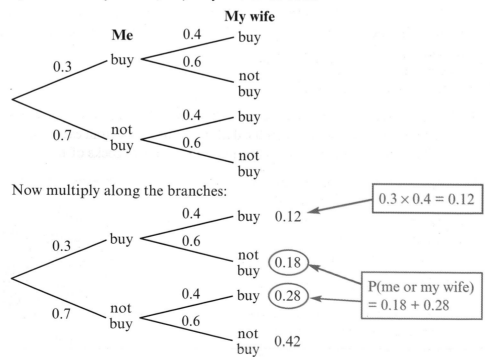

a) P(we both buy tickets) = 0.12
b) P(only one of us does) = 0.18 + 0.28
$$= 0.46$$

Warning!
Make sure that you understand when to multiply and when to add probabilities.
You **multiply** along the branches – e.g. 0.3×0.6 to get 0.18 at the end.
You **add** in order to combine alternative end points – e.g. $0.18 + 0.28$.

We can multiply the probabilities in this case because we have
assumed that my decision about whether to buy a ticket is
independent of my wife's decision.

Exercise 37.2

Solve each of these problems with the aid of a clearly labelled tree diagram.
You can assume that the events are independent.

1 ✔ The probability that Usha can finish the crossword in her daily newspaper in under
half an hour is 0.6. Calculate the probability that, on two randomly chosen days,
Usha is able to finish both crosswords in under half an hour each.

2 The probability that Tom forgets to bring his calculator to a mathematics lesson is
0.25. Find the probability that, in two successive lessons, Tom forgets his calculator:
a) on both occasions; **b)** only once.

3 When Boris goes shopping he visits the baker's with probability $\frac{3}{20}$ while the
corresponding figure for Doris is $\frac{7}{20}$. They are both going shopping tomorrow.
Calculate the probability that at least one of them will visit the baker's.

4 ✔ The probability that a Christmas cracker detonates successfully is 0.8. Three
crackers are chosen at random. Calculate the probability that exactly two of them
detonate properly.

5 On my journey to work I have to drive through two sets of traffic lights. The
probability that I find the first set on red is 0.2, but the probability that the second set
is red is 0.7. Find the probability that, on a randomly chosen journey:
a) both sets are red; **b)** only the first set is red; **c)** exactly one set is red.

6 A cereal manufacturer places a plastic toy inside each cereal packet. When a packet is
chosen at random the probability that it contains a submarine is 0.3, while the
probability of an aircraft is 0.45. The only other possibility is that the toy is a tractor.
a) Calculate the probability of obtaining a tractor.
b) Two packets are chosen at random. Calculate the probability of obtaining exactly
one submarine.
c) Three packets are chosen at random. Calculate the probability of obtaining at
least one aircraft.

7 A newspaper reckons that a quarter of the voters in a certain area support the Progressive Party. Four people are chosen at random and asked which party they support. Calculate the probability that exactly one of them supports the Progressive Party.

8 When a certain type of rocket is used to launch a satellite there is a 5% chance that the launch will be unsuccessful.
   a) Express the probability 5% as a decimal.
   b) Four launches are planned. Find the probability that only three of them are successful.

9 In a multiple-choice test there are five suggested answers to each question. Only one answer is right. I decide to guess the answers to the last three questions.
   a) Explain why the probability of guessing an answer correctly is 0.2.
   b) Find the probability that I guess all three correctly.
   c) Find the probability that I guess only one of the answers correctly.

10 ✔ When United play a match at home they reckon to win, draw or lose with probabilities 0.5, 0.3 and 0.2 respectively. United are due to play their next two matches at home. Find the probability that they will:
   a) win both matches;   **b)** win only one of them, and draw the other;
   c) lose both matches.

Summary

In this Unit you have learnt how to use a sample space diagram for the probability of a combined event, and a tree diagram for a sequence of events. In using tree diagrams you multiply the probabilities as you work along the branches.

You have also deduced the value of a missing probability by using the principle that the probabilities describing all the alternative outcomes to an experiment must always add up to 1.

Review Exercise 37

1 When I play chess against a certain friend the result is that I either win, draw or lose. I win a game with probability 0.4 and draw with probability 0.35.
   a) Calculate the probability that I lose a game.
   b) Calculate the probability that I lose three games in a row.

2 In a game of Paper, Scissors, Stone I am equally likely to win, draw or lose. I play two games. Find the probability that :
   a) I win the first game;
   b) I win both games;
   c) I do not win either game.

3 Two fair dice are thrown. Draw a sample space diagram to show the 36 equally likely outcomes, and use your diagram to find:
a) the probability that the total is 10;
b) the probability that the total is less than 5;
c) the probability that at least one of the dice shows a 6.

4 One bag contains a red ball, a blue ball and a yellow ball, while a second bag contains two red balls and one yellow ball. Two balls are randomly chosen, one from each bag. Draw a sample space diagram, and use it find the probability that
a) both balls are red;
b) at least one ball is red;
c) both balls are the same colour.

5 A computer game produces letters which I have to arrange to make a word. The letters are classed as either vowels or consonants. When a letter is chosen the probability of getting a vowel is 0.3.
a) Write down the probability of getting a consonant.
b) Draw a tree diagram to show the results of choosing two letters.
c) Find the probability that when two letters are chosen, the first one is a vowel and the second is a consonant.
d) Find the probability that when two letters are chosen, one is a vowel and the other is a consonant.

6 Two ordinary dice are renumbered so that they each carry the values 1, 1, 1, 1, 1, 6 on their faces. Both dice are thrown together.
a) Draw a sample space diagram to show the possible outcomes.
b) Find the probability that the total is 7.
c) Find the probability that the total is even.

7* Three coins are tossed. One of the possible outcomes is heads on the first coin, heads on the second and tails on the third. This is written HHT.

First coin	Second coin	Third coin
H	H	T

a) Copy and complete this table to show all the possible outcomes:
b) Find the probability of getting three heads.
c) Find the probability of getting two heads and one tail (in any order).

8* When I throw a dart at a board the probability that I hit the bull is 0.1. I throw three darts altogether. Draw a tree diagram to show the three throws, and use it to find the probability that I obtain:
a) no bull;   **b)** three bulls;   **c)** exactly one bull.

9* A ball is chosen at random from a bag, and then replaced. A second ball is then chosen at random. The probability that **both** balls are red is 0.36.

a) Calculate the probability that the first ball is red.

b) The bag contains 20 balls in total. Each ball is either red or green. How many green balls must there be in the bag?

10*A drawer contains six socks, of which two are blue. Peter decides to pick two socks out without turning the light on. He takes out one sock and puts it on, then takes out a second sock and puts it on. Peter reckons that the probability of getting a pair of blue socks is

$$P = \tfrac{2}{6} \times \tfrac{2}{6} = \tfrac{4}{36} = \tfrac{1}{9}.$$

Unfortunately Peter's calculation is wrong.

a) Explain briefly why Peter's calculation is wrong.

b) Work out the correct answer to this problem.

Level 6 Review

Exercise 1 *Do this exercise as mental arithmetic – do not write down any working.*

1 Write 3.141 592 6 correct to 4 decimal places.

2 Write 76.031 correct to 3 significant figures.

3 Write 450.2713 correct to 4 significant figures.

4 Write 76.2099 correct to 1 decimal place.

5 Arrange in order of size, smallest first: 6.18, 6.03, 6.3, 6.01, 6.099.

6 Find the next two numbers : 5, 8, 11, 14, __, __

7 Find the next two numbers : 5, 6, 8, 11, __, __

8 Find $\frac{3}{4}$ of £120.

9 Express 0.8 as a percentage.

10 Express $\frac{1}{4}$ as a percentage.

11 Express 0.325 as a percentage.

12 Express $\frac{7}{10}$ as a percentage.

13 Write 62% as a decimal.

14 Write down the multiplying factor for a 6% increase.

15 Write down the multiplying factor for a 4% decrease.

16 Express the ratio 25 : 15 in its simplest form.

17 Find the first three terms in the number pattern described by $u_n = 3n - 1$.

18 Find the first three terms in the number pattern described by
$u_{n+1} = 3u_n - 1$ and $u_n = 1$.

19 Find x if $x + 11 = 7$.

20 Find y if $2y + 1 = 19$.

Exercise 2 *Do this exercise as mental arithmetic – do not write down any working.*

1 £24 is to be shared out in the ratio 5 : 3. Find the value of the larger share.

2 500 francs is to be shared out in the ratio 5 : 3 : 2. Find the value of the smallest share.

3 Increase £25 by 10%.

4 My bus fare was 80p but has increased by 5%. What is the new fare?

5 Carpet costing £15 per square metre has been reduced by 10%. What is the new price?

6 There are 36 children in a dance club and $\frac{2}{3}$ of them are girls. How many girls are there?

7 A square has sides of length 9 cm. What is its area?

8 A rectangle measures 12 cm by 5 cm. What is its area?

9 A quadrilateral has four equal sides but no right angles. What type of quadrilateral is it?

10 How many mirror lines does a kite have?

11 How many mirror lines does a square have?

12 Every day the number of bacteria in a colony doubles. Today there are 6000. How many will there be in three days' time?

13 Six cans of drink cost £1.50. How much will 15 cans cost?

14 Three of the angles in a quadrilateral add up to 280°. State the size of the fourth angle.

15 What name is given to a 2-D mathematical shape with six straight edges?

16 What name is given to a 2-D mathematical shape with eight straight edges?

17 What name is given to a 3-D mathematical solid with eight flat faces?

18 The perimeter of a square is 20 cm. What is its area?

19 Find x if $\frac{x}{4} = 5$.

20 Find y if $20 = 3y - 1$.

Exercise 3 *You should show all necessary working in this exercise.*

1 Find a term-to-term rule for this number pattern: 3, 7, 11, 15, …

2 Find a position-to-term rule for this number pattern: 2, 3, 5, 9, 17, …

3 Express 31 as a percentage of 50.

4 Express 70 cm as a percentage of 2 m.

5 Express 350 g as a percentage of half a kilogram.

6 A company employs 350 people, but today 21 of them are away. What percentage are away?

7 Three chemicals are mixed by combining 450 grams of A with 350 g of B and 250 g of C. Write this as a ratio in its simplest form.

8 Solve the equation $5x + 3 = 3x + 11$.

9 Solve the equation $x + 13 = 5x - 7$.

10 Solve the equation $7x - 2 = 68 - 3x$.

11 A triangle has a base of 16 cm and height 10 cm. Find its area.

12 The diagonals of a rhombus are of lengths 24 cm and 10 cm. Find its area.

13 Two dice are thrown. Calculate the probability that the total score is at least 7.

14 When I play chess against Boris I either win, draw or lose. The probability that I win is 0.2 and the probability of a draw is 0.3. Find the probability that I lose, and say which one of us is the better player.

15 The angles in a certain quadrilateral are 140°, 100°, 20°, 100° (in order as you go around it). Gary says 'This shape must be a kite'. Explain carefully whether Gary is right or wrong.

16 The angles in a certain quadrilateral are 80°, 100°, 80°, 100° (in order as you go around it). Lucy says 'This shape must be a parallelogram'. Explain carefully whether Lucy is right or wrong.

In questions **17–20** you are given some *Logo* code. Describe as accurately as you can the shape which is drawn in each case.

17 repeat 4 [fd 80 rt 90]

18 repeat 2 [fd 80 rt 130 fd 50 rt 50]

19 repeat 5 [fd 90 rt 72]

20 repeat 5 [fd 90 rt 144]

Exercise 4

1 The equation $x^2 - 9x + 4 = 0$ has a solution between $x = 8$ and $x = 9$.

Use trial and improvement to find its value correct to 1 decimal place.

2 The equation $x^3 + x - 4 = 0$ has a solution between $x = 1$ and $x = 2$.

Use trial and improvement to find its value correct to 2 decimal places.

3 Copy and complete this table, in which x and y are related by the formula $y = x^2 + 3x - 1$.

x	−3	−2	−1	0	1	2	3
x^2	9	4			1		
$3x$	−9		−3		3		
-1	−1	−1		−1		−1	− 1
y	−1	−3			3		

Draw coordinate axes in which x can run from −3 to 3 and y from −3 to 17. Plot the points, and join them up with a smooth curve.

Use your graph to obtain a value of x when $y = 0$.

4 The diagram shows an object and its image after enlargement. Make a copy of this diagram on squared paper, and use it to find
a) the coordinates of the centre of enlargement;
b) the scale factor of the enlargement.

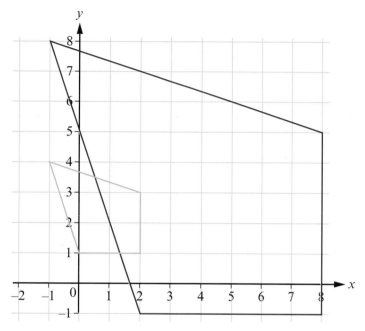

5 The recipe for a *Bûche de Noël* includes the following:

6 eggs

5 ounces (150 grams) caster sugar

2 ounces (50 grams) cocoa powder

a) The recipe is for 8 people. Avril wants to change the recipe so that it serves 12 people. Calculate the quantities required for Avril's recipe, using grams rather than ounces.
b) The recipe appears to contain an error, because 150 grams is three times 50 grams, but 5 ounces is not three times 2 ounces. Can you explain the cause of this apparent error?

6 The four angles in a quadrilateral are $x + 5$, $2x + 15$, $3x + 10$ and $5x$. Set up an equation, and solve it to find the value of x. Hence find the sizes of the four angles.

7 Find the missing angles represented by letters:

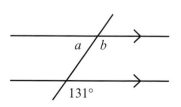
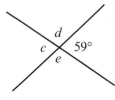
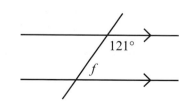

8 A circle has a diameter of 16 cm. Find its circumference.

9 A circle has a radius of 21 cm. Find its area.

10 A circle has a circumference of 90 m. Find its diameter.

11 A circle has an area of 45 cm². Find its diameter.

12 Look at these four scatter diagrams.

Write down the letter of the one which shows:

a) strong positive correlation;
b) no correlation;
c) weak negative correlation.

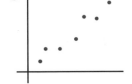

13 Here is one vertex of a regular polygon.

144°

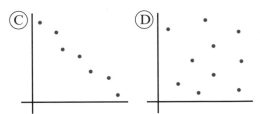

Calculate the number of sides which this polygon must have.

14 Explain why the diagram below could not represent one vertex of a regular polygon.

154°

15 The table shows the times taken by boys and girls in running a cross-country race:

Time taken, t minutes	Number of boys	Number of girls
$10 \leq t < 11$	1	
$11 \leq t < 12$	4	1
$12 \leq t < 13$	11	4
$13 \leq t < 14$	12	10
$14 \leq t < 15$	7	13
$15 \leq t < 16$	1	8
$16 \leq t < 17$	0	2

a) How many boys took part in the race altogether?
b) How many girls took part?
c) Illustrate the data with two frequency polygons, both drawn on the same set of axes.
d) Describe briefly any differences between the two sets of data.

Answers to ✔ questions

Unit 1 Place value and powers of 10

Exercise 1.1
2 13 593   **9** 20 003
14 Sixty-three thousand, two hundred and seven
20 Thirty-two thousand and sixty-seven

Exercise 1.2
3 96 615   **8** 2808   **14** 21 804   **17** 19 217

Exercise 1.3
5 637 000   **6** 2390   **15** 83 000   **16** 6400

Unit 2 Number patterns

Exercise 2.1
1 32   **8** 24

Exercise 2.2
3 9, 18, 27, 36   **9** No   **14** Yes   **18** 1, 2, 4, 8, 16

Exercise 2.3
5 73 is prime   **6** 59   **7** 41, 43, 47   **8** 27 is composite

Exercise 2.4
3 Start at 6, go up 5 at a time: 26, 31
5 Start at 100, go down 3 at a time: 85, 82
8 Start at 1, multiply by 2 each time: 32, 64

Unit 3 Fractions and percentages

Exercise 3.1
3 $\frac{5}{9}$ **10** $\frac{5}{16}$

Exercise 3.2
3 $\frac{8}{18}, \frac{12}{27}, \frac{16}{36}$ (other possibilities also)   **6** 44   **10** $\frac{6}{7}$

Exercise 3.3
2 60%

Unit 4 Working with decimals

Exercise 4.1
3 1.9　　　　　**10** 4.3　　　　　**15** 6.39　　　　　**17** 5.67

Exercise 4.2
1 32.5 cm　　　　**8** 0.13 m

Exercise 4.3
4 62.8　　　　　**5** 3.5　　　　　**13** 54.19　　　　**14** 33.24
20 £16.99

Exercise 4.4
2 3.003, 3.01, 3.209, 3.3, 3.01　　　　**6** 0.42, 0.415, 0.4, 0.37, 0.365

Unit 5 Coordinates

Exercise 5.1
1 a) (4, 3)　　　　**b)** (3, 2)　　　　**c)** (2, 4)

Exercise 5.2
1

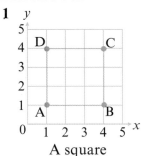

A square

4 a)

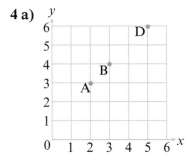

4 b) (4, 5)

Unit 6 2-D shapes and 3-D models

Exercise 6.1
1

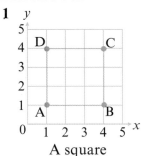

Exercise 6.2

2  rotation through 90°

Unit 7 3-D Models

Exercise 7.1

1 Four (equilateral) triangles   **2** Six squares   **3** Twelve pentagons

Unit 8 Units and scales

Exercise 8.1

1 15 cm 5 mm

Exercise 8.2

1 c) centimetres (or millimetres)   **j)** kilometres   **2 f)** grams

Exercise 8.3

1 6.6   **3** 10.4   **4** 5.75 ($5\frac{3}{4}$)

Unit 9 Perimeter and area

Exercise 9.1

3 26 cm   **9** 12.0 cm

Exercise 9.2

3 12 cm²

Exercise 9.3

1 45 cm²

Unit 10 Looking at data

Exercise 10.1

1 Mode 23, range 9

Exercise 10.2

1 a)

Amount	0	10	20	50
Frequency	3	6	5	3

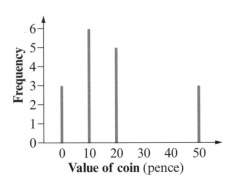

Exercise 10.3

2 a)

Mark	Frequency
00–09	0
10–19	2
20–29	0
30–39	6
40–49	10
50–59	16
60–69	5
70–79	8
80–89	2
90–99	1

b)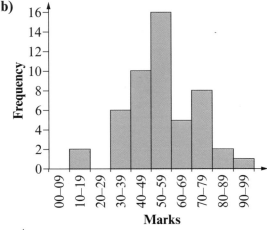

c) 50–59   **d)** 23

Unit 11 Decimals and negative numbers

Exercise 11.1

1 c) 10.006   **2 a)** Sixty-nine point two five

7 63.63   **14** 424.19

Exercise 11.2

5 484.5   **7** 9.007   **13** 9.85   **17** 1719.63

Exercise 11.3

4 –7.5, –7.33, 14.05, 14.66   **7** –11

9 –7   **15** 16

Exercise 11.4

2 £7.92   **7** £5.84

Unit 12 Multiplication and division without a calculator

Exercise 12.1

2 15 228   **8** 31 744   **17** 243 873   **19** 50 625

Exercise 12.2

2 5284   **9** 275   **18** 999

Unit 13 Fractions and percentages

Exercise 13.1

2 $\frac{2}{3}$ **10** $\frac{1}{5}$

Exercise 13.2

9 93   **12** 305

Exercise 13.3

1 630   **7** $420   **11** 324   **18** 108

Exercise 13.4

6 62.5%   **8** 36.4%   **10** 71.4%   **17** 14%

Exercise 13.5

7 $\frac{1}{40}$ **14** $\frac{3}{20}$ **17** $\frac{13}{50}$ **19** $\frac{1}{6}$

Unit 14 Ratio and direct proportion

Exercise 14.1

1 3:4   **8** 2:3   **9** 1:1.25   **13** 1.75:1

Exercise 14.2

2 210 g, 240 g   **7** 30 cm

Exercise 14.3

2 £1.92

Unit 15 Rounding and estimation

Exercise 15.1

1 160   **8** 210 000   **9** 40 000   **14** 70 000

Exercise 15.2

1 1200   **7** 200   **10** 1400 g   **19** 600 scripts

Exercise 15.3

6 Right   **7** Wrong, should be 755

Unit 16 Algebra

Exercise 16.2
3 53   **6** 20   **11** 62   **18** –1

Exercise 16.3
5 –10.589, –10.6   **8** 30, 30   **14** 3112   **20** 1.881

Exercise 16.4
2 $2x - 5$ **9** $(x + 3) \div 2$ **14** 21 pounds, $9 + 2x$ pounds
18 £1100, £$1500 - 50t$

Exercise 16.5
3 c) $4m + 6n$ **6 a)** $7y^3$ **6 c)** $9b^2 + 7b$

Unit 17 Coordinates in all four quadrants

Exercise 17.1
2 square   **3** Trapezium

Exercise 17.2
1 P (6, 4)   Q (–4, 5)   R (4, –3)   S (–7, –7)   T (3, –6)   U (–9, 3)

Unit 18 Geometry of 2–D shapes

Exercise 18.1
1 Acute   **2** Obtuse   **3** Right-angled

Exercise 18.2
1 53°   **3** 105°   **5** 348°

Exercise 18.3
1 80°   **3** 135°

Exercise 18.4
1 48°   **3** 54°

Exercise 18.5
3 106°   **5** 34°   **19** 115°   **20** 63°

Unit 19 Symmetry and congruence

Exercise 19.1
1 Order 4   **4** Order 2   **5** Order 3   **6** Order 5

Exercise 19.2
2 No symmetry   **4** Translation symmetry
7 Rotational symmetry of order 8   **9** Reflection symmetry

Exercise 19.3
1 A and D   **2** B and E

Unit 20 Metric and imperial measures

Exercise 20.1
4 560 km   **7** 120 g

Exercise 20.2
3 137 cm   **7** 253 ml
13 420 kg. Less than 500 kg, so the lift can take them.

Unit 21 Areas of squares and rectangles

Exercise 21.1
1 16 cm^2 **5** 81 cm^2 **10** 7.84 cm^2 **12** 26.0 cm^2

Exercise 21.2
1 20 cm^2 **5** 18 cm^2 **10** 17.5 cm^2 **12** 22.3 cm^2

Unit 22 Averages and frequency diagrams

Exercise 22.1
2 8.375, 8   **4** 8.05, 5.9   **12** 0.5, 5
20 66.8 g, yes, as 66.8 > 65

Exercise 22.2
1 5, 7   **7** 6.5, 3

Exercise 22.3
3 a) 30 throws   **b)** The mode is 2.

Exercise 22.4
1 The two stations have a similar average (median) temperature, but station B has a greater range.
4 The range is similar for each group, but the trainees earn about £16 000 less than the fully qualified accountants.

Unit 23 Pie charts and line graphs

4

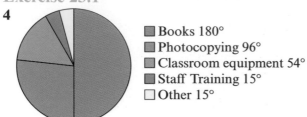

■ Books 180°
■ Photocopying 96°
■ Classroom equipment 54°
■ Staff Training 15°
☐ Other 15°

1 Line graph

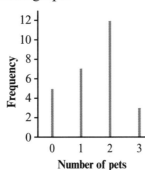

2 Time series graph

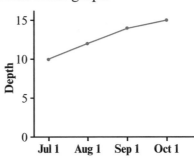

Unit 24 Theoretical and experimental probability

3 Impossible   **7** Unlikely   **9** Reasonably likely

2 a) $\frac{5}{18}$ **b)** $\frac{6}{18}$ or $\frac{1}{3}$ **c)** 0

7 a) $\frac{3}{6}$ or $\frac{1}{2}$ **b)** $\frac{1}{6}$ **c)** $\frac{2}{6}$ or $\frac{1}{3}$ **d)** $\frac{2}{6}$ or $\frac{1}{3}$

5 a) $\frac{5}{100}$ or $\frac{1}{20}$ **b)** $\frac{40}{100}$ or $\frac{2}{5}$

Unit 25 Rounding and approximation

2 104.8   **6** 12.20   **10** 46.20
15 4.21, 4.201, 4.021, 1.24, 1.024   **20** −3.6, −2.14, −1.44, 0.26, 0.77

3 2.791   **10** 0.19

2 0.3 (or 1.9)   **8** 7.3   **9** 3.07 and 0.90

Unit 26 Number patterns

Exercise 26.1

3 Starts at 16 and goes up 3 at a time, 31, 34
4 Starts at 11 and goes down 2 at a time, 1, −1
7 Starts at 1 and goes up 2, then 3, then 4 etc, 21, 28 (triangular numbers)

Exercise 26.2

3 2, 6, 10, 14, 18   **6** 8, 6, 4, 2, 0   **10** 1, 4, 9, 16, 25   **12** 1, 3, 7, 15, 31, 63
18 1, 2, 4, 7, 11, 16

Exercise 26.3

2 25, 28. $u_n = 3n + 7$ **8** −5, −8. $u_n = 13 − 3n$
12 Not linear. Goes up by 2, then 3, then 4 etc.
13 Linear. $u_n = 3n + 18$

Unit 27 Fractions, decimals and percentages

Exercise 27.2

1 c) $\frac{19}{24}$ **j)** $\frac{1}{2}$ **2 a)** 80%   **g)** 37%

Exercise 27.3

1 a) 0.375   **j)** 4.6429   **2 a)** $\frac{22}{25}$ **e)** $3\frac{16}{25}$

Exercise 27.4

1 b) 70%   **f)** 620%   **2 b)** $0.\dot{3}$ **h)** 0.075

Exercise 27.5

1 b) 371   **e)** £936   **5 a)** 1.12   **b)** £18.50

Exercise 27.6

1 b) 3:4   **h)** 20:13:11   **3 a)** 3:5:12   **b)** $\frac{3}{4}$ hour

Unit 28 Linear equations

Exercise 28.1

3 $x = −7$ **8** $x = 7$ **11** $x = 33$ **13** $x = 23$

Exercise 28.2

3 $x = 7$ **9** $x = 3$ **13** $x = 6$ **19** $x = 2.5$

Exercise 28.3

2 $x = 8$ **7** $x = 7$ **15** $x = 3.25$ **20** $x = −1.4$

Exercise 28.4

3 28   **6** 12

Unit 29 Functions and graphs

Exercise 29.1

2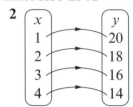

7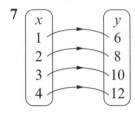

12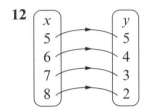

15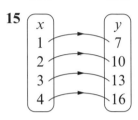

20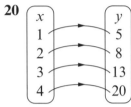

Exercise 29.2

2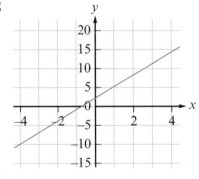

8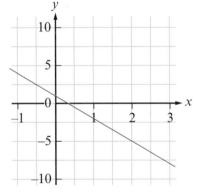

Exercise 29.3

1

x	−4	−3	−2	−1	0	1	2	3
x^2	16	9	4	1	0	1	4	9
+4x	−16	−12	−8	−4	0	4	8	12
−3	−3	−3	−3	−3	−3	−3	−3	−3
y	−3	−6	−7	−6	−3	2	9	18

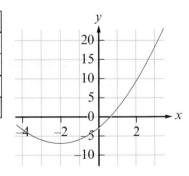

6

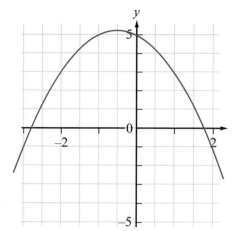

Unit 30 Quadrilaterals and angles

Exercise 30.1

1

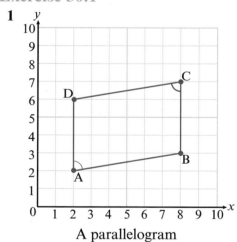

A parallelogram

4

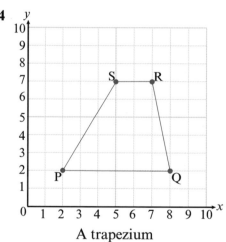

A trapezium

Exercise 30.2

2 $b = 93°$ (angles on a straight line)
   $d = 67°$ (angles on a straight line)
3 $e = 100°$ (angles on a straight line)
12 $s = 90°$ (angles on a straight line)
   $u = 30°$ (Z–angles)

$c = 113°$ (angles in a quadrilateral)

$f = 100°$ (opposite angles of a kite)
$t = 60°$ (Z–angles)

Exercise 30.3

1 $a = 10°$ **3** $c = 38°$ **6** $g = 14°$

Unit 31 Making shapes using *Logo*

As these questions are self-checking on a computer there are no key answers to this Unit.

Unit 32 Area and volume

Exercise 32.1
1 a) 156 cm²   **f)** 71.5 cm²   **3** 319 cm²   **4** 218.5 cm²

Exercise 32.2
2 98 cm²   **4** 108 cm²   **5** 35 cm²   **8** 100.75 cm²

Exercise 32.3
1 184 cm²   **3** 408 cm²

Exercise 32.4
1 560 cm³   **4** 570.18 cm³

Unit 33 The circle: area and circumference

Exercise 33.1
3 31.4 km   **8** 59.7 m   **13** 134.5 mm   **18** 76.97 km

Exercise 33.2
3 78.5 km²   **7** 154 km²   **13** 1439 mm²   **15** 706.9 cm²

Exercise 33.3
2 3.18 inches   **3** 3.34 mm

Unit 34 Enlargement and reflection

As these questions are extended drawings there are no key answers to this Unit.

Unit 35 Frequency diagrams and pie charts

Exercise 35.1
1 Discrete   **7** Continuous   **8** Discrete

Exercise 35.2
3 a)

Age	$0 \leq x < 5$	$5 \leq x < 10$	$10 \leq x < 15$	$15 \leq x < 20$
Frequency	3	0	7	14

b) The storm probably took place 2 years ago.

Exercise 35.3

2

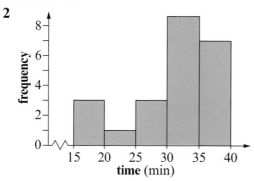 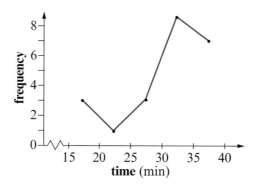

Exercise 35.4

1

Country	Great Britain	France	Germany	Other
Angle	172°	82°	41°	65°

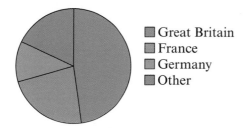

- Great Britain
- France
- Germany
- Other

Unit 36 Scatter diagrams and other graphs

Exercise 36.1

1 Strong positive correlation
3 Weak positive correlation
5 Weak negative correlation
7 a) Plant A probably died.
b)

2 No correlation
4 Strong negative correlation

c) The height and temperature show strong positive correlation.

Exercise 36.2

1 b) About 70 km (actually 72)   **c)** About 88 miles (actually 87.5)
5 a) 20.2 hectares   **c)** 37 acres
  d) 6 hectares

Exercise 36.3

2 a)

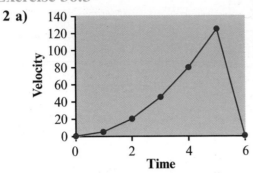

b) 101 m/s
c) 2.8 sec
d) It lands between 5 and 6 seconds after being dropped.

Unit 37 Probability

Exercise 37.1

3 $\frac{1}{9}$ **6 a)** $\frac{1}{6}$ **b)** $\frac{1}{4}$

10 a) $\frac{1}{9}$ **b)** $\frac{1}{18}$ **c)** $\frac{1}{4}$ **d)** $\frac{1}{6}$

Exercise 37.2

1 0.36   **4** 0.384
10 a) 0.25   **b)** 0.3   **c)** 0.04

Index

Index